Metamorphosis:

The Butterfly Experience

Metamorphosis:

The Butterfly Experience

Alicia Cass

ISBN: 0991030702
ISBN 13: 9780991030705

The Butterfly

I would like to thank God who is the Author and Finisher of my Faith. Without Him there is no Metamorphosis and without that process I have no testimony.

As I wrote this book my reality hit, so many of my friends were dead, still on drugs, incarcerated, and worst of all still stuck in the same life style. As my pen hit the paper my tears began to write my story. My heart was overwhelmed because it meant going back to my childhood and opening a dark door in the attic of my heart. This door had been locked and bolted with hurt, pain and secrecy for over 40 years. This day meant going through the threshold and becoming vulnerable with myself. It meant exposing my ills, stripping and becoming naked. It meant forgiving those whom I thought I had forgiven and most of all forgiving myself. As I was writing I had an emotional breakdown. I couldn't pull it together. At first, I didn't understand. I thought I was delivered and free from some of my pain and issues, but then I realized I never had a chance to truly grieve. Grieve; over my childhood innocence being stolen, grieve over my family hurt, grieve over not having a mother, grieve over a father that could not show me love. Simply put, I could grieve BECAUSE IT WAS MY TIME. This night I allowed myself to cry and for the very first time, to keep crying. Throughout all the trauma and loss in my life, I have always had the ability to keep pushing with no time to cry or mourn. This night, for the first time, I didn't have the ability to keep it pushing. I was *Amazed*! It was the first time that I allowed myself to be vulnerable with me.

Dedication

This book is dedicated to those that have experienced childhood trauma, sexual, physical, emotional or domestic abuse, the foster care system, violence, loss or just the everyday ups and downs of life. I want you to allow the cocoon to strengthen you, because it is within the cocoon (struggle) that your wings are developed. I want you to know that while you can't see your wings they are visible to others. Know and believe that it is never too late to emerge from your cocoon. Once your Metamorphosis occurs know that you no longer crawl on the ground of uncertainty, unable to see past the weeds. Don't allow others to classify you as a caterpillar, because YOU'RE NOT. You have beat the odds and transformed into the Beautiful Butterfly YOU were destined to be. You now have a High View, So Fly...

Table of Contents

The Butterfly · v

Chapter 1   Mama's Dead· ·1
Chapter 2   Short-term Freedom · 11
Chapter 3   The Deer and Lion · 15
Chapter 4   Middle Passage · 19
Chapter 5   Different Family, Same Dysfunction · · · · · · · · · · · ·24
Chapter 6   Hello Hell ·35
Chapter 7   Birth of a New Family · · · · · · · · · · · · · · · · · · 44
Chapter 8   Foster Care: Big Pimpin' Foster Mamas · · · · · · · · ·55
Chapter 9   Time to Grow Up · 72
Chapter 10   Hood Boot Camp 101 · · · · · · · · · · · · · · · · · ·78
Chapter 11   Stepped Up My Hood Game · · · · · · · · · · · ·84
Chapter 12   Survive or Die Period! · · · · · · · · · · · · · · · · · 100
Chapter 13   Tennis Shoes · 105
Chapter 14   Hood Loss · 113
Chapter 15   The Homeless is Homeless · · · · · · · · · · · · · · 121
Chapter 16   Longing for the Hood · · · · · · · · · · · · · · · · · 129
Chapter 17   Time was Running Out · · · · · · · · · · · · · · · · 136
Chapter 18   Grim Reaper: Death Came · · · · · · · · · · · · · · 141

Chapter 19   The Connection · 147
Chapter 20   Gate Hopping · 154
Chapter 21   Loss is the New Normal · · · · · · · · · · · · · · · · 163
Chapter 22   Family Life · 175
Chapter 23   New Man, Old Enemy · · · · · · · · · · · · · · · · 185
Chapter 24   Out of the Frying Pan into the Oven · · · · · · · · · 193
Chapter 25   War· 205
Chapter 26   Civil War· 212
Chapter 27   Mad, Homeless, and Pregnant · · · · · · · · · · · 218
Chapter 28   Something is in the Air · · · · · · · · · · · · · · · 230
Chapter 29   Metamorphosis · 243

Acknowledgments · 251
Bio · 253

Alicia,

As I was praying for you and asking God how can I be a blessing to you for Mother's Day, the image of a butterfly came to me. I could not understand this until I was putting away some jewelry, and I saw the butterfly pin that I've had for some time, and it became very clear.

The butterfly is one of God's most beautiful creations. The cycles of it's life that it must go through, to become that beautiful butterfly is so like the transformation of your life.

So, my adopted daughter, I give you this Butterfly with love, because I know with God's help you will touch so many lives with the love of God, as a Butterfly touches the petals of flowers, the branches of trees, and the rocks in a stream. Thank You for adopting me as your Mother.

HAPPY MOTHER'S DAY

God Bless You
Sister Lonnie

Chapter 1

Mama's Dead

Wake up! Wake up! That is all I can remember about my mother. I was four years old when she died. We were a family of seven who lived in a two-bedroom apartment, three girls and two boys It was 1975 and my father, Robert White was 29 and my mother, Barbara was 27. They had been married for 10 years. My father was from Mississippi and my mother was from California. My father had always planned to marry my mother and said he really loved her. My mother got pregnant at 16 and my father was 19. It was then that my mother's father told my father that his future wedding plans were now expedited. They got married when my mother was six months pregnant. Looking at their wedding picture my father was smiling, but my mother wasn't. During the wedding ceremony my grandfather cried and after he told my father, "If you ain't go treat her right, bring her back home."

At the time of my mother's death my sister Annette was the oldest, she was 10, Edwin 9, Curtis 8, Sandi 6 and I was 4. My mother died of a heart attack while I was in the house with her alone. She died 2 months after her 27th birthday. My father was at work, and my brothers and sisters were at school. God only knows how long I wandered around the house while her dead body lay on the couch. My mom worked off and on as sales clerk. She stayed at home to care for me because my parents couldn't afford day care.

I can still see the apartment. When you first walked into the living room, the small couch sat against the wall. My mother's body stayed on that couch for hours. The couch was white with green flowers and it was made with suede material. The walls were white and we had suede drapes that were black and white with the same flower print. The two bedrooms were on the right of the living room and off the living room to the left was the kitchen. We had a white table with yellow chairs and on top of the table was a lemon design. When I got older, my Great Aunt Helene told me that when she talked to me that day, I told her that my mommy would not wake up. I don't remember. I remember my grandmother coming over and shouting for my mother to get up, as she laid motionless on the couch. I remember my sisters and brothers and me sitting at the kitchen table when I said, "She's dead." Now, looking back, I don't know if I really knew what that meant, or if I had just heard my grandmother say it. I don't remember much else about my mother except my father made it very clear she was his wife and we had caused her to die. *We were kids—what could we have done to kill our mother?* Whenever my father spoke of my mother he always referred to her as his wife, and so it was as if I never had a mother.

No one talked much about her or even told me about her. *Was it too painful?* In the process of writing this book my beautiful Aunt Helene passed. As my family sat at the hospital discussing the mortuary that they would use for Aunt Helene, my Aunt Letty said she wouldn't use Simpson's Funeral Home because they were horrible. Aunt Letty said when my mother died she went to view the body. When she saw her body, it had embalming fluid coming from her mouth, Aunt Letty ran out screaming. My Aunt Letty was my mom's baby sister she didn't care for my father. Heck, none of my mother's sisters liked my father. My Aunt Jo told me that the family blamed my father for my mother's death. I assumed it was because my mother was advised by her doctor's not to have more than 2 kids due to her heart condition and at 22 she had 5. As I sat there listening, she stopped. It was as if she did not want to relive the memory of what happened. After 39 years, she still could not finish the story. My other Aunt Jo quickly agreed they did a horrible job on my mother's body, but they did not say what else happened. This was the first time I had heard anything about my mother's death. As bad as I wanted to know what happened, I also did not want to squeeze old wounds that clearly were still infected.

Growing up, every now and then, my oldest sister would tell wonderful stories of how my mother protected her "bad" kids, meaning us. Annette would tell me how my father would try to whip us and my mother would not have it. Physical fights would break out and, according to my sister's recollections, my mother held her own. My dad wasn't always the winner. After my mother's death, that would all change. She wasn't there to protect us anymore. Before then, I didn't remember my father spanking me much. When his wife Barbara (as he called her) died, it seemed as if he was going to make up for all the whippings he could not give us when she was alive, especially the ones he thought we deserved for killing his wife. My father wasn't a very tall man, but he had big hands and he always seemed angry. He didn't really talk to us, he only talked at us. As we got older, he continuously reminded us that we killed his wife. As a young child, I had no idea what he was talking about. Hell, I didn't even know his wife.

After my mother's death, we moved from the apartment to a house on 73rd and Hoover Street. It was on a big lot that had two houses, we lived in the back house. It was also next door to the grocery store. Because of the location we had a lot of shady people walking by and through our yard to go to the store. It was one of the worst neighborhoods, which only made our lives a living hell. When we went outside, it seemed that all the trouble happened on our front door step. Crime was everywhere. This frustrated my father and he took it out on us, as if we had made him move into that neighborhood. My father would complain and fuss at us, because he said the neighborhood was bad. We didn't understand what crime was, we just knew that he said it wasn't safe.

Within the first couple of months of living on this street, I made my first enemy. In fact, I never knew her name. All I know is that one day

I was riding my Big Wheel down the street and a couple of girls, a little older than me, were sitting on their front porch. As I turned around to head back up the street to my house, one of the girls gave me a mean look. She then came running toward their front gate. As I began to peddle harder, the other girl followed suit. Even as an adult, I remember that day. I was scared as I peddled my way to my yard while the girls chased after me. I jumped off my Big Wheel and ran as fast as I could into the house. I was just hoping that the first Big Wheel jacking didn't start with me. I looked out the window happy to see my Big Wheel was still there. After that day, I learned the parameters of the street. You don't go that far if you're by yourself. *You're probably thinking "What?!" Well, nothing.* I wouldn't have dared tell my father what happened. My father would whip us for anything he could think of and as far as I was concerned, I wasn't going to give him yet another reason or opportunity. I did not want to get whipped for allowing myself to be jumped and having my Big Wheel jacked.

My father was very violent and over the years, his logic and rationale for his method of discipline would prove to be not only crazy but also stupid. This was a result of his upbringing. My father and his sister my aunt Mae were raised by their father, grandpa Willie and stepmother grandma Janie because my grandmother Gussie was in a mental institution in Mississippi. My grandmother had been there since my father was a young boy. Grandpa Willie and grandma Janie were physically abusive to my father and aunt. He was so abusive that my great grandfather Cougar shot my grandfather and left him in the woods for dead. Once my grandfather recovered he fled to California with my father and aunt. As I was saying one night, my sister and I were playing in the living room, I was flying the paper airplane I made. During a flight, it hit my father. He politely gave my paper airplane back, not saying a word. The next night, I was running in the living room being chased by my puppy, Sheena. Trying not to get bitten, I accidentally ran into my father as I jumped onto the couch. My father gave me a whipping with an extension cord for running into him. He also said, "I know you hit me on purpose the night before with that paper airplane. So I'm just giving you the whipping you should have already got the night before."

My brother Curtis and I got the most beatings. I got beat for being bad and fighting. My father always told me fight. The times I did fight I got a whipping for doing what he said. Curtis got beat for being slow, because he could not follow directions well. Curtis was mentally challenged. Although he was 8, he had the mentality of a 5-year-old. Before my mother died she had Curtis in a school for kids with special needs and after her death my father removed him from the school.

When my father beat us with an extension cord, it was considered a two-part beating. Part one was the actual whipping and the second part was the worst because after the beating, he would bathe us and put Noxzema skin cream on the bruises and lashes. The Noxzema made the bruises hurt worst. It smelled strong and burned like nobody's business. The bruises lasted for days. I was 5 when I got my first two-part beating.

The house we moved in was small. It had two bedrooms and one bathroom. My sister Sandi and I shared a bedroom and bed. I remember many nights I was afraid to go to the bathroom by myself. I would look at the coats hanging on the door and they looked like shadowy people. I wasn't about to walk past the coats, so I just put my head under the covers and peed the bed. In the mornings when my father came in and found that the bed was wet, one of us had to confess. It wasn't going to be me. My sister would beg me to confess, so she didn't get whipped, too. Poor girl, she got many whippings because I wouldn't dare open my mouth. One morning after I wet the bed, I was trying to take the sheets off when my sister caught me. "Dad said whoever tells the truth, this time, will not get a whipping," she said. With that, she crossed her heart and hoped to die if she was telling a lie. Well, she should have dropped dead because she sure was lying. I marched into my father's room ready and willingly confessed with pride because at school I was taught not to lie. I thought I was doing the right thing. After my confession, my father took his thick brown leather belt that he pulled so graciously from his waist and began to beat me. After my beating that morning, I went into the room with my sister and asked, "What happened?" She replied, "I had my fingers crossed behind my back." That was one lesson I learned very early, if you're going to tell a lie, stick with your lie even until death—don't ever tell the truth or confess. That beating bred a liar.

I remember my father's belt because it had a big buckle on it that made noise when it wasn't buckled. Every time I heard the buckle clinking whether he was putting it on to get dressed or undoing it to whip us I began to cry. I became pre-conditioned to believe that whenever I heard the clinking sound, I was going to get beat. There were many mornings that my sister and I were in the living room looking for socks in the laundry basket when we heard the clinking, immediately we stopped and began to cry. We did not know what was next. I remember my father buckling his belt and looking at us as if we had lost our minds. We were terrified of that man. Didn't he know that we lived in fear on a daily basis? When my father whipped us, he always left marks and bruises. *I'm sorry. Did you say mercy? What's that?* He never showed us any even when we begged as if our very lives depended on it.

Getting beat for wetting the bed had become a regular occurrence for me. It just made me violent. As my dad beat me, I evolved into a little bully in kindergarten. I was learning how to prey on others; the funny thing was I was a tiny girl. I was probably the tiniest thing on the play yard. I didn't look intimidating I was really skinny and I looked 3 years old instead of 4. I wore two pony tails with ribbons and barrettes on the end. I wore bell bottom jeans and a green plaid coat, some bully right? Yet, I would terrorize the other kids. I had a reputation for biting and fighting.

My father had a lady friend; she would bring her sons by to play. We all went to the Wanda Mikes Day Care Center. We were one of the first families to enroll. His lady friend had a son named Shawn. Shawn was known for being the baddest boy on the Kindergarten playground. We claimed we were cousins. One day, cousin Shawn decided that he did not have enough kids to bully. Shawn decided he was going to pick on me and pushed me to the ground. Once I got up off the ground, I bit into his arm like a pit bull and wouldn't let go. I could hear the playground teacher yelling my name telling me to let go, but I didn't. The teacher was sitting in a chair on the other side of the play yard. When she saw I wouldn't let go, out of breath two yard teachers finally made their way to the scene of the crime. As one teacher pulled my teeth from his arm, Shawn took off running. I stood there with skin in my teeth. I'll never forget Shawn running fast and hard on the big playground. I didn't know where he was going and I didn't care. I felt good about the fight, because I won. Immediately, I was sent to the principal's office. The principal, Ms. Cooper, knew me by name. I would have a thousand more of those meetings, and I think she knew it. As she called my father, I sat proudly because I was taught that if someone hits you, you better hit them back. I remember Ms. Cooper hanging up the phone then fussing at me. She called the playground teacher into her office because she was disgusted with my father's response. My father was actually proud that I bit Shawn. I can't say that I remember Shawn or his mother coming back to our house after that.

Violence was a part of my culture. Whether in my home or in the neighborhood, it just was. The entire neighborhood of criminals walked through our yard because we lived next to the local grocery store's parking lot. One evening my father went to the washhouse and left my sister and me home alone. We were sitting in the living room watching TV when we heard someone messing with our front window. Our porch had two sides of long, pullout windows on both sides of the front door. We could hear someone taking the windows out one by one. We were terrified. We stood there holding hands and crying. Finally, my sister got the phone and called our Uncle Denny. The burglar did not know that a five and seven-year-old were alone in the house. Uncle Denny came over, scared the burglar away, and then waited for my dad to get home. When my father came home, he thanked my uncle and as soon as my uncle left, beat us for calling him. I guess the only way we were not going to get into trouble, was if the burglar murdered us. Outside of that, there was no excuse for calling my uncle. I thank God no one ever tried to break in again while we were there alone. Quite frankly, we would not have called for help. We would've probably just ended up dead— anything to avoid his belt and the extension cord.

The neighborhood we lived in was producing the most notorious gang members in the city. Everyone was poor and trying to get over on the next person. We fit the perfect mold: motherless kids whose father beat us and left us at home alone at night to go to welding school. Someone was always bullying my brothers Curtis and Edwin or trying to break into our house. When we were home alone some of the older neighborhood boys would come by and bang and kick our back door, as we sat terrified at the kitchen table. They kicked the back door yelling, "Curtis and Edwin are going to get their asses kicked when they come out of the house." I never understood why they kicked on our door because my brothers did not hang out or fight. We didn't want those boys to get into our house, nor did we want our father to stay with us at the house. Can't say we felt safe either way.

Unfortunately for my brothers, they couldn't hide forever. One day one of their main bullies, Keith, finally caught my brother Curtis standing in front of our porch. As my sister and I were playing, he walked up to my brother and started pushing and hitting him in the face. We sat there in fear as my brother just stood there not daring to hit him back. Clarence, the neighbor that lived in the front house saw what was happening and shouted out his window for Keith to leave my brother alone. When Keith turned cussing at Clarence; my brother picked up a stick and hit Keith in the face knocking him to the ground. My sister and I began screaming, "Run, Curtis run!" As he took off running, Keith got up from the ground screaming about what he was going to do when he caught my brother. Curtis stayed in the house for weeks after that trying to avoid Keith.

Keith was a constant bully to both of my brothers. Once, he had Curtis steal his own birthday present. When my brother stole the watch from my father he did not know it was his birthday gift. Keith instructed him to bring him something or else he was going to get beat up. Keith was older and bigger. And he had the 'hood to back him. My brother was younger, smaller and mentally challenged. My brother didn't have any real friends that I can remember because they called him slow. He was actually in what was called the "special ed class" at school. All they did was make leather belts and sun visors, or that's all I saw. Everybody knew the kids in Curtis' class were special. My brother didn't have a father to go to for help so he did what he could to make Keith leave him alone. When we were grown, somebody shot and killed Keith. When I heard the news I wasn't a bit sad. Even though all the years had passed, I still hated him in my heart and was glad he was dead.

Being afraid and beaten had become a part of everyday life. One afternoon my father was whipping my brother, and for some strange reason, Curtis decided to fight back. They were in the living room and, as my father was hitting my brother, they both fell over that little couch. When the fight was over, my brother had a broken arm and a black eye. After that beating, my father dropped Curtis off on my grandmother's porch so weak and hurt, he could barely walk. My grandmother called the ambulance. My brother was in the hospital for a week.

My father's rage had appeared on many occasions. That wasn't Curtis' last beating. One afternoon Curtis was getting beat when he decided to make a run for it. He opened the front door and ran down the street in nothing but his underwear. Curtis ran to our neighbor Felicia's house. Her mother was Ms. Dorothy. Ms. Dorothy saw my brother running down the street in his underwear. When Curtis came running, she gave him some of her daughter's pants. Ms. Dorothy brought my brother back home later that day. I don't know if she had a conversation with my father or not but the police never came to our house. I believe she felt sorry for me because she would let me come to her house as much as she could.

Throughout our lives, every now and then, my oldest brother Edwin would get a whipping, but they were few and far between. Edwin was my father's favorite it was rare for him to get beat. One night we were in our living room and I'm not sure what happened with the second in command. I remember my father was about to whip Edwin. As civilians, we were in awe. My father went to grab Edwin, he told my father, "If you whip me, I'm gonna call the police." My brother could barely get the words out of his mouth when my father reached down, grabbed him by the ankles and flipped him upside down. We sat in fear as my father held my brother upside down in midair slamming his head on the floor. My father kept yelling, "Call the police!" *You know he never did, right?* Later that day, my father told us we could get out of his house. We packed our stuff and said we were going to run away. My father took us to my grandmother's house three blocks away.

Chapter 2

Short-term Freedom

My grandmother, what can I say, except, my grandmother! My mother's mother was a hot mess to say the least. Thelma Jamma Beasley was her name, but we called her Ma, pronounced Muh. She weighed a hundred pounds soaking wet. Although she was a little woman, she didn't take any mess. The neighbors called her Bee. *You wonder why she was called Bee? Well, here is one opinion about it.* One night when we were at my grandmother's house, she was cussing at us as usual. My cousin Tee leaned over and whispered, "I know why they call her Bee." I asked, "Why?" And he proudly said, "Because she's a bitch." We laughed so hard it caught her attention and she turned and looked at us with death in her eyes. She knew we were laughing at her.

We heard bitch and other curse words on a regular basis at Ma's house. When I told Ma of the beatings, she gave grandmotherly advice and it went like this, "When your brother tries to get you into trouble, beat yourself up and go lay in the streets and let someone call the police. Then say he did it." I was never sure why she did not give that advice about my father, maybe because she thought my brother betrayed us. *Yes, that was grandmother's advice.* We stayed with my grandmother for a couple of days during our running away spree.

When we stayed at Ma's house, we saw a little bit of everything. Ma and her sister Helene were the life of 76th street. They were always drinking and partying. My grandfather floated through the house never touching a drink or dancing. *Poor grandpa.* Ma and Grandpa were the odd couple. She was a drunk and a party animal and grandpa was a hardworking man who took care of his kids and now grandkids. Maybe that's why they had separate bedrooms. The craziest thing grandpa ever did while watching us was if we didn't behave, he'd threaten to handcuff us. We thought it was the funniest thing. One summer day, my cousin Christine called his bluff. She wouldn't behave, so he took her to the bathroom and handcuffed her to the soap rack that was against the wall in the bathtub. After Christine's arrest, he made the rest of us go to bed. We lay on the bed with tears rolling down our eyes from laughter. He came in the room and asked, "Who's next?" We played sleep and waited for him to go into his room. When he did, we got up from the bed and peeped our heads in the bathroom. Christine was sitting in the bathtub handcuffed to the soap rack. We made faces at her and ran back in the room laughing until our stomachs' cramped. I loved my Grandpa. He never hit me.

When my grandmother had company over, she would call for Sandi and me to dance on her living room table. My sister didn't really like getting on the table to dance, but I did. I got on the table for the drunks and danced. Ma would tell me to whip it. "Whip it" meant as you danced on the table you hit your vagina with your hand and shouted, "Whip it!" I learned how to "whip it" by the time I was five.

Ma also gave us Ambassador since it was her favorite drink. It came in a dark green bottle. The first time I drank with Ma, I was about 5 years old; it burned my throat. After that, she did not have me as a willing volunteer to sip with her. Ma would tell the other kids to single out one person. That was the person we would chase and force to drink a shot of Ambassador. Ma also gave us cigarettes to smoke. She taught me how to blow smoke through my nose. Funny, one time she caught my brother smoking on the side of her house. She was angry because he had stolen her cigarettes. *Well, no need to fret.* She marched him right into the house and had him sit at the dining room table. Ma laid out a whole pack of cigarettes and told Curtis to smoke them as we watched. *I'm assuming the lesson was to not smoke without her.* Ma had Curtis put three cigarettes in his mouth at one time. He coughed as tears ran down his face. *I was never sure if he was crying or if it was just all that smoke in his eyes.*

After our stay at Ma's house, it was time to go back home. We weren't home long before my father beat my older sister, Annette, for cooking eggs in grease. He held a pillow over her face as he beat her so no one would hear her scream. After the beating he left a bruise on her arm. It was Saturday and Annette prayed the bruise would not go away before school on Monday. She knew if she had a bruise she would have to go to MacLaren Hall. MacLaren Hall was a child protection institution for abused, unwanted, abandoned, orphaned, and neglected children. Monday when she went to school, she showed Mr. Sherman, the vice principal, her bruise. She got what she prayed for. She went to MacLaren Hall, never to live with my father again.

After our return from grandmother's house, my father told us if we did not want to call him dad, we could call him Mr. White. We did what Edwin did—we called him Mr. White. It didn't last long. We went back to calling him, dad. The resistance had fallen. When my father went to school at night, he left Edwin in charge. Whatever Edwin said was law. If you made him mad, or even if you didn't make him mad, he got you a beating just because he could. My father would not believe anything anyone else said only Edwin. Who, by the way, was a pathological liar.

Now that Annette was out of the house my older brother Edwin abused his power to get what he wanted out of us including molesting us. I can remember the first time I saw my brother Edwin touch my sister Sandi. I was in the living room watching TV. When I went into the room; my brother was getting from on top of my sister. My brother told me to go back into the living room and they were just playing. Little did I know there would be many years of him and other family members "just playing" with the younger girls in my family. The next day I was down the street playing with an older girl named Kim. She asked, "Where is your brother?" I answered, "He's playing on top of my sister." Kim could not wait until she saw my brother that day. When she did, she confronted him. My brother said I was a liar. I didn't see anything wrong with me telling Kim. *After all, weren't they playing?* My sister also denied that she was playing, but she never called me a liar. *From that day on, Edwin would be the hunter luring the dumb deer in for the slaughter.*

Chapter 3

The Deer and Lion

My earliest memory of my brother touching me was when I was about 4 1/2 years old. He would come into my room and say he wanted to play house. At the end of the game, he always ended up on top of me grinding and humping me. As we got older, he began to become more aggressive. He would follow me around the house and trap me in the room by myself. He had all kinds of excuses to get me alone. He asked if I would walk to the store with him. He would take me in the backyard to touch me. *It's so sad. I was a tiny girl, nothing but a baby.* I remember the first time he exposed his dick to me. I was disgusted. I didn't know what to think about it except, yuck! As I got older, I got smarter. I didn't stay anywhere with him by myself if I could help it. I tried being his friend so that he would leave me alone. Of course that never worked. He didn't want a nagging little sister that idolized her big brother. He wanted a victim.

When he realized I was avoiding him, he began to harass me more. He would tear down my self-esteem with his words. He was grooming me for many years of abuse. As he tore me down mentally and emotionally, he trained me to comply with whatever he asked. Everyone in the house bowed down to him. I was about six when he tried to put his dick into my mouth. I told him I did not want that thing in my face. He just kept grabbing me trying to make me have oral sex.

During that particular attempt he was unsuccessful and eventually gave up because, as a six-year-old, I didn't know what to think --let alone what to do. Who would have thought that some of my first sexual experiences would be unwanted and with family members? *Yes, I said "members." We'll get to that later.* My lack of not knowing how and unwillingness to perform oral sex did not deter him for long. As I got older, he would corner me into the room alone and lay on top of me. As he began to hump me, he exposed his dick and white stuff shot all over my legs. I was disgusted. It was sticky and felt funny. When I asked him what it was, he said he should've used the bathroom. I had no idea what semen was. I thought this white stuff appeared because he forgot to pee. I didn't have anyone to tell. I was being stalked in my own house. The coldest part of it all was he would verbally harass me all day. He would talk about how big my head was and how skinny I was. He would have my sister Sandi laughing for hours as he talked about me. Where I come from it's called, "bagging." This only made me do what he wanted so he could leave me alone. It didn't work.

This happened off and on until I was about 12 years old. *I guess you're wondering why not tell? I wondered the same thing. It's called guilt, shame, humiliation, no self-identity and no self-worth. Ladies and gentlemen, once someone strips away these important elements, they can get you to do anything they want.* Remember, my first lesson in self-deprecation began at 4 ½, and it wouldn't be the last one.

As the years went on, my family would help me create a new identity, one they wouldn't like. Many days I sat on my bed thinking. *You're too old not to have said no. Who cares if no one believes you?* Edwin would always say that I was a hoe. I came to the conclusion that if I was a hoe, he did his part into putting me on the road to "hoe-ville." I did not know how to love myself or what real love or intimacy was or what it was supposed to feel like. He robbed me of the ability to have natural sexual orgasms because I was touched too early. Sex in my eyes was dirty, nasty and something that you did in the dark with no emotion. You just lay on your back, kept your mouth shut, got up, washed off and acted as if it never happened.

For over 30 years, I was robbed of the ability to love and to be loved. It was just business. Do what you need to do and get the hell off of me. *FYI, men, a woman can lay down with you anytime and get nothing out of it because she's been stripped of emotions and trained from childhood to just lay there unattached.* In my latter promiscuous years, I would tell people I've slept with men and got nothing out of it. The general response was, "That's IMPOSSIBLE!" *Hey, people! "It's POSSIBLE."* Throughout my life, I would have boyfriends ask me questions about my sexuality. Who was your first? Have you ever tried oral sex? When was the first time you tried oral sex? And all I could think of was the fact that my first experiences with sex had begun when I was just a preschooler. *How sad.*

My Aunt Joan or JoJo for short always told me to watch out for strangers and not to get into a car with men I did not know. She was adamant about it. When I became an adult, some family members were talking, and I had heard that her grandfather molested her when she was a little girl. *Poor JoJo.* In those days, we didn't have the Internet; we had the weirdo in the van. She would say, "Look out for the strange man trying to lure you into his van by promising you a puppy." When I was little, I would walk to school trying to avoid any weird or creepy looking man in a van. While the whole time, the creepy weirdo lived in my house, ate at the same table, watched the same TV, and shared my bloodline. *Hey, Auntie JoJo, you forgot the most important warning: watch out for the related stranger in your own house, trying to lure you into the bedroom, bathroom, or backyard, with trust, power, control, shame, guilt and humiliation. No van, no puppy! I guess she could not bring herself to tell me that the weirdo lived amongst her and shared her bloodline: her grandfather and my great grandfather!*

At least with the outside weirdo, you could try and run somewhere safe, but for me there was nowhere to run, no one to run to. This weirdo was daddy's favorite pet and he knew it. One of the toughest things about being molested by a family member is you're still together at family gatherings, Christmas, and birthdays. I learned to cope. Coping meant act as if it never happened. This was just my life and there was nothing I could do about it. I went on as if he, they, had done nothing. *Can't say nothing, don't say nothing, don't feel nothing, ain't gon' be nothing.*

The molesting stopped as I was gaining a new family. A family that would back me and reinforce that I didn't have to take shit from nobody.

Chapter 4

Middle Passage

My family stayed on 73rd until I was in the second grade. We would not live there anymore because of what I told the school nurse. One night I had gotten a whipping and the next day I went to school as usual. In those days, we were checked for Scoliosis in our underwear. I went into a room in the nurse's office for my test and she noticed the lashes and bruises. She asked what happened and I told her my father had whipped me. The exam stopped. She told me to get dressed and to have a seat. I sat in her office and waited to go back to class. As I waited, two police officers came and spoke with the nurse. She had called them. One officer asked if he could talk to me. I sat amazed because I had never been that close to someone with blue eyes. He was very nice. After our talk, Sandi and I were put in the back of the police car and were taken to MacLaren Hall.

I remember we were scared. We did not know what to expect. In MacLaren Hall, things were different, and the food was nasty. They put us in a room with other kids and walked us to a closet to give us clean underwear and clothes. Later that night as I was lying down I heard a girl crying. In the morning, she had a white baby doll. The next night I began to cry. I have never been sure if I was sad or I wanted that white baby doll, but I got one. My sister told me, "You only cried to get that doll." *Thinking about it, gotta love me.* There was an older girl in our room that made sure I got my doll. She also made a necklace of beads for me. She tied it with fish string to make sure it didn't come off. I don't remember her name, but I had the necklace on my neck long after we left MacLaren Hall. Eventually, they had to cut it off my neck because it was pinching the front of my throat. *As I touch my throat I still have the mark on the front of my neck under my Adam's apple.*

After MacLaren Hall, Sandi and I went to live with my Aunt Letty. My brother Curtis went with my grandmother and brother Edwin went with my Aunt Darlene. My oldest sister Annette went with my beautiful Aunt Joan. Annette lucked up because Aunt JoJo didn't have any children, lived in a beautiful home and was a flight attendant. I always wanted to live with Aunt JoJo. She was beautiful and sophisticated. It wasn't until I began this book that I found out my older sister lived with my father's sister, Aunt Mae, for over a year before going to Aunt JoJo's. Annette stayed in MacLaren Hall for over two months before going to Auntie Mae's house. Annette said that over 12 social workers questioned her throughout her stay, with the hopes she would change her story and go home. Annette was adamant that after that last beating she received, she would never return. I was surprised that Aunt Mae took Annette in considering she did whatever my father wanted.

My Aunt Mae had three kids at the time, Ronnie 10, Denise 8 and Jr. 6 and a husband who was a career criminal. Annette said that her stay with dear Aunt Mae was short lived because my Uncle Jay was getting out of prison and Aunt Mae said she had to go. Annette was built like a grown woman; which meant she couldn't stay. *You can put it together, right?* My aunt said there would be no more room once my uncle came home. *I did the math. If your man is coming home and he's sleeping in your room, where's the addition?* Years later, I would spend many summers at my Aunt Mae's and she always let me stay. *Recently, I did the new math.* As a teenager, I was 80 pounds soaking wet and flat chested as they came. *No threat.* She had plenty of room for me. As a kid, I never thought twice about why I was the only girl that went to Aunt Mae's house. *As I sit and*

laugh now, I thought I was special, and I guess I was. Because of my petite size, they didn't need more room.

Aunt Letty was my mother's baby sister. She had two young kids Angel 4, Bebe 2, and a husband. Sandi and I moved into her two-bedroom apartment. Her husband loved music and he was really sweet to us. They called him Bud. I'm not sure how long we lived with my aunt before Bud died, but it wasn't long. They said he drowned in a swimming pool. We were all really sad that he died. I guess he was the first real man figure in our lives. We went to view Bud's body, but were not allowed to go to his funeral.

After Bud died we went from that apartment to living in the back of my grandmother's house. *You remember Ma, right?* Ma had two houses on a lot. One in the front and one in the back. Over the years, different family members lived in one or the other. At this time, Ma lived in the front house and now, since my aunt had no husband, we moved into the back house. It was a one-bedroom house. *Can you believe it?* There were five of us living there. If you sneezed, you could hear it in the other room. My Aunt Darlene, lived two houses down and Ma's sister Helene lived up the street. One night when Aunt Darlene and her husband were fighting, all the kids busted down the screen door and ran to Ma's house. That's how close they lived from one another. I guess it was convenient that all my family lived on the same street that way the dysfunction could continue as normal.

During this grieving stage, we sat in that tiny house listening to music all day. The music brought some comfort to us all. I remember my aunt being extremely sad. She cried all day, so we went to Ma's house to give her space.

During this time, I was a second grader and Ms. Cindy Mann was my teacher. I loved Ms. Mann—she was so sweet. I loved music. She introduced this black kid to James Taylor. The class would sing "Short People Got No Reason to Live" and "Shower the People You Love with Love." It was a long way from "Ain't that a Bitch" the song Edwin taught me. Ms. Mann would record the entire class singing because she wanted her mother to hear it. As it turned out, my voice was the loudest on the recording so it was suggested that the class redo the recording and that I sit in the back. After the second recording, Ms. Mann told me I was still the loudest one singing. She took a special liking to me and asked my aunt if I could spend the night at her house. My uncle had recently died and I believe my aunt allowed me to go because she was overwhelmed. I wasn't allowed to tell any of the other kids. I went to Ms. Mann's apartment and I loved it. I didn't want to go back home. She invited her brother over to eat with us and we went swimming in her pool.

Later that night, as we were getting ready for bed, we were in her bathroom when Ms. Mann asked about my hair. She had a picture of my class and noticed my hair was different. *You may be asking yourself, "What's different?"* Because we went swimming, my hair was not the same as in the photo. Ms. Mann asked, "How did you get your hair to look like the picture?" I proudly traumatized her by telling about the pressing comb. I explained to her that it was a metal comb that you put on the stove in the fire and then put it in your hair. She was shocked. For black people, that's what we did. We put a flaming hot comb in our hair to straighten it out, still do.

As Ms. Mann stood behind me in the bathroom, she put some brown cream on her face. I smiled because she looked like me. She then told me, "I wish I could look like you." *I believed she loved me.*

The last memory I have of Ms. Mann is when I went to summer camp with her. At the end of camp, I remember sitting on her lap and she was crying. She told me she would miss me. At first, I didn't understand. She explained she would not be coming back to the school. As Ms. Mann cried, she put a ring on my finger. It had the initial M on it. Ms. Mann told me she never wanted me to forget her. I left for home sad that day never to see Ms. Mann again. When I returned home, I lost her ring at Aunt JoJo's house. I looked for the ring the entire time I was at her house. I never found it. I was sad. I had now lost Ms. Mann twice. Funny, years later as a young adult, I went back to my aunt's house, still hoping to find that ring. Over the years, I tried to find Ms. Mann but never did. *Ms. Cindy Mann, after all, these years, I have never forgotten all the love that you showed me. I still love and think of you. Always have, always will.*

Chapter 5

Different Family, Same Dysfunction

Soon after my uncle's death, my aunt began dating again. We moved into a bigger house and shortly after, my aunt met my soon-to-be Uncle Jerome. I loved my uncle. He was my favorite. My aunt introduced him to us by saying, "If he ever does anything wrong, you tell me and he's out of here." Years later, I wanted to ask, did that statement count for her? Because she was stricter than my uncle. My aunt fussed and my uncle gave speeches. When Aunt Letty met Jerome, she had four girls all under the age of ten. He eventually moved in with us. Uncle Jerome loved his music. He had a singing group. His group sang in nightclubs. His friends would come over to practice. After they left for their gigs, my sister, cousin and I would imitate the group. As for Ma, she did not care for Uncle Jerome. I knew she loved my Uncle Bud. I wasn't sure if she didn't like Uncle Jerome because he had a mediocre job parking cars at the civic center or just because she was plain evil.

My uncle became very attached to my youngest cousin, Bebe. She was just a baby and she started calling him daddy. He treated her as if she was his daughter. He treated us all as if we were his kids. Ma was mad that Bebe called Uncle Jerome daddy. Every time we were at her house, she would ask Bebe who her father was. Bebe would say, "Jerome." Ma would go into a full rage explaining to her that Bud was her father. *Think about it, who would interrogate a baby? To answer that question quickly— Ma.* This happened off and on for some time.

On the weekends when Aunt Letty and Uncle Jerome went to the club, we stayed at Ma and Grandpa's house. Ma would have us get on the table and sing, "A Change is Gonna Come" by Sam Cooke. That was the family's anthem. Every girl was to know that song. As we sang, Ma drank and my grandfather shot dice with the boys.

We had a few characters in the family. My Granduncle Ray, Ma's younger brother, also lived in the house. He slept in the back room with my brother. The little room was small, dark and gloomy and reeked of pee. *Drunken pee.* When you entered that room, the smell of ammonia burned your nose hair. I often wondered how they both slept back there. Uncle Ray was a drunk. Whenever we came over he couldn't stand the noise. *I guess kids and hangovers didn't go together.* I remember that us grandkids had no respect for Ray. When he talked, he repeated himself. He would tell us to do certain things; we would mock him by repeating exactly what he said exactly how he had said it. I'm not sure if that was his speech or the pluck. *"What's pluck?"* Why that was his alcohol that he kept in a brown paper bag as if we didn't know what it was. Quite frankly, he wasn't trying to hide it. Every day he sat at the dining room table and drank his pluck.

In those days, folks loved to sit on the front porch. One of Ma's rules was you didn't sit on the porch and drink. I never understood that rule considering by the end of the night she would act a drunken plum fool and my aunts would have to tie her up. All the neighbors would witness her behavior. *I guess it was the principle. Go figure.*

This particular day my uncle decided he would sit on the porch, defying Ma, drinking his pluck. Ma didn't notice he was drinking because I was showing her my new green stamp book. I was telling her how I decided to collect stamps after a presentation in my classroom. As I was talking, she peeped out the door and saw my uncle sipping from his bag.

She went to the front door and told my uncle to get into the house because the neighbors could see him. I'm not sure if my uncle was tired of being bossed around or just plain drunk, but he slurred, "How can you talk? You're a drunk bitch." *Poor Ray.* Ma snatched my stamp book out of my hand and threw it at my uncle's feet. Uncle Ray had bad feet from a trucking accident. Ma then began to pick up cans off the porch that Ray had collected and threw them at his feet. He squealed, "Please stop!" To make matters worse, she had the nerve to whip him. *Yes, whip him.* My granduncle was a senior citizen still getting spanked by his older sister.

Ma could be a nice person sometimes, but by the end of the day, she was a different person...*a drunken person.* In the mornings, we would go to her house before school. She would be sipping coffee and eating her buttermilk cookies that came in a green bag. By the end of the day, she was cursing everybody out, my grandpa included.

Grandpa loved collecting guns, knives, cigarette lighters and diamond jewelry. He would sit at the dining room table and clean his items while Ma cussed away. One Saturday afternoon I was sitting at the dining room table watching my grandpa clean his cigarette lighters. As he was refilling them with lighter fluid, his hand caught on fire. I jumped up from the table and called Ma from the kitchen. She came to the door only to find grandpa still sitting at the table. He was slowly getting up. She began to yell to him that his hand was on fire as if he didn't know. Grandpa walked to the bathroom. As he shook his hand, the flames became bigger. We both followed while Ma yelled for him to hurry up. He was in no hurry; maybe he thought he would be consumed by the flames and wouldn't have to hear her mouth again. Surprisingly, he did not have a burn on his hand. The fire had burned on top of the lighter fluid. Grandpa was tough. I guess he had to be, to be married to Ma. Now don't get me wrong Ma was tough, too. *You ask how tough?*

Sometimes, when Sandi and I went to her house, we would take care of her wounds. *You're asking if she fell and hurt herself? Oh no!* The wounds we nursed did not come from having an accident like most elderly people. These were "Crazy Bee" wounds. There were days that Ma got drunk and transformed into Bee. When this happened, she would fight with my aunts. One night, Ma was fighting with my aunts and Sandi and I ran out the side door. Right behind us, my aunts managed to get Ma to the side door and pushed her out. Ma took her hand and punched out the small window near the door she was thrown out of. Later that night, we had to pick glass from her hand. She never went to the hospital. *Sadly, I never thought of it as dysfunctional until much later. Weren't all grandmas like that—cursing, kicking and screaming? Weren't all grandkids having a good time smoking and drinking with their grandmother?*

Although anything could happen at my grandparents' house, we wanted nothing more than to go there. After school, our time was split between going to Wanda Mike's Day Care Center and Ma's house. We asked Aunt Letty if we could stop going to the center. We wanted to be at Ma's house; that's where all the action was. Aunt Letty told us she would talk with my father because he was paying for us to go there.

I had a couple of reasons why I did not want to go anymore. One, I thought I was too big and two I stayed in trouble. While attending the daycare center I had plenty of fights and I bullied lots of kids. I had a particular person that I bullied. Her name was Tasha. My family believed in fighting and not bullying, but I did both. Although fighting was my main gig, I was also in the extortion business. I was in the first grade when I decided that I could get material goods out of the people I bullied. I had Tasha bringing me jewelry and money. *Mind you, it was only a few quarters and costume jewelry but, in my day, a few quarters went a long way.* Tasha brought what she could and I went home and lied about where I got it. I told Aunt Letty that a friend gave me the jewelry. My situation was strange. I was a bully, but didn't want to see other kids bullied, except the ones I bullied. *I thought that would give you a mind bender.*

There is one person from the center that has stuck in my head after all these years. Her name was Debra Rae and we had a strange "mean girl" relationship before the "mean girl" concept began. Every day that I came to the daycare center I would take Debra Rae into the boy's bathroom and beat her up. She would hang with me at the center and did as I said. At the end of the day, my sister and I would leave the center to walk to Ma's house. Debra Rae would come out running across the play yard to the gate and, as I was walking, she would start cursing. She would kick the gate and call me names. She would tell me she was going to beat me up tomorrow. I couldn't believe it. *Didn't I just beat you up this morning?* I would be furious. Debra Rae knew I couldn't get to her because she was safe behind the gate. I guess she was saying all the things she couldn't while I was punching her in the face.

As she cursed, I began to cry. *You ask, why cry? Didn't I win the morning fight? Didn't I have the belt for winning the most daycare fights in the boys' bathroom? Was my title not undisputed?* I cried because I had rage and now the gate separated us, putting restrictions on me. In plain and simple terms, I couldn't get to her. I cried all the way to Ma's house. My sister asked, "Why are you crying? Didn't you already beat the girl up?" It wasn't enough and when I got to Ma's house, I cried myself to sleep. All I thought about was how I was going to beat her up the next day. *What did Debra Rae do that I wanted to get her back so badly? Well, she had the nerve to make me control myself. Or, might I say, the situation made me control myself. In my mind, that, in and of itself, was a reason to get her. I don't believe I was even angry about her calling me names.*

The next morning like clockwork, when I showed up at the center I made it my business to find Debra Rae. I took her in the boys' bathroom and the rematch was on. To be honest, it was never a rematch—she wasn't a real fighter. I gave her a chance to get a belt that I knew she had no skills to retrieve. I was a more experienced fighter. After all, I was being beat at home, so to fight someone a little bigger than me was cake. *The funny thing about our strange relationship was she wouldn't stop tormenting me and I wouldn't stop beating her up.* This went on until I left the daycare center.

Later in life, I would call certain situations the "Debra Rae." The "Debra Rae" translates to the following, when someone talks trash and acts like they want to fight until you catch them from behind the gate and you find out that they really don't. The "Debra Rae" represented situations that I could not control. I had uncontrolled anger, and when I couldn't act on it, I would rage all the more. As an adult, I have walked away from Debra Rae situations and I cried, literally.

I learned there were gates in life that separated me from the "Debra Rae" scenarios and I wasn't happy. Debra Rae showed that at an early age, I had problems accepting the fact that sometimes you just had to walk away and work situations out peacefully. I did not know how to deal with all the anger and hostility. I did not know how to walk away, so I let it out. I did not hold my anger in, to my own detriment. I have had many fights where I was scared to death and had the opportunity to walk away, but didn't. I fought anyway.

I was unsuccessful in dealing with the Debra Rae scenarios so, in turn, I began gate hopping. I no longer waited for a situation to present itself again. I went over the gates. I crossed many boundaries and got into situations that I could have avoided. Later on, when I joined my gang, hopping gates proved to be an excellent skill. *Did I say, gang?*

While at the daycare, I was frequently sent to the principal's office. I always thought Miss Cooper didn't like kids or that she was mean or maybe she just didn't like me. I had a teacher that was very nice named Ms. Rene. She worked in my room, the yellow room. I must have been having a bad day when I decided at the age of seven to call Ms. Rene a bitch. She asked me what I said and I said it again. Ms. Rene called my aunt. When I got home that butt warrant was waiting for me. I got the whipping of my life. But, even after the whipping, I wasn't sorry. That night my aunt gave my sister specific instructions. Sandi was to march me to Ms. Rene and I was supposed to apologize. The next day my sister took me to Ms. Rene. As Ms. Rene was putting supplies into the cabinet my sister told me to say I was sorry. I stood with my arms crossed, mad. I wasn't sorry. My sister threatened to tell my aunt if I didn't apologize. I apologized.

As I walked away, I simply said, "Bitch."

Ms. Rene turned from the cabinet "What did you say?

Sandi nervously said, "Nothing."

I believe my sister heard exactly what I said. She never told my aunt.

After tireless asking, we were finally released from the daycare. We were free and, on our way out, we had a family fight. There was a family of five girls. For some reason, I didn't get along with the two my age. They were twins. Maybe it was the fact that I fought with everyone my age. Tension had been building between us. On our last day, my brothers decided to come to the center to walk with us and the family fight was on. I fought both twins while each of my siblings fought a sibling. We were way more experienced in the violence department. We kicked their butts and we were proud. As we walked to Ma's house happy and thinking no one can mess with us, Ma came on the front porch irritated, "The daycare just called. Every last one of you have to go back." Our victory was short lived since we had to return to the center to answer for our barbaric behavior. After the center's interrogation of what happened, we went back to Ma's house. When we returned her first question, was "Who won?" And, of course, we proudly exclaimed in unison, "We did!" We were never punished for fighting. My family had the "Ghetto Fight Policy." It stated that if someone hits you, you better hit them back or your butt is in trouble when you get home. So, in other words, if you don't fight in the streets you would have one by the time you made it home. *There was no conflict resolution; you didn't walk away; you resolved it with your fist, and they didn't want to hear about you losing.*

It's strange; my family had other crazy policies. For example, if we went to a relative's house, we were not supposed to ask for or accept food. If a family member offered food, we were trained to say no. There were times when I went to my aunt's house and she asked if I wanted food. As my stomach growled, I replied, "I'm not hungry." Aunt Letty would give me the evil eye. *You ask, what's the evil eye? Well, that's the Mama stare that every mother has. One squint of the eyes and you knew if you moved or breathed wrong, you were going to get your butt whipped when you got home.* My Aunt Letty didn't have to say a word; I knew not to take any food. We broke that rule only once. It was during Easter break when my sister was watching my cousins and me. Before my aunt left for work, she gave specific instructions: don't go outside and don't hide eggs in her house. She didn't mention the "don't ask for food" policy. She didn't think she had to.

As the day progressed things were going really well. We baked a cake for Aunt Letty. We even had that Easter egg hunt she told us we couldn't have. We waited anxiously for Aunt Letty to come home. It was getting late and we were hungry. We decided to call my grandmother to see if Aunt Letty had stopped by her house. It was not unusual for her to stop there first because that was her routine. We told Ma we were hungry and she said she would bring food. Ma also said not to tell my aunt. She didn't have to remind us, we weren't crazy. We knew the "Family Food Policy."

We waited hoping Aunt Letty wouldn't beat Ma to our house. Ma and Aunt Darlene showed up with McDonalds. We were rescued. Ma told us to make sure to hide the wrappers. Just as Ma left, not 10 minutes passed when we heard my aunt coming through the door. We began to panic, we scattered like rats in a trashcan. We hid the food under our beds. Aunt Letty came in and immediately went to her room. We weren't sure how we were going to finish the food and that's when she came from her room with a belt. *What the heck? Was this chick psychic?* Aunt Letty stopped by Ma's house and the person they should've told not to say anything was my grandfather. Grandpa didn't know he was in on a secret mission. When Aunt Letty got there, he innocently told her we had called and said we were hungry and that Ma and Aunt Darlene had taken us food. That was the first time I saw my sister Sandi get a whipping from my aunt.

As we were sitting on our beds, my aunt came back into the room and said we could eat if we still had food. *How did she know? Maybe it was the smell of Happy Meals throughout our room.* We took our food from under the bed. Sandi was so upset she threw her food in the trash. McDonald's wasn't the only thing Aunt Letty would end up smelling. A couple of days after the food incident she noticed a bad odor. It was the eggs we hid. We left some behind the curtains in the living room. We got a whole week of punishment. *Some Easter break that turned out to be...*

We continued to live with my aunt until we noticed subtle changes. I believe the change was with us; we began to feel different. We were not her natural children. When we were younger, we had no clue. It wasn't until we got older that we noticed the obvious. "It's nothing," she said to me personally. But it was the look she had on her face. She was young. Was she tired of taking care of her dead sister's kids? After all, no one expects a 27-year-old mother to suddenly die. With the tension, we began to visit my father more often. He had moved into what was called "The Jungle." We did not know why it was called the jungle until we went to visit and a group of boys jumped my brothers and chased them home. It was one of the worst neighborhoods with every kind of dangerous animal you could find and that's why it was called "The Jungle." On one of our visits to my father's apartment, he wanted us to go to dinner. He said he had someone that wanted to meet us. My father took us to an Italian restaurant. His friend met us there with her daughter. Her name was Ann and she had a little girl named Beatrice. We kept staring because it was something wrong with the way Beatrice walked. Ann explained Beatrice was born with her intestine inside out and required surgery. We had no idea what that meant. Later on, we learned that Ann forgot to mention Beatrice was a drug-exposed baby. I guess Ann thought trying to explain to a 10 and 12-year-old that she was on and off crack cocaine for years would have been difficult. My father didn't introduce Ann as his girlfriend. While we were at his apartment, I noticed Ann was caressing his face. I knew then, I didn't like her. Not long after that, Ann became pregnant. I was angry, who was my father to have a baby? In my eyes, he was old and plus he had a thousand kids already. *Us!*

My dad and Ann moved into a house in Carson. When we went to visit he had a surprise. His daughter was born. *You noticed I said his daughter because she wasn't my sister. In fact, I hated her. Who can hate a baby? Me!* My sister Sandi sat on the couch and held her. I didn't want to see her let alone hold her. It was no secret I hated that baby. I told everyone I could. I told my sisters, cousins, and the rest of my family. My father knew not to leave me with his daughter or she may not be alive when he returned.

After my father's daughter was born, I had no interest in going to his house. So, he came and visited us.

My father wasn't the only one whose living situation changed. We moved to Hawthorne into a 3-bedroom apartment. We hated that apartment. It had nowhere for us to play, so unless we went to Ma's house we were stuck in the house all day. One afternoon Sandi was pressing our cousin Angel's hair in a chair in the kitchen right next to the stove. Angel nodded asleep and her hair went into the flames. I saw her hair begin to catch fire. I jumped up from the table and ran down the hallway to my aunt's rooms screaming, "Angel's hair is on fire!" My cousin came running down the hallway with her hair completely on fire. My aunt put her in the shower to put the flames out. I remember my cousin came home with all her hair shaved off and a burn on the top of her ear. It was almost the summer, so she did not have to go back to school. My sister and I did not know what to say or think. We already felt uncomfortable living there and now this had happened. It wasn't long before we moved back in with my father. By that time, he had moved into another apartment. Ann was no longer living with him. I was glad. Ann would be the sweetest person during the day and later that night she was tweaking. *What's tweaking? Tweaking is when someone is on crack co-caine, and they're paranoid and looking out of windows, looking on the floor for more dope and cleaning up until all hours of the night.* At that time, I didn't know what tweaking was, I just thought she was plain crazy. On top of her tweaking, she dressed provocatively. When my Aunt Helene called, I would tell her that Ann was a prostitute. My aunt loved to hear me say the word "prostitute" as she laughed over the phone. She would ask me to tell her the difference between a prostitute and a hoe? I would say, "A prostitute gets paid and a hoe gives it up for free." She thought it was the funniest thing coming out of the mouth of a kid. Ann would wear skin-tight disco pants, tube tops with no bra, super high heels and a bunch of makeup. She contradicted my father. He was a construction worker who got up at 5:00 a.m. to go to work and didn't drink or party. *Talk about the odd couple.*

I didn't have any respect for Ann. I didn't know her and to be quite honest I didn't know my father either. While we lived in this two-bedroom apartment, it never dawned on me that Ann didn't have her own baby, Sheri. Sheri and I were years apart and yet I hated her. *You ask why?* I watched my father treat her with love. *Wait a minute. Her mother is a hoe who is on drugs and you treat her nicely?* He was mean as hell and unloving to his wife's kids. The wife he claimed *we* killed. The wife he loved so much.

Chapter 6

Hello Hell

In the midst of moving back in with my father, the molesting started again. My brother let me know that he came back first, and technically my father took us back in because my aunt no longer wanted us. He would tease me that my aunt didn't want me in her house. *Hell, nobody wanted me.* Once again, we were left at home with my brothers for the summer. Edwin followed me and trapped me in the room. He would have me lay on the bed, pull his dick out and as he humped and grinded on me white stuff got all over my legs. I was disgusted and told him I didn't want to play house with him. He told me he forgot to use the bathroom and it was going to be all right. Every time he wanted to play house I told him I didn't want to play and I didn't like that nasty white stuff on my legs. He said the white stuff came out because he forgot to use the bathroom. He would say, "Alicia, I'm going to the bathroom so that white stuff won't come out." He would leave me in the room and go to the bathroom. I would just sit there hoping he didn't come back. *You know he came back.* His going to the bathroom didn't work because the white stuff still came out. After he was done, he would then peek out the room door and slide back into the living room like a snake. As if nothing happened. I just sat on the bed feeling nasty and dirty, not knowing if this white stuff was going to come off my legs.

I felt humiliated and shameful with no one to tell. When I would finally come out the room he would have the nerve to look at me as if I wronged him by showing my face. I would go into the bathroom to scrub that stuff off me.

Edwin made sure I knew he was the king of the house because my father left him in charge. On one of his days of bullying me, I stood up to him over the TV. He grabbed me by my arm and pushed me out the front door. When I tried to get back in, he opened the door and took a cup of water, poured it on top of my hair, and shoved me out of the doorway. I can't say how long he left me locked out of the house wet. I just stood outside. My sister didn't open the door either. That was his way of telling me he did what the hell he wanted because he was in charge. *I clearly had nowhere else to live, nowhere to go, and no one to talk to. I just existed, not even living.*

From time to time, Aunt JoJo would send letters and presents. During this time in my life, I needed hope and the letters provided it. I always wished JoJo was my mother. After I had taken the presents out of the boxes, I kept the boxes in my drawer. *Those empty boxes from JoJo meant the world to me.*

I loved everything about my aunt. She was gorgeous and I loved nothing more than going to her house in Altadena. She lived in a nice house with a fireplace and her dog, Rip. Rip was a German shepherd that had the nerve to understand German. Rip wasn't like the kind of dogs we were used to having. Our dog stayed tied on a chain in the back-yard never to see the likes of being walked. *Considering where we lived our dog wasn't safe no way.* Whenever we got on the 110 Freeway, we knew we were on our way to Jo's house. As we came through the tunnels, we were transported into the twilight zone. In the twilight zone a.k.a. Jo's neigh-borhood, she had white neighbors and no drunks hanging out. There were green trees and it was so quiet around 6:00 p.m., that you could hear the crickets. Where we stayed all you heard were people arguing and police or ambulance sirens.

Going to Jo's house was one of my most special events. I waited for the opportunity when we could go and just sit in front of the fireplace. It was always heartbreaking when I had to go home. When it was time to leave, I would pack my bags slowly as if that was going to prolong the inevitable. The car was always quiet as I took the trip back to reality. All I could do was hope to get back there as soon as possible

Once at Ma's house, Aunt JoJo came to visit. Happily, I sat with her on the couch. Unlike the other adults that made the children leave the room when they began to talk, she let me stay. She was talking with Ma and caressing my arm. I felt so special. I sat there thinking how I was being touched, and I kept telling myself I can trust her. In my mind, all I wanted to do was tell her. *She is the one that said look out for the stranger.* Finally, I called her name and when she answered me, my mouth couldn't move. I said nothing. I had her full attention and I couldn't get the words to come out. I didn't have the nerve to tell her that I was being touched. *After all, it was my fault, plus I was bad.* I looked up at her and told her I loved her, and she said it back. *After our, "I love you" exchange I slipped back into the black hole in my mind, in my life.*

Life went on in my father's apartment, and my brother continued to intimidate and rule his way. The kids in the neighborhood thought he was a king. My brother Edwin had the gift of gab, meaning he could talk his way into or out of just about anything. He could tell the biggest lies and have you believing it until you had to say to yourself, "Wait I was there and that's not what happened." He awed everyone in the neighborhood. Edwin had just turned 18 when my father decided to get him karate lessons. Let me tell you Edwin dressed the part. He had the full karate outfit and shoes to match. In my house, we all loved to watch karate movies. We would stay up until midnight waiting for them to come on TV. The funniest part was when the characters spoke their lips never matched what they said. We didn't care. We must have watched every movie from "Kung Fu Monkey" to "Enter the Dragon" with Bruce Lee. *By the way, did I mention that my brother Edwin thought he was Bruce Lee?*

One evening, Edwin was ruling the house when Curtis decided that was the night he was going to speak up. They were arguing over the bed. Because Curtis was a little slow; Edwin always took advantage of the situation with his mouth. As they were arguing, my father burst into the room and told them to take the fight to the streets. *Isn't that what any responsible parent would say?* Remember my family had that "Ghetto Fight Policy" in full force, so Bruce Lee and Curtis took it to the streets. As my brothers were arguing, the neighbors began to look out their windows. I knew what they were thinking; Curtis was about to get the Bruce Lee beat down of his life, after all, Edwin knew karate. They argued for a while and something surprising happened, Curtis got tired of being bullied, so Bruce Lee met Muhammad Ali for the first time. I tell you, it was a battle of cultures. *You asked me who won between Ali and Lee bout?* Well as Bruce was getting into his karate stance Muhammad punched with accuracy. By the time Bruce Lee went into another position, Muhammad had already punched again. Bruce tried to regroup and get his kick ready when Muhammad punched and punched some more. Muhammad was bigger, faster, and angrier. It could've been all those days of being harassed, but the Greatest was truly just that, at least, that night he was. Could you believe it a free pay-per-view fight in the middle of 92nd and Orchard Street? Muhammad won the belt that night. Every kid that could make it to their window watched free of charge. The neighborhood was shocked because my brother Edwin was held in high regard especially wearing that karate suit. Embarrassed Bruce went into the house. My brother Curtis was a little afraid because he did not know what my brother Edwin a.k.a., Bruce Lee was up to. And when Curtis went into the house he noticed his bed was made up, and he pulled back the covers and saw that Edwin had cut an extension cord leaving the wires exposed and had laid it on a wet towel under the cover and plugged it into the wall. Once Curtis saw the not-so-well-put-together booby trap, he decided to go and stay at my aunt's house for the night. My sister and I got on the phone and called everybody we knew. I dialed and she was in the background validating my account of history being made.

King Edwin had been dethroned for a brief time. Every kid on our block that could sneak on the phone was calling our house. They couldn't believe Curtis had beat Edwin up. Kathy from across the street said she had been trying to get through to our phone for over an hour. I guess it was busy from me calling my family members. After Bruce Lee's defeat, he was quiet for a few days, but it didn't last long as he was back to harassing Curtis and everybody else the next week. I never thought Curtis was physically scared of Edwin, but Edwin intimidated him with his mouth. You would think after that great karate defeat Bruce Lee wouldn't have a word to say; be it in Chinese or English, but, unfortunately, that wasn't the case. I tell you, it has been well over 30 years, and I still laugh when I think about the battle of Ali and Lee.

I'm not sure what happened, but the next day my father came home and said we had to live with my aunt until our house was ready. *Whatever that meant.* My father, Edwin and Curtis moved in with my Aunt Mae. Sandi and I moved in with my Aunt Darlene. Aunt Darlene had three kids of her own Tee 14, Earl 13, Christine 10 and my oldest sister Annette now lived there also. We all lived in my grandmother's three-bedroom, one bathroom house, and now my grandfather lived in the back house. We stayed with Aunt Darlene waiting for our house to get ready. We still were not sure what my father meant. He didn't talk to us kids; we weren't real people. I was about to graduate from the 6th grade. I was excited because I was going to go to Bethune Middle School with Sandi. Sandi was always a bit mature for her age and she did not want to hang with me. Living with Darlene, we found ourselves as indentured servants. My sister Annette was always cleaning and watching my cousins. My two cousins were in the 7th and 8th grade and they were already smoking cigarettes and doing drugs. They would steal my aunt's money, and everyone in the house knew they did it. After my aunt's money came up missing, she would make her usual public announcement that if her money did not come back she was going to put everyone out except her daughter, Christine. When she made her announcements I would think in my head, *"Lady, you know your badass kids have your money."* But, I couldn't say it YET...

My cousins were trifling. When my sister Annette went to sleep my cousin Earl tried to go in her bra and take her money. Annette had a job as a teenager and had to resort to keeping her money in her bra like an old lady. That was the only way they were not going to get it. Tee and Earl made us feel bad for living with their mother. Their favorite phrases were "Your daddy did not want y'all" and "Y'all here with my mama."

My cousins Earl and Tee took advantage of this, too. Both of my cousins started molesting me. They started by making me feel as if my aunt was going to put my sister and me out, and we wouldn't have any place to go. I often wondered if they touched Sandi. I would not dare to ask, after all, Tee was her best friend. I was 12 going to the 7th grade, and I was not fully developed. In the black culture, girls at that age were full and developed, at least, my two sisters were. So my cousins teased me about being skinny and flat chested and, as a result, it ended in them touching me and relentlessly sucking all over my body. There were times I had marks and I did not want anyone to see them or question me about being with a boy when I hadn't. One morning after I came out of the bathroom stuffing my bra with tissue, my cousin began teasing me. I walked away embarrassed because it was stuffed because both my cousins had me in the room at one time, and they had sucked my breasts so hard they had swollen up and one was more swollen than the other. The odd part about what was happening when they touched me sexually I didn't fight back. But if they touched me physically I would. Maybe this was because I didn't think I was worth much. After all, my own brother had been touching me for as long as I could remember.

My grandmother told us if someone hits you, you better hit them back or else you're going to get beat. She never said if someone touched you, you better fight back. She taught me how to fight physically, but not mentally. My brother was older and bigger and even when he hit me I hit back, but I did not fight back when it came to being touched. I would never let anyone hit me without a fight. Earl and I fought all the time.

After every fight, my aunt would kindly tell me how mannish I was and that I was always starting fights, not that her son was bigger, older and hit girls. My aunt and her kids did not want us there. We felt the same. The tension in the house was rising and it was only a matter of time before a civil war broke out.

I approached my last field trip of the school year and I asked my sister if I could use her Polaroid camera. I bought film and was ready for my trip. *I told you war was in the air.* When Tee saw I had the camera he tried to take it and I refused. He told me it was his I told him he wasn't going to get it, plus he was probably going to sell it for drugs like he did everything else.

We kept arguing until I went into the room and got Annette. She would settle the argument. As Annette stood her ground, the argument escalated and Tee became angrier. Tee attempted to take the camera out of her hand, but he was not strong enough and Annette pushed him.

The civil war had officially started as he yelled from the top of his lungs, "That's why your Mama is a dead bitch!"

Before I could blink, Annette took a full swing and socked him in the face knocking him out. Tee flew over the couch with his sister Christine yelling and crying. And of course, my mannish self told her, "Shut the hell up!"

As Tee was trying to gain consciousness he was rambling "Y'all jumped me. I'm going to tell my Mama y'all jumped me."

Sandi, who didn't fight, tried to help him. He kept insisting the troops ambushed him, so what did we do? Just that, Annette and I jumped him. Annette was beating him as he tried to pin her to the floor when she bit a plug out of his stomach. Tee was screaming for help. As he was screaming, I was socking him in the head. Earl tried to get in it, but he saw that I had Annette fighting with me, so he did the next best thing and just stood there. Christine went and got grandpa. As we were on the floor tussling, kicking, scratching and biting grandpa came into the room from the back door with no shoes, no shirt, a pair of pants, and a gun in his hand. All I recall him saying was "stop this shit now!" The sad part was we weren't afraid of the gun. We only stopped because we loved and respected grandpa. We got off the floor still locked to one another like 3 pitbull dogs and my grandpa pulled us apart. As grandpa was talking to Annette, my cousin got his BB gun and pointed at us. Grandpa took the BB gun from Tee. We went to the neighbor Ms. Gloria's house. We both knew we couldn't live there long especially after Aunt Darlene found out we beat up her son. When Aunt Darlene came home it was hell to pay for all three of us jumping Tee. At least, that was his recollection. She tried to make us feel bad. *I had dreamed about him getting his ass whipped, I was happy.*

Aunt Darlene's guilt trip worked on Annette. Even as a teenager she was a faithful churchgoer. She tried to be the peacekeeper in our unfortunate situation. Maybe it was because she had the understanding that we had nowhere else to go. In fact, one of my most memorable moments was Annette dragging me to church with her. Annette was attending Vacation Bible School and she asked if I would go with her, and I had agreed. That was until she jacked up my hair on the day we were supposed to go, so I refused. Well, my good old aunt told me I had to go because I said I was going. *As if she cared if I knew Jesus.* I got into Annette's car with angry tears streaming down my face, *Yes, all this because I didn't want to go to church.* When we got there, I refused to get out of her car. Annette told me she was locking her car and I could not sit in it. I got out and we walked up to the church. I told her, "You can't make me go in." I kept my word. I stood in the front of the church looking like the Tasmanian devil, hair a mess, tears flowing, with my arms folded in protest. Everyone that passed by me got a mean look.

I'm not sure how long I was out there, but the lesson had already started and I was still refusing to come in. Papa, the Pastor of the church, came out and approached me. Papa did not ask me to go in bible study, but to work. *Yes, I said work.* He asked a 12-year-old to come in to handle some work he needed done. I followed this nice stranger into his office. He had me sit at his desk and handed me the church's checkbook and a list of names and amounts. Papa stated he needed me to do the payroll for vacation bible study. *How Papa knew a 12-year-old could fill out checks, I don't know.* After church, Annette was looking for me. She probably thought I ran off. Annette came to Papa's office to find me smiling and completing my work. She could have passed out. After that, Annette never had to drag me to church again. I completed Vacation Bible School. *The scripture that I learned from Vacation Bible School was, "Come follow me and I will make you fishers of men."*

Chapter 7

Birth of a New Family

Eventually, my father found a house on 85th between Figueroa and Hoover, and it was time to move back in with him. The house had two bedrooms and one bathroom, so it was ok. Sandi and I were excited that we were going to have a room. That was until my father decided his boys were more important and gave them the room. My father put a bed in the dining room for us and that's where we slept. When my Aunt Mae came by to see the house she told my father that his living set up was crazy and that girls needed their privacy. But everybody knew my brother Edwin was his favorite, and there was no way in the world he was going to let his favorite son sleep in the dining room.

Of course, once we moved back with our father, it was a different house but the same situation. The molestation began, again. My brother began stalking me. He would follow me around the house, kind of like a lion following a deer, waiting for the deer to make a crucial mistake. Sandi began watching me, and she noticed it. She would always ask me where was I going? How long was I going to be gone? Little did I know she was watching out for me because she knew something wasn't right. Right before we moved out from my aunt's house, I overheard a conversation between her and my cousin Tee as they were walking home from school. I heard her tell Tee that my brother had been touching her. Tee told her that my brother had also tried to touch him, and he declined and that he called my brother tutti-frutti. Looking back, Tee was actually disgusted. That's ironic considering he was touching family members himself. But I guess it was no harm since we were girls in his sick mind. The more they talked the more I tried to listen and the faster they walked. Finally, my sister turned around, "What do you want?"

"Nothing," I said, trying to play it off. I believe she knew I was listening, so they didn't finish the conversation. However, later on, it led to her protecting me. She did the best she could.

One of the first incidents that happened at our new house was that as I was going to the back yard to the garage my brother followed me outside. "Alicia, what are you looking for?" he said in a nice, calm and creepy voice. I did not answer because I knew in my heart what he really wanted. He was not interested in helping me. He grabbed my hand and said, "Alicia, this is going to be the last time. I promise." I was 12 and he was 17 and all I was thinking was if I do this one last time he will leave me alone forever. He told me to get into my father's old pickup truck. He molested me there.

I remember laying on the front seat with the same thing happening. That white stuff on my legs and now on my vagina. I still didn't know what it was. I went to wipe it off and he yelled out, "No, you can get pregnant!" I had no idea what he was talking about. I asked, "Pregnant?" I had no idea how you got pregnant. I did not have the birds and bees talk with anyone. Where I came from the streets taught the birds and bees. As of that day, I hadn't had my formal lesson. I got out of the truck disgusted as I went back in the house. When I came to the door Sandi was waiting and the first thing she asked, "Where were you?" As I began to lie she told me she had been looking everywhere for me.

Scared and nervous, I told her "Down the street with Tina."

"I already called Tina's house. You weren't there."

"I went to the store."

"The store was closed," she replied impatiently.

After I ran out of lies, I stood there nervously. She was like my mother and I did not want her to be mad at me. Somehow, in my heart, I knew she knew but I was too scared and embarrassed to tell her. I was too ashamed because I didn't say no again.

"Don't you go anywhere by yourself ever again. Now, get in the house."

With my head down, I shamefully walked in the house. Right when I got in, my brother came through the door behind me. I watched her give him a look that said *I know what you did*. From that day on, she did her best to cover me.

Unfortunately, Sandi couldn't always protect me. One day while everyone was gone; Edwin was on the phone with Tina from down the street. She was now his girlfriend. I thought *since he has a girlfriend he will leave me alone*. As I walked into the kitchen, he hung up the phone and followed me. He bumped up against me like it was an accident. He then trapped me against the wall. I want to go down on you. *What does that mean? I thought this was over.*

He quickly pulled my pants down and started kissing my vagina. I stood against the wall thinking *yuckkkk!* He asked, "Do you like it?"

I said, "No."

He asked me again, "Does it feel good?"

Again, I said, "No!" *Was he really expecting me to change my mind?*

After he saw that I was not moving and scared that someone would walk in, he pulled down his pants. "Kiss me down there," he suggested.

I looked at him and said, "I don't want to."

He started rubbing my leg and he grabbed my hand. He said, "It's ok, it's the last time."

I got on my knees. He pulled his dick out and put it in my face. I wouldn't touch it. He angrily hissed, "Stop playing." He grabbed me by the back of my neck to guide my head. I still refused.

Was I less willing because I was older or just scared someone would walk in? I can't say. That was the last time he touched me. You ask me if he stopped trying?

Oh no. There were many times he had that look on his face. But, there was a new look I had on my face, I was no longer nervous or scared.

I was running with a new crowd. We fought and robbed. *Did he see my transformation?* One day while his girlfriend Tina was over, I came in and sat on the couch.

He hissed, "Don't sit so hard on the couch."

I told him "I do what the hell I want to do."

He yelled, "Sit on the couch like that again, I'll hit you."

So, I intentionally got up, then sat down hard. He politely got up off the couch, picked me up and slammed me onto the floor. I got up, socked him in the chest and sat back on the couch harder. He picked me up again and threw me to the floor. I got back up, socked him in the chest then sat on the couch even harder. This went on until Tina couldn't take anymore. "Stop throwing her on the floor!" Although I couldn't win, I wouldn't stop fighting back. That day was the last day he had put his hands on me physically or sexually. *Damn it, I had morphed. I was mean as hell, mad, angry, vengeful and bitter. And he knew it.*

During this time, I was ending the 7th grade and summer had come. I had new friends on my street and we all played baseball in the large empty field across the street. Those baseball games brought everyone outside. Another game we liked playing was called hooker fights. We went to the corner, mostly on Friday nights, to watch the hookers fist fight over who was going to stand on the corner. We loved to watch the hookers fight over the corner because that usually meant money and jewelry would fall to the ground. Like scavengers, we picked up whatever fell. *You asked did I say that? YES, I did.* We lived on 85th off Figueroa -- the hooker capital of the area. When it rained, the hookers wore bathing suits and raincoats.

I never thought the hooker game would be played in my house. One day I was sitting in the living room with my neighbor Lamont when my father walked in. Nothing was strange about the time because he worked at night in security. This time, there was someone behind him.

She wasn't crazy Ann. She was a prostitute. *What the hell?* My father had picked up a prostitute on his way in from work.

As she followed him to his bedroom, he politely turned to Lamont and me and said, "Hey, I want you guys to meet Peaches." *Peaches?* I thought I was going to die from embarrassment. He walked her to his room to handle business. I sat there in shock.

Lamont looked at me and in a soft voice said, "Imma go home Licia." I nodded in agreement. That was not the last time my father would bring a prostitute home as if he was on a casual date.

I tried not to be in the house. I usually just hung out down the street at Tina's house. As a matter of fact, all the kids hung out at Tina's house. I didn't want to be home, between the molester and my father bringing his regular prostitutes home-- it was crazy.

Once school started back, I was hanging tough with the homies known as the Hoovers. The majority of us grew up together and went to Loren Miller Elementary School. We started claiming the set then. I started claiming Hoover right after 6th grade. Some of the most unlikely kids started bangin. From the fat kid that was teased to some of the nerds; I guess everyone was looking to belong somewhere. We had a crew that went to Bethune Middle School. The only problem with this was that our gang was in the enemy's neighborhood. It was in middle school that I got my name Babyface. I was first called Babyface by Devance a.k.a. Green Eyes. I hated that name and I hated looking young. It brought him no better joy than to tease me with the song "Baby Face." I didn't want the cute baby face because I was tough. Or so I thought. School wasn't on the top of my priority list, but I went. I had many fights at school and got into lots of trouble. My dad always had to come pick me up. I had no respect for my father. Why would I stop fighting? He didn't care about me and if he did, he didn't show it. My father just housed us—no emotion and no love. One weekend I was outside playing tag with the neighbor Lamont. While trying to get away, I ran across a hole that I thought was flat ground. I heard something snap. I couldn't move my leg anymore and horrible pains shot up my leg. The next morning, when it was time to go to school, my leg was swollen and I could not walk. I asked my father to take me to the doctor. He replied, "You and your siblings planned to hurt your knee so you wouldn't have to go to school. You're going to school." *Was this man on drugs? What siblings? They were all older than I was. They weren't outside playing tag.* I was in so much pain and my knee was so swollen it wouldn't bend. He still refused to take me to the doctor. His fatherly advice, "Go to school and next time don't injure yourself to stay home." *Ok, I'm going to say it again-- was this man on drugs?*

So that morning in pain with tears rolling down my face, my father watched as I limped out the house with the help of my sister. I limped to the bus stop and caught the bus to my aunt's house. *Did she know I was there, No!* Her son Tee ditched every day and we all knew it. So I went there for the day. Sandi came and got me after school to help me home. This went on for about a week until my Aunt JoJo heard about it. Jo called the school and told them my father was neglecting me. The school contacted my father. He had two options, take me to the doctor or get into trouble. He took me to the doctor. I had fractured my patella. On the way home from the doctor he angrily said, "I never said your knee wasn't hurt. I knew you did it on purpose." *Ok, last time was this man on drugs?*

My father did not take care of the needs of his daughters. As young girls, he showed us no affection or emotion. We never had the birds and bees talk. When I started to develop, I sent my sister Sandi to ask him to buy me a bra. He looked at her, laughed and said, "For what?" Hurt and embarrassed I wouldn't dare ask for personal products. *Thinking back, if it wasn't for the fact that I was trying to ditch school, I don't know how I would've handled my menstrual cycle.*

I went to school and was trying to get out, so I went to the nurse with a fake stomachache. The nurse called my father. His rule was— the only way we could stay home was if you were sick. But, we had to go to school sick and the nurse had to send us back home. *You got that right; we had to leave home, go to school sick and then we could stay home. Yes, I know your brain*

hurts from that logic. You can imagine my headache. Just take a break, put the book down and shake your head. Ok like I was saying. I told the nurse I was sick and she called Aunt JoJo. As I sat in the office waiting to be picked up, I was so excited. We always went to eat and I enjoyed her company. When Aunt Jo arrived at the school, I was happy to see her. I got into her nice car and as she was driving, we took a detour. *Where was she going?* She pulled into Thrifty's drug store. *I'm about to get ice cream. Nothing was better for an ailing stomach then Thrifty's ice cream.* When we went in, she took me down an unfamiliar aisle. *What's this? Stayfree maxi pads, tampons and vaginal wipes.* I began screaming in my head. *This isn't ICE CREAM!* My Aunt JoJo thought I had come of age. All I wanted to do was ditch school and stay home. Aunt Jo piled the counter with pads, women's vaginal wipes, and panty liners. I was looking around hoping no one I knew would see me. She then gave a 50-hour talk about how to use pads. *LADY WHERE'S THE ICE CREAM!*

My day was gone and I still didn't get any ice cream. She dropped me off with my brown bag and a smile. *Lady, do you really think you did something for me?* I just wanted to skip school in peace, watch He-Man and Boy George and Michael Jackson music videos. A perfectly good ditch day was ruined. The next day when I returned to school, my sister Sandi's friend, Tee Tee approached me with a huge smile on her face and said, "Congratulations." I looked at her like I didn't know what she was talking about. She said it again with a smile on her face, "Congratulations." Once again, I acted dumb. She said, "Nevermind" as she walked off frustrated. I guess she wanted to welcome me into the tribe of the girls with periods and celebrate with tampon stories. I knew what she was talking about, but I was not a member of the Kotex club. I knew my sister told her. So much for trying to ditch. At least, that time some good came from it, because I would have never asked my father for tampons.

I also tried to ditch, because as Hoovers we were surrounded by our enemies. At Bethune my little crew had to stick together. My crew was Lisa, Poo, Lady, Skinny, Kitty and Donald. I started carrying a knife to school because we were outnumbered by our gang's enemy the EC's. Up until this point, I had never carried a knife before, but I was ready to use it.

In that year, I had another transition. That year I met Birdie. Her real name was Felicia. She was a light-skinned, pretty girl that everybody seemed to respect and fear. I didn't know her. People began to tell me she was from my same gang, but a different set. They were also saying she was one bad chick and she could fight like a dude. Looking at her, I couldn't see it. Birdie was a beautiful girl, no rough edges. I had the honor of witnessing her skills first hand in the cafeteria. I watched her beat up a bigger girl named Sherelle.

At lunch one day she asked, "Where do you live?"

"I live on 85th but I am from 74(Seven-Foe)."

"Why do you claim 74(Seven-Foe)?"

"My family grew up in 4(Foe) Hood and we had just moved in the 80's."

"Well you should be from 83 (Eight-Tray), cause that's where you live." We instantly became friends. Not long after I started, claiming Eight Tray and we began to walk home together.

The girls in the neighborhood knew even if Birdie didn't win, that chick would fight you head up, one-on-one until she did. What made people afraid of her was the fact she was not afraid to lose. If she was afraid we never knew it. As time went on the homies had names to distinguish Felicia from Alicia. They called her Fatal and me Crazy.

Years later that fight or die spirit cost her, her life. Birdie had a younger boyfriend that she would beat up all the time. One day he told her that the next time she beat him he would kill her. No one took him seriously. He was 16 and he was not from our hood long. Unfortunately, he kept his word. He shot Birdie, she was pregnant and when she was killed, she left three kids behind. Birdie was 23.

Summer was coming and this was the time that I would go and stay with Aunt Mae so I could be with my cousin Denise. The thing about this was she lived in Blood hood. Bloods and Crips were enemy's. My cousins knew I was a Crip and they were Bloods. My cousin Denise and

I would sit on the corner and sell weed. She introduced me to selling drugs when I was 12. I wore a black headscarf tied around my head. My cousin Ronnie said I was going to get killed because I was wearing it. I did not see anything wrong. I wasn't disrespecting his hood because my rag was black, not blue, but in his eyes, anything that wasn't red was disrespectful.

That was the last summer I went to stay there. I stopped asking to go to my aunt's house because I was running tough with my crew. Also going to my aunt's house was also starting to be a problem. When I got back home, one of the lil homies brought it to the big homies attention that I was hanging in Blood hood. They wanted to know what was up? I also never wore red or burgundy. When I came back from my aunt's that summer she had bought me a burgundy vest. When I wore it, a lil homie started questioning my loyalty. You know there was always a messy person in the crew, and in our crew, it was Lil Moe. *Funny Lil Moe's girl Dawn wore red, burgundy, or any other color she wanted. But this was off limits for those of us who claimed to be frontline soldiers.* Lil Moe had the homies mad at me. One homie warned me, "Homegirl be careful, watch your back. That's all I can tell you." About a week later, my homie Lil C asked me to walk to the 74 (Seven-Foe) hood with him. I didn't think anything of it. We always mobbed together. That day something was different as we were walking he kept taking strange cuts. Cuts are routes in our hood that no one knew about except those that lived there. We were taking new alley routes. As we were walking down the alley, he kept looking around as if he was making sure no one saw us. Lil C then started holding my hand as if he was leading me somewhere. That's when it dawned on me. He was looking for a spot to take me to rape me.

Once I figured that out, I played it off. I told him, "I need to stop by my Aunt's on 76th street." I went into her house my heart was beating fast. *Ain't this some shit? This fool is trying to get me.* I stayed in the house for a while. I came back out and told him, "My Aunt won't let me come back outside." Lil C said, "I'll wait." He waited outside for a while. When he saw I wasn't coming back out; he finally left. The next day, my cousin confided in me that Lil C was going to rape me and he was suspicious over who could have warned me. I never brought the subject up and I never went anywhere with him again or trusted him for that matter.

Things kept escalating in my hood over my loyalty, so I stopped going to my aunt's house. Not that I was scared, but I wanted my hood more than my family, after all, my hood was my family.

In my house, things were tense and my father was angrier. He was mad about everything. *The funny thing about my father was his thinking was stupid and it only made sense to him.* I was playing in the house with Lamont when we broke our large window in the living room. I knew I was going to get beat. Lamont sat and waited with me to explain to my father what happened. *As if that was going to help.* When my father showed up, we explained what happened. He wasn't mad, no whipping. A few weeks later Sandi and I were bringing groceries in the house when I dropped a jar of spaghetti sauce. He cussed me out. *Window, jar of spaghetti sauce; go figure.* The same night my sister cut her ankle on the trash bag with the broken spaghetti jar. I don't know what happened to spark his anger; it may have been the fact he would have to take her to the doctor. When I came back into the kitchen, he had my sister cornered against the kitchen counter slapping her unmercifully as she tried to cover her face.

After that, we went to spend the night at Tina's house. Her mother Joannie agreed that we could stay for a couple of days until things settled down. We went back home, but unfortunately, that would not be the last of my father's rage. The last and final beating that pushed us out of my father's house went like this—we had a broken sink in the bathroom that wasn't fastened to the wall correctly. The night before school I sat on the sink to look in the mirror doing my hair and wouldn't you know it the sink fell. *Mind you I didn't even weigh 80 pounds.* When it hit the floor, I just stood there, and as I looked at the sink, my father heard the noise. He came running into the bathroom in a full rage. He didn't even give me a chance to explain what happened. He snatched me by my blouse, drug me into the living room, slammed me on the floor and started beating me. I tried to cover my face and hold him off, but I couldn't.

I tried to kick so he wouldn't beat me anymore, but he pushed my legs over my head and put his weight on me. Not only could I not kick anymore, I couldn't breathe. The more I screamed, "I can't breathe!" The more he beat me. A million things went through my head…hate, rage, and helplessness. *Why did we come back? Was his sink more important than me? Did he ever want us after my mother died? Was he still angry that we killed his wife? Hadn't he forgiven us? We loved her, too.* As my mind was racing, I felt as if I was about to blackout. He snatched me up by my blouse, stood me to my feet to face him and hit me again. Just as he went to swing me back to the floor, he lost his grip, and just like my brother years before I ran out the door. I guess I finally had the courage that my brother had and that was to run and not just stand there and allow him to beat me. *Why was he beating me, anyway? For sitting on a broken sink that he didn't secure to a wall?* I finally had the courage to run and kept running. I ran down the street to Tina's house. *I was never going back home. I hated his guts.*

Later that evening he told my sister, Sandi, she could go as well. We both ended up staying at Tina's house. *Funny thing, he never told my two brothers to leave.* We stayed at Tina's house for about a week before her mother Joannie called Children's Services. Tina's house was already full with her family. There was definitely no room for us, so Children's Services came to pick us up. That day we cried as we hugged Tina. We didn't know where we were going or how long it would be before we saw her again. I wasn't concerned about seeing my family again, and since I was having trouble with my lil' homies about my Blood affiliations, maybe foster care wasn't that bad after all.

Chapter 8

Foster Care: Big Pimpin' Foster Mamas

The first foster home we arrived at was in San Bernardino with a white family. They were nice to us but, of course, I felt out of place. *You asked me was I out of place because of their lack of cultural sensitivity? Oh no, I was out of place because it was stability.* There were no police sirens, it was just plain old silent. Our mattress was not in the dining area of the house. I couldn't rip and run up and down the street. No gangs. No homies. It had always been Sandi and me, but it was really just the two of us now. It was summer, so we weren't in school. We stayed a little longer in that foster home because we refused to be separated. That made it more difficult to place two sibling, teen-aged girls. We didn't want to talk to our father. All I was thinking about was getting to the phone to call Aunt Jo. I was sure if I could call her she'd come get me. I knew she was a very busy flight attendant, but I was willing to behave. I guess I was trying to believe in my heart that maybe, after all, these years somebody wanted me-wanted us! That's what I held on to as we stayed with this family waiting to find out where we would go.

While we were at this foster home, I decided if I was going to live with Aunt Jo I had to get myself together. I was going to be a fashion designer.

When I told the foster mother, she bought me graph paper and my designing began. I drew prom dresses. After all I was a changed person and I was going to my prom. At this foster home we had a swimming pool. We didn't have to catch the bus to the public swimming pool and wait for my father's prostitute girlfriend to get us. Because our stay was longer than expected, the foster family took in another girl. Their adult son moved out of his room. I didn't want him to move out, he was cute. Our new girl did not speak English. She was already getting on my nerves. *You people ask so many questions. I hear you asking why? Was it because she could not communicate in English?* Although she didn't speak English well, she understood my sister's language of LOVE. I was angry because I began to notice my sister mothering her. *Hold up, wait a minute, we didn't know this chick.* I don't want to share my sister with her, so I politely gave her my rules, "Rule #1 - don't bug or become close with my sister. Rule #2 - don't touch my graphing paper. Rule #3 - follow the first two rules and you'll be alright."

My sister didn't care about any rules I gave, she gave me her same instructions that she'd given me all my young life, "Alicia be nice." I was more than willing to be nice if homegirl followed my rules. Of course, you know she didn't. It was a hot day and Sandi was in the pool. I didn't go swimming because I had to watch this new girl. She couldn't swim so she just sat around the pool, while my sister attempted to talk with her. I sat by the pool mad. She's breaking rule #1. Why was my sister fraternizing with my newly found enemy? Angry, I went to my room and sat on my bed. *What did I find?* Some of my graph paper was missing out of my designing book. I guess the new girl wanted to draw, too. That's all I needed to get her. She gave me a reason; she broke my made up rules. My sister couldn't save her from my wrath. I went outside, nice and calm but angry. The new girl was standing by the pool smiling trying to talk to my sister. I walked up slowly and asked her about my paper. She looked at me as if she didn't understand. I didn't give her time to figure it out. I kicked her in the pool, eight feet to be exact.

All I heard was a splash and Sandi screaming my name. The girl was screaming, too. Sandi went into lifeguard mode and saved her. I was actually disappointed that she did not drown. As Sandi pulled her to the side of the pool to safety, she was saying, "You bitch! You bitch!" I didn't care that she was calling me a bitch in her broken English. I made my point. Poor Sandi gave me that mother's disappointed look. As if to say, when will I learn? In response to her look, my unremorseful attitude simply conveyed not anytime soon. Although I didn't want my sister to be disappointed, her look of disapproval was not having the same effect on me as before.

We stayed at that foster home until they found someone willing to take both of us. We went to Raylene Place in Pomona, California. *It's funny how to this day that is the only foster home address I remember.* When we pulled up in the front of the home it was beautiful. It did not look anything like where we lived. The yard was nice. There were no drug addicts or prostitutes on the corner. Our caseworker, Mr. Walker, walked into the home and introduced us to our foster mother. *When I saw her, my first thought was, ain't she too old to have kids?* He then gave the foster mother the scoop on us. Sandi was the good one and I was the bad one. As he spoke with her, we looked around in awe. Her home was immaculate. She had the most beautiful and clean furniture that we had ever seen. We hit the jackpot. The foster mother said her husband was not home and she called for her daughter Reina to come out and meet us. Reina came out of her bedroom, gave us a fake smile and a fake wave, and disappeared back into the hallway. The foster mother excused herself to go to her room. This was an ample time for Mr. Walker to give us his social worker pep talk. Just as soon as the foster mother was out of sight his smile turned into a stern look, he looked directly at me and said, "Keep your mouth shut. You should be glad that someone took you in."

Thank God for those caring social workers. This was the moment I decided I would never become a social worker. The foster mother came back into the room and wrapped up things with Mr. Walker. She said, "My name is Jeri. You can call me, Mama." All her foster kids called her Mama. Mama gave us a tour of her home. It had three bedrooms, two bathrooms, and a den. Mama said she did not do this, meaning taking foster kids in for the money, but out of the goodness of her heart.

The first room Sandi would share with another girl. *Wait, I thought we were going to be together?* Mama said she had made an exception and took the both of us in, so I had to share a room with her daughter Reina. I stood there. *Oh just great, I get the prison cell with the fake chick.* Sandi's new roommate name was Lenora. She was at work. Mama walked me to Reina's room, and she had already locked her door. Mama knocked, "Let Alicia in." She opened the door abruptly with a fake smile on her face. *Was she going to kill me in the middle of the night because she had to share her room with a foster girl? If she was going to try it, it was going to be all bad for her because I brought my "Ghetto Fight Policy" with me. Like American Express, I never left home without it.* Reina looked at me, "Well, come in." She had two beds in her room. It was clear the other bed had never been slept in. I put my stuff on the bed and hurried out to go back to the room with Sandi. Mama wanted to continue the tour of the house. She took us to the den, "This is where you can watch TV. You are not allowed in my living room. Don't sit on my furniture in there. Don't go into the refrigerator without asking." She then walked us to the garage to show us the deep freezer. Of course, it was locked. *Who locked food away from kids? Didn't she get paid to keep us? Oh, yeah, it was out of the goodness of her heart, no worries I would soon test that theory.*

Although she had confined us to certain parts of her house and locked up her food, she said something that caught my attention, she was going to be our Mama. She didn't even know me. She had my rap sheet from my parole officer, I mean social worker, Mr. Walker. It contained my felonies and convictions of bad behavior and she still wanted to be my Mama. *Are you kidding? Who cares about food and solitary confinement? Heck, lock the stove too, I had a Mama old and all.* At that point in my life, I was so wounded I was willing to take her mothering conditions. *FYI when an abused child lets you in right away that means that child is really hurt. Normally, the response is just the opposite. Be careful to keep your word and you'll have no problems.*

Later that night Lenora came home from work when she walked through the door Mama, met her and said "The new girls are here. Come introduce yourself." When Lenora came into the room we were surprised. Lenora was not black; she was Hispanic. I had never seen a black family caring for a Hispanic girl. Lenora kindly welcomed us. She called me "Lil Bit" because of my slim frame.

Mama told us, "My son Brandon lives next door with his wife, Roz. From time to time, he would be popping in to check on you." *Cool more family.* "You girls get acquainted," Mama instructed as she left the room.

Lenora then gave us the rundown of the house. The first thing she told us, "Never be alone with Mama's son Brandon. He's a pervert." She would not say why he was perverted, but I was listening because I had lived with plenty of perverts. She would never have to tell me twice. She then let us know, "Reina is a selfish brat. Stay out of her way, you'll be ok. I have a job so I can have more things, but mainly to stay out of this house. Out of the way. By the way, I'm happy that you're here. We'll go to the same school, Pomona High School."

Mama came back and peeked in to see how the prisoners were doing. She said, "Pops is home." I asked, "Who is Pops?" Lenora laughed, "That's Mama's husband." We went into the den to meet him. Pops was a tall, big, light-skinned man with green eyes as old as the Egyptian pyramids. Pops made Mama look like a 20-year-old.

Over the next few days, we became close with Lenora. I stayed in the room with her and Sandi until it was time to go to bed. Reina locked her door every day, so I had to stay in another part of the house until she returned home. Since Reina was 18, that meant she could return any time she wanted. She didn't come home at regular hours like the rest of us. I didn't mind because I sat in the den and watched the new TV channel that came out that was just for blacks, BET. One afternoon, I was sitting in the den when Mama, came in. She said she had something she wanted to show us. Mama pulled out her photo albums. She wanted to show us her former foster kids. When she opened the books, to tell us how she did this for love and not money, I could not help but notice the pictures were super old. *In the words of Janet Jackson, what had she done for foster kids lately?*

Mama showed pictures of her trips to Las Vegas. She proudly shared, "My foster daughter Deb still comes around." After she left the room, I looked at Sandi, "these pictures are old as hell." Before I could finish, she told me, "Be quiet." *Was she buying the hype that Mr. Walker sold; to shut up and be happy someone took us in?* I gave Sandi a smile. *She knew that meant another time sister.* Mama came back in and continued to brag about how well she took care of her foster kids. She reminded us that she did it out of the goodness of her heart. *I'm sorry didn't she say that already? Yea, I know I'm just repeating it over and over like she did.* Mama owned a dry cleaners, a hair shop and she showed us her clean Cadillac. *JACKPOT!* Mama was old, but she was styling. Mama told us we could go to the beauty shop with her. We were excited. We didn't know anybody that owned a business. Mama also said she cooked, so we would eat well. We weren't there for a week before it was my birthday. I turned 14. She cooked to celebrate. When we sat down to eat, I began to look for the tacos, spaghetti or French fries.

I asked Mama, "What's this?" Mama smiled. I saw greens and some other meat that was not in my vocabulary. *Where were the chili fries or McDonalds?* Mama politely said, "I cooked you collard greens and corn bread." As I looked around the table, Sandi had her fake smile on. She gave me the look to put mine on. Sandi knew I didn't own one. The night we arrived Sandi told me she never wanted to see my father again and my behavior would determine if we stayed because we did not want to be split up. I thought about what she told me, so I put on a fake smile. But I didn't eat the food. *I wanted to tell Mama not all black people ate soul food.* After dinner was over, I heard Sandi in the kitchen explaining to Mama that my father bought food out a lot and we were not used to a home cooked meal. *Was she explaining to the prison official why I didn't eat my rations? It wouldn't be the last time she would have to explain my behavior.*

Being in this foster home was different. I was determined to try to make this work. Not entirely for me, but for Sandi. I felt I owed it to her not to get us sent back to my father. *After all, he didn't want us anyway.*

I was excited because it was almost time for school shopping. I didn't get anything for my birthday except greens, cornbread and neck bones. That week Mama took us shopping at the second-hand store and gave us hand-me-downs. *Wasn't she well off?* She was a little upset because I was too skinny for the hand-me-downs. For the first time in my life, I was happy to be super skinny. I asked Mama if she could buy Sandi and me fluorescent neon shirts. That was the style. She repeated her Foster Mother's National Anthem. *Please join me and stand on your feet ladies and gentlemen, remove your caps and sing, "I do this out of the goodness of my heart."* All that was missing at this point was a larger audience. Mama bought me bell-bottom pants. We all know in 1984 bell-bottom pants were not in style. That's why they were so cheap. I started to complain but I didn't want to get us kicked out. I took my bell-bottoms, Sandi ended up with a lot more of the hand-me-downs.

The good thing about living with Mama was we became friends with her son's in-laws. Brandon's wife Roz had two teenage sisters visiting them from out of town for the summer, Jackie and Spanky. We hung out together listening to Prince. They had a common bond -- nobody liked Brandon. I had not yet discovered that Mama was crazy, too. Jackie hinted around about Mama, but she saw I was still in the honeymoon stage of the relationship. Mama hadn't showed her hand just yet. Jackie warned, "Don't be around Brandon by yourself." *What was up with this pervert?* I was the youngest out of the girls and everyone was looking out for me. When Lenora got home, that evening I told her I wanted to know about Brandon.

Lenora took me in the room and closed the door. "When I first came to Mama's house, Brandon was making his rounds. Meaning letting himself in. Once he knew I was home alone, he tried to rape me."

My mouth was wide open, "Why isn't he in jail?"

"I told Mama, but she didn't do nothing. That's when I knew I wasn't protected in foster care either. Always put the chain on the front door so when Brandon tries to let himself in he can't." *I was ready; he wasn't going to get me.*

A few days later when Mama went to work at the cleaners I was in the room with Sandi when we heard the door. "Oh no, was it Brandon?" We got up and ran into the living room. It was not Brandon; it was Reina. She was in her bra and panties. We looked at each other in amazement. She opened the door for her boyfriend, Andre. Lenora, Sandi, and I stood there in shock, as she threw her arms around him. Reina looked back at us with a mean snarl, "WHAT?" We all giggled because Andre was clearly embarrassed. I'm sure he was not expecting four girls to greet him. Andre tried to politely push her arms off. Reina didn't move. Didn't' Andre know this was her Mama's house? We were just prisoners; oops I mean foster kids. Sad thing was Andre was really nice. How did she get him? Oh yeah, she answered doors in her underwear.

Starting high school went well… except my bell-bottoms. We made friends but the unexpected happened. How would I explain Lenora? I was embarrassed that I was in foster care because our father beat us. How would I explain that I lived with a Hispanic girl? So I came up with the best lie ever. My mama had taken Lenora and her family in because they were homeless. So sad, Lenora was telling everyone we were sisters. Didn't she know we were two different colors? She didn't care; she loved me. I never asked her how she explained the black and Hispanic thing.

I also started stealing Reina's change out of a glass jar on her dresser. Stealing was not my gift. But, since Mama would never give us money for school and I was embarrassed to keep using the county food tickets I took her change. *Back in the day if you got free lunch, you would get teased. I was tired of lying to my friends that I lost my money or that I wasn't hungry.* I stole her change and when it was time to eat at school I asked Sandi, "What do you want?"

Reluctantly she asked, "Where did you get money?"

"Don't worry about it. We're eating today."

This would not be the last time we lied about money. The school had a Disney Land trip and this was my first time going. I was excited. Mama gave us a good old $10 each. When we got to Disney Land, we both played like we lost our money. Our friend Leslie Brown, we called Leslie B, bought our food. *How embarrassing.* Mama told us if we wanted money we had to earn it. She told us we could go to her shop on the weekends to wash hair and clean up. So we began to get up at 6 a.m. on Saturdays to go with Mama. Washing hair was better than selling drugs. Everybody came to get their hair done on Saturdays. We stayed there from 6 a.m. to midnight. After our first couple of trips of working, we figured out Mama wasn't going to pay us.

When we asked about our money, she sang her anthem. I figured out she was a liar not just about paying us, but also about becoming our Mama. *It was on now!*

I told her "I don't want to go to the shop anymore."

Mama said, "You still have to go because Pops isn't home. "You can't stay in the house by yourself."

That was her magical way of getting me to go. I went, but I didn't do anything. Sandi still worked although she knew she was not going to get a dime. The next day, I sat at the kitchen table telling Sandi that Mama was a lying bitch.

She called Sandi into her room, "Tell Licia I can hear her."

Sandi came back to the table. "Lower your voice. Mama can hear you."

"I want her to hear. She's a lying bitch and a thief, too."

After Mama lied and stole from us, I decided to finally call home. First I called Aunt Jo to ask if she could take me in. When I called, the phone just rang. *Was she out of town?* I hung up. Desperately I took the phone in the bathroom and called again. This time, she answered. I practically begged her to come to her house. I explained to her everything that was going on and she asked to speak to Mama. *Didn't she believe me?* She said she couldn't do it. When I realized she wasn't going to take me in, I hung up the phone in her face. I then called home and spoke with my brother Curtis. He was happy to hear from me. I told him where we were living. He sounded excited for us. I didn't tell him how we were really living. I then called Annette. She told me she was getting married. *Who could she have been marrying?* In my neighborhood that's what the majority of girls did, they took the first prince or frog that came along. Anything to get out of their home situations, and at last, my sister had found her frog.

We had been in the foster home for a whole year before we saw Annette. We did not want to see anyone else, and we definitely didn't want to see or speak to my father. The more I spoke with Annette, the more I was longing for home. Not my father's house, my homies. I missed walking home from school re-enacting Michaels Jackson's *Thriller.* I missed going down the street to Tina's house. Living in that foster home was weighing on me. I was away from my friends, my neighborhood, and my environment. One evening I had fallen asleep in Sandi's room. I was in her room because she had a radio and we would both wait to hear songs on the LA radio stations. I also was in her room because Reina locked me out of her room. It was then I heard my favorite song, I hadn't heard in months. I jumped out of my sleep and started singing "FLYYY Girl." Fly Girl was a song by The Boogie Boys. Sandi and Lenora jumped up they thought I was crazy. I sang until the song went off. Then something unusual happened. I began to cry.

Sandi grabbed me. I started yelling, "I can't take it anymore! I hate it here! I hate Mama! I hate Reina, I hate Brandon! I hate the neighborhood! I hate it all!"

In the midst of my crying, all my sister could do was hold me. *At 14, was I having a nervous breakdown? I was isolated from everybody and everything I had known and nobody cared especially Mr. Walker and Mama.*

The next day Mama said she had good news. We were allowed to go to LA for my sister's wedding. My sister wanted us to be her bride's maids. Mama didn't want me to go. She said she was letting me go out of the goodness of her heart. Mama said we would catch the bus from her cleaners because she was not driving us to LA and my father would bring us back. I couldn't stand my father, but I was willing to get in the car with him as long as I got to go to LA. Sandi refused to go. She still did not want to see my father.

Once I got to LA my first stop was my sister's house. I was excited to see her. When I got to her house, she opened the door I froze in amazement. *Who was this? My sister had put on so much weight I did not recognize her. Annette was happy to see me.* After visiting with my sister, I got to see Tina, my friends and, of course, I hit my hood. The homies had not seen me in a year. It was rumored that I turned Blood and was living in the Blood neighborhood. Another rumor was I moved back south. I didn't care I was just glad to see them. I stayed with Tina until it was time to go back. I didn't want to leave. I didn't want to go back with Mama and for the first time in my life, I didn't mind if I was separated from Sandi.

Over the next couple of weekends, I went to LA. Eventually, I figured out how to catch the bus from my school. Soon I started ditching school catching the bus to LA. Sandi knew, she just didn't say anything. After some time, Sandi started to go to LA with me. She wanted to be in the wedding. When we went to LA at the end of every weekend, they always had to look for me. I was never at my father's house. I was with my homies. The more I went to LA the harder it was to go back to Pomona. One of my last weekends in LA, I had a fight with an old "frenemy" Tasha. Before I left for foster care, I used to bully Tasha at school. She was scared of me. But while I was gone, Tasha was hanging with my enemy Kendra. They called her Firecracker because she was hot in the pants with the boys.

My weekend was coming to a sad halt. As I walked down my father's street, I walked by Tasha's gate. She was leaning on the gate with Kendra. She gave me a dirty look. I instantly gave her a mean look back. *Had she forgotten I use to punk her every day?* I saw Kendra whispering in Tasha's ear. Then she said, "Tasha don't be scared of her."

Before Kendra could say another word; I reached over the gate and hit Tasha in her face. They weren't expecting that. The fight was on. I think Tasha thought Kendra was going to help, but Kendra wasn't crazy. Kendra didn't like me, but she was too scared to fight me so she pumped Tasha up to do it. Tasha was in for the fight of her life. We fought like two animals, or at least, I did. Tasha didn't know I had my "Ghetto Fight Policy" handy as always. As we were fighting, others came to cheer the fight on. I grabbed Tasha by her shirt and snatched off her gold chain. She screamed, "My father gave me that chain!" Everyone knew her father, Stoney, had just died of an overdose. I didn't care. All was fair in war. Sandi was on her routine to find me to go back to Pomona, when she heard Tasha screaming and the crowd cheering, she came running. Sandi pushed through the crowd to see Tasha and me rolling on the ground. Sandi yelled, "Stop it!" Just as she was about to break up the fight, Tasha bit me on my left breast. I started to bleed badly. Sandi then gave me her blessing to beat Tasha up. I got Tasha back. I bit her on the side of her face right over her eye. After that, she couldn't see and she didn't want to fight no more. I wouldn't let her out of the fight. Finally, Sandi grabbed me. We both had forgotten we had to go back to the foster home. When Sandi grabbed me, she asked, "What happened?" Before I could explain she said, "Nevermind." She knew it didn't matter anyway.

As we walked to my father's I attempted to fix my clothes. Before I stepped on the porch, he walked out the house agitated. He asked, "What took you so long?" He knew I had been in a fight. That's the one thing about the ghetto, news traveled faster than the Internet. "Had a fight with Tasha." He wasn't a bit surprised and he didn't give me a lecture. I went into the bathroom to doctor up my bite wound. It was deep. Tasha's teeth marks were big. My breast was bleeding and swollen. Tasha's teeth marks are forever engraved on my left breast.

When I got back to Mama's house nothing was said about my brawl, so I thought everything was cool. That was until the following weekend. As usual, we rode to the cleaners to catch the bus to go to LA. That's when Mama looked at me, "You aren't going anywhere." *Who in the hell was she talking to? My bags were packed. I was ready to see the homies.*

Mama then sprang her list of evidence, "I know every weekend Sandi has to look for you to come home. And I know you had a fight and got bit."

What's the problem? She didn't get bit! "What's your point?"

"You have to stay at the cleaners."

Free child labor? I don't think so sister. I politely turned to Sandi, "Let's go." Sandi, of course, tried to get me to stay. As we walked out of the cleaners with our bags Mama screamed, "If you leave, you can't come back to my house."

REALLY? Did she think my heart was sad? I was going to my real family, the streets, and was glad about it.

We walked to the bus stop, Mama drove behind us screaming, "If you leave, you can't come back." *I know what you're thinking-- didn't she say that already?* While we sat at the bus stop, Sandi once again tried to get me to go back. I refused. Mama pulled up in her Cadillac to give me one more opportunity to go back to her child slave shop and return home with her. I sat at the bus stop ignoring her waiting for my chariot, the bus. I went to LA and had the time of my life. I didn't care or think about where I was going to live. Sandi ensured me that she was going to stay in Pomona with Mama and graduate. I had no arguments with her. I understood it was now time for us to part ways. I loved my sister, but our time together had come to an end. When I went back that Sunday you better believe Mama was waiting for me. That next day, Mr. Walker was there to pick me up. He wore a disappointed look on his face as if to say, "Didn't I tell you not to mess this up?" I put my clothes in a trash bag. Mr. Walker took me to a foster home in Pasadena, on Calaveras Street. As we pulled up to this shack, he said with a smirk, "You see where you have to live now?" I didn't care. I didn't want to live in Pomona no way. *Funny thing Mr. Walker did not tell this foster mother about my rap sheet. I guess he saw her living conditions and didn't feel he even had to sell me on this foster mother. Looking at the condition of her house, she was going to accept any kid she could get.*

This foster mother was old, too. In fact, she had a trach in her throat. When she talked she had to cover the hole up. *At this point, was I surprised?*

Absolutely not. Foster care was big business. Just house kids you don't care for and you could get paid big money. This foster mother had two other girls that she had adopted that lived with her. In fact, she adopted all four siblings, but one was in jail. This foster mother didn't have a luxury car or own any businesses. She had a small three-bedroom, one-bathroom shack on a lot with two other houses. Ours was in the back. When I got there, her youngest foster daughter introduced herself as Janet. She was 17. Janet had an older sister, Michelle, she was 21. Michelle had a two-year-old son Gary; he was bad. Janet said Michelle was not supposed to be living in the house, but the foster mother would not put her out because she had nowhere else to go. In foster care once you turned 18, you were not supposed to be living in the home. My plans did not include staying in this shack until I was 18. I had a family, my homies. I met my roommate Tracey. She was cool. Tracey had a big smile with a large gap in her mouth with a shape that killed for days. In fact, she knew it and she used it to her advantage.

Tracey and I stayed up late nights talking about what landed us in foster care because it was like the prison system and you were the criminal. Tracey said, "I can't go home because I testified against my father."

I told her, "So did I."

She looked at me and said, "It was a different testimony. My whole family is mad at me. My father had been raping me for years and I finally told. My mother chose to stay with my father, so I can't go back home. My father raped my sister, too, but my sister lied in court and said it didn't happen and went back home."

Tracey told me she was worried because she was going to be 18 soon and she had nowhere to go. In the middle of the conversation she looked at me with love in her eyes. She reminded me of my sister Sandi. *Did I remind her of her little sister? Did she try and protect her sister from their father like Sandi tried to protect me from our brother Edwin?* Tracey, like Sandi and Lenora, took care of me. She gave me money when she got it from men. *Yes, I said, men.* Tracey dated older men, because of her shape she caught any man she wanted and, as a result, she used it to survive and to look after me. Tracey loved me. It's amazing this list of abused girls tried their best to look after me, to love me, to protect me. *Was it because no one had protected them?*

In that home it was small and crazy. It wasn't long before I broke the house rules. This foster mother like Mama made soul food. One of her rules was after she cooked don't go into her kitchen and cook or eat again. *Was she crazy? I didn't eat greens, hog mogs or neck bones!* So, I did exactly what she said not to do. One evening, after the foster mother cooked her dinner that stank up the house, I waited and went in and cooked bacon and eggs. She was angry. I explained to her I didn't eat that stuff; unlike Mama she did not sing the foster mothers national anthem; she just said those were her rules. I didn't care. I knew I wasn't going to be there long because I started having visits with my father. *Had I forgiven him? Of course, not, I wanted to get back to LA.* I saw Sandi when we went to court. She was doing fine. She was worried about me. I always convinced her that I was ok.

In this foster home, we had a foster girl war going on and the foster mother had no idea. Tracey and Michelle did not get along because Tracey took Michelle's soon to be boyfriend Marcus, before he could say yes to Michelle he went for Tracey. Marcus had a job and a car, and with that being said, so did Tracey. The tension in the house was thick, but Michelle was scared of Tracey. There was tension between Michelle and me because I was Tracey's favorite and also I was a recipient of Marcus' money. Michelle and I usually got into arguments when Tracey was not there. I always told her, "You and your bad son ain't supposed to be here no way. Y'all supposed to be in the street." This usually made her shut up. Maybe she thought I was going to tell Mr. Walker, my social worker. Janelle was the foster mother's informant. She stayed in the room with the foster mother because there was no room in the house. Janelle also helped her because she was old and sickly. Janelle was not close with her sister Michelle, so she didn't get in the middle of the war.

I had two fights while I was there. The last fight got me thrown out. I had the first fight with another girl that came after me, her name was Ellen.

We did not get along because of a boy that lived down the hill from us. He liked me, she liked him and I liked Dominique at my school. I know drama. Since she thought I stood in the way of her would-be boyfriend there was tension between us. One night I decided to end it once and for all. I demanded Ellen to do my dishes and she refused. *What? Didn't she hear what I said?* I demanded she do my dishes and she said no again. I then explained to the poor girl how it went. After my debriefing, she still refused. I explained the pecking order. I was the chick in charge of our age group in the house. Ellen didn't care. She had back up, Michelle. So what did I do; what I did best— started fighting. Before anyone could get to the kitchen we were fighting and dishes were flying everywhere. The foster mother and Janet came running in. Janet broke the fight up.

The foster mother took me to her room, "I will not have any more trouble. If you do anything else, you will have to go. *I didn't care. My plans were to go back home to my father's.* My hood.

Things were also escalating because Tracey had just turned 18 and she had to go. She moved out that week. *I had lost Sandi again. Angry and hurt I argued with everybody in the house.*

Michelle and Ellen became good friends and they were in the best of spirits, and it just made me angrier. Michelle allowed her son Gary to get into my hair stuff again. *Did she think because Tracey was gone I wouldn't hold my own?* The argument started in the bathroom. The fight broke out in the living room. *I was mad. Sandi was gone Tracey was gone and now Michelle thought she was going to punk me.* As we were tussling on the couch, the foster mother came running out screaming, "That's it! You have to go." *I didn't care, I kept fighting. Michelle got all my pent up anger.* Janet was outside with her boyfriend Charlie, he was also a grown man. *Side note, does anyone see the trend of grown men dating young, abused girls?*

Janet pulled me off Michelle and walked me outside. She said, "I don't like my sister's ways, but you can't beat her up." At that moment, I thought I was going to have to fight her, too. Then she started laughing because she realized her sister got beat up by a kid. That fight was my ticket out of that foster home. The foster mother let me know that Michelle was her daughter and I wasn't.

The next day, I went back to my father's house. He didn't have a relationship with me. There was an unspoken rule— don't ask for hugs, kisses or attention because you're not getting it. I was cool with it. He hadn't given me love in the past, so what was new? I was glad to be back in the hood.

Chapter 9

Time to Grow Up

Things were different on 85th or the 5 as we called it. I noticed a super fine looking man who lived next door. *Where did he come from?* It was Big Bone he had been away for the two years we lived on the street, he was in jail. What can I say about Big Bone? He was brown skinned with green eyes and had a killer smile. Bone was from Hoover. He was 18 and I was 15, but that didn't stop me from looking. Every time I thought I heard him coming out of his house I would go to my front door and pretend I was about to leave the house. Finally, one day he spoke. He was fine. *Surely, I'm going to die if he likes me.* I started hanging outside his gate talking with him. One day while I was hanging on his gate waiting for him to come outside, Tina and Jav walked up and started talking about sex. I hadn't had sex, only molested and fondled. *How does one of the baddest girls tell folks she's still a virgin? And quite honestly because I was molested I didn't really want to have sex!* Tina was bragging about having sex, and I joined in with my lying self, and Jav called me on it. Jav knew I was lying. He started asking hard questions that I didn't have the answers to. He asked the basics at first. How did it feel? He asked me how many times did I cum? *What's that?* I shouted none of your business. Which translated that I was clueless, because in all actuality I had no idea what he was talking about. Bone heard him teasing. The one thing I can say about the homies, they can smell a fraud a mile away. They knew when you weren't supposed to be hanging in the hood and whether or not they could get you. It was not long before I was I hanging with Bone and ended up in his house. When he got me in his room, he knew I had no idea what to do. I kept fronting like I knew what I was doing. As I lay on Bone's bed, I was praying his mother, Mrs. Jon, didn't come home from church. *Yes, I said church.* I was hoping she would not come in with her bible and find two sinners naked. I was also nervous that I did not know what to expect or feel. *How long was this supposed to last? On TV it went on forever.* I laid back with my fake smile and as he got on top of me. He started trying to penetrate me. It was not working. He looked down at me with a smile as if to say, "I knew it! Your lying ass never had none." Scared, I kept my fake smile on as if I was enjoying it. There was no joy; it was painful. After a long struggle, he finally penetrated me. He looked down at me and asked me an important question, "Did you get yours?" *Get what? What was I supposed to get? Of course, I had no idea what he was talking about.* I smiled and softly said, "Yes." He smiled back. I guess that was his go-ahead that he could get his and he did. After this ordeal, I still had no idea what he was talking about or what just happened. He rolled off me, held me and we talked about random things. I was still confused, in pain and praying his Mama didn't walk in. *Some first time....*

The next big event after I got back home from foster care was I was going to go to school. I wanted to go to school in the Valley, the one that didn't have gang members. That was until I got there. So, I asked my father if he would enroll me in a school in the Valley. I knew I couldn't go to any high school in my neighborhood. They were all enemy schools. My father was from Mississippi. He had no idea what an enemy school was nor did he care. I could not explain to him that my home school was in Blood hood. My cousins were Blood's, and that didn't mean anything to me. I didn't want to go there and you know he sent me there anyway. For the most part, the Bloods were cool with me because some of them remembered me from the summers that I spent with my aunt. They knew I was a Crip. They had one rule; respect their hood. I didn't like the school at all. I had no interest in school. I had just come back from foster care. I had no relationship with my father, and I had to worry about getting jumped every day. *Yeah, this made school fun.* I did have one teacher there that actually cared about her gang-affiliated students, Mary Hoover. She was a white lady who got it and I do mean she got it. Being in her English class was the first time I heard a teacher cuss. If a student was disrespectful, she was there to meet them half way. All the students loved her, just not her name. Mrs. Hoover picked up that I loved to read. She gave me books and took an interest in me. Unfortunately, my gang ties and homies were more important than reading. I began ditching again; then stopped going altogether. *I know you're not surprised.* I started hanging with an older girl named Cassey. She moved on 85th when I was in foster care. At the time, Cassey was 18 with a 1-year-old son named Keith and was also pregnant with her second child. I started helping Cassey. I watched her son Keith, because she didn't want anyone to know, she was pregnant again, especially Keith's father, because she knew this baby wasn't his. One day after coming from Cassey's house, my father tried to be a dad. He said he thought Cassey was too old for me to hang with. *Were my ears playing tricks on me? Let me get this straight he beat me, I had to go into foster care, and now he's concerned about me hanging with an older girl? Go to hell old man. I hang with who I want.* I continued to hang with my newfound friend. Heck, I even helped Cassey deliver her second son Andre. She went into labor and the paramedics didn't make it on time. So, she had Andre at home in her bed. As I held him in a sheet, I was ready to die from seeing all that blood.

While hanging out I had a fake curfew, meaning I could be down to Tina's house until 10 p.m. But, because my father worked nights, I no longer went to Tina's, I was on 82nd and Hoover at the spot with the homies. At the time, I didn't know what a spot was. I was 15 and it was 1986. A spot was where dope was being sold. I hung in a particular spot. It was called the Dungeon. The Dungeon was a set of duplexes that were between 82nd and 83rd and Hoover. *The funny thing was the dope spot was right next to a church.* The man that lived in the duplex was named Ronald Petrie. He told us to call him Petrie or Star Child. Petrie was a dope fiend from Chicago. That's how a bunch of young gang members got to hang out at his house. Petrie's drug of choice was heroin and up until that time, I had only sold weed with my cousin Denise. Now I was watching Petrie push balloons out of the spot. The balloons had heroin in them, so when the police came you could swallow it or put it up in your butt literally.

When summer came, I was hanging at the spot more than with Cassey. She came to the spot to tell me she was being evicted. Big Keith had taken Lil Keith. He figured out that Andre was not his son. She was now left with Andre and on the verge of being homeless because Keith no longer paid her rent. When I sold weed, I tried to help her out by buying Andre little things here and there. Cassey, had a knack for sleeping with guys. That's how she got what she wanted and got her bills paid. She was sleeping with some of the biggest dope dealers at that time. *I guess you are asking why was she on the verge of being homeless then?* It's called Hood Protocol. There was the wifey, the girlfriend, and the hoodrat. The wifey and girlfriend were pretty much taken care of. But, the hoodrats were only good to sleep with when you felt like it. The hoodrat would get a couple of dollars now and then. Hoodrats didn't get their rent paid all the time -- if at all. Because of this pecking order, hoodrats slept with more than one homie. *Mind you, the homies (men) that did the same thing weren't considered hoodrats, but "The Man" because they had a bunch of women. Gangsta life is parallel to society, men have status and honor, and women are just tramps.*

At first, when I saw Cassey's hoodrat tendencies, I didn't give it a second thought, after all, she was training me to be a hoodrat. One day I slept with a much older and ugly (might I add) guy named, Little Jay. He had been liking me for a while. So, he finally pressured me into going to a motel. He said he just wanted to kick it. We didn't have to do anything that I didn't want to do. *Yeah right.* In those days, going to expensive motels was thought to be something. Places like the Snooty Fox and the Mustang Motel were where the ballers, those that had money, took their women. I went to the motel with Little Jay and Cassey, who went with his homie. I had sex and didn't want to. Embarrassed, I went to Cassey's house the next day. As I told her what happened, she looked at me with confusion on her face. She asked me the question that would set the tone for the majority of my young life. "Did anybody see you go to the motel with him?"

I was looking at her to say, umm you?

"Did he have a camera in his underwear?"

I wasn't expecting questions. I needed help. I replied, "No."

Now I had a confused look on my face. With a confident smile, she shared the key to hood life. Simply put, she said, "Just lie. It will always be your word against a man's."

I stood there as if I had never been told to lie before. My grandmother's famous advice was "If you're going to tell a lie stick to it." Did Ma's words have some truth? I thought there must be something to this advice, so I took it. Instead of saying no to sexual advances, I slept with man after man then lied about it later. *I had already been stripped as a child of self-worth and self-esteem, so this seemed to be the most logical thing to do.* So in between sleeping with guys and hanging out I noticed that a few of my homegirls had the same problem, they were molested at home. We all had an unspoken agreement; we'd rather have control over the men we slept with. At the end of the day we were still being used. I guess it was the fact that we understood people in the street using us, but family? That was the ultimate betrayal and heartbreak.

Around this time, I started hanging with Keisha. She had been in a foster home down the street from my father. She was placed in foster care because something was wrong with her mother. She never said exactly why she was taken from her mother, but it was the 80's and the crack boom had swept the hood. One night when we were hanging, I decided to have a little to drink and to smoke some weed. *Mind you, I come from a family of crazy. Meaning, we didn't need drugs to act foolish.* I don't remember getting high or drink. When I woke up in the dope spot, I realized it was well after 10:00 p.m. That meant my father was already home and he knew I was not down the street at Tina's house. I told Keisha I wanted to call home first. I was not just going to go home in case my father tried something. Keisha walked with me to the phone booth on the corner of 85th and Hoover. I had already told Keisha who was a runaway herself, that if it didn't sound right I wasn't going home.

I called my father. The phone rang for what seemed like forever. I was about to hang up when he answered. The operator said, "You have a collect call from Alicia. Will you accept?"

"No."

I politely hung the phone up. Keisha asked, "What happened?"

"He didn't accept the call. I don't trust him. I'm not going home."

I translated that his refusal to accept my collect call to mean it wasn't safe to go home. Keisha looked surprised. I guess she didn't believe me. After all, I had never run away before or stayed out all night. Keisha and I walked down Hoover Street in silence. I had now just entered into her world as a 15-year-old runaway. Both of us were running from abusive homes and adverse family situations. *Those were the longest couple of blocks I had ever walked.*

I went back to the Dungeon and knocked. Petrie let me in. Keisha didn't stay with me because she had a place to go. When young girls were runaways, they usually slept with older men to have a place to stay. Keisha had an older man. I was new to the game of street hustle, but I would soon become a professional of how to survive in the drug-infested ghetto. The next day Cassey came looking for me in the spot. I explained to her what happened. I knew I couldn't stay with her since she was being evicted and my father might call the police on me. I didn't know what to do except I wasn't going back even if he answered a phone call. Since I couldn't be seen on 85th anymore Cassey started hanging out with me in the spot. I didn't consider myself a runway; I felt that I had no family that could help me. The next day I called my brother to say that I was alright and if he talked to Sandi to let her know I was ok.

Chapter 10

Hood Boot Camp 101

It was now survival time. Petrie allowed a group of us to stay in his place, but he couldn't provide food, so we did what we could. We went to ABC market and stole food to eat. The older homies started to notice me more because I was always in trouble.

One day, as I was sitting in the Dungeon with my homegirl Brenda a man came through the door. Brenda greeted him, "What's up Lil Dog?"

Lil Dog or "Dog" as she called him, had been in jail for a minute and was making his rounds through the neighborhood. Dog looked at me and gave Brenda a look and he asked, "Who's the new booty?"

Brenda said, "That's Alicia, she used to be from The Foe, but she turned Tray since her father moved in the hood." I had met Brenda when I first got back from foster care. Brenda was already hanging in eight Tray hood before I ran away. Brenda explained that she knew me because I used to date her play cousin Shaun, and plus we lived around the corner from each other.

I was 15 and it didn't help that I looked 12. They were having a side conversation. I heard her say, "Don't worry she's down. She's 15."

Dog came over to me and asked me how old I was. With my smart mouth and bad attitude, I replied, "Fifteen." *As if to say I was 30.* He immediately laughed. He knew I had to have heart or was just plain stupid to say that to an ex-convict who had just gotten out of jail. My heart was beating fast, but I wasn't going to show him that I was nervous. After a week of staying in the Dungeon, Dog and I became good friends.

Two incidents solidified our relationship. The first was a mission that we went on that went bad. One night our regular group of deviants was on the way to steal food from ABC market. This time, Dog went just because. Dog was older; he didn't have to steal food. He went just to see who had heart. There were about seven of us walking down Hoover Street, as we crossed the light on Manchester, Lil Wade who was leading the pack decided to deviate from the plan. A man was crossing the light going in the opposite direction. I'm assuming it was at that point Lil Wade thought it was a good idea to rob him. Without saying a word, Lil Wade grabbed the man's shirt, slammed him on the ground and tried to take his wallet. The man then flipped Lil Wade on the ground. Lil Wade and the man started tussling in the crosswalk. Lil Wade started yelling, "He stabbing me!" What Lil Wade didn't know was the man had a knife for an occasion such as this. Before the man could stab him again, I ran over, kicked the man in the head and jumped in the fight. Dog stood in amazement. I guess he thought the boys in the crowd would help first, but instead it was the one he called the "new booty."

I didn't think about getting stabbed. I just knew Lil Wade needed help. When you're in the hood and family is in trouble, whether they started it or not, you help. We managed to get the knife and money from the man. Afterwards, we headed back to the Dungeon to see how bad Lil Wade's stab wounds were. We didn't have to steal food after all. We had enough money to eat that night, but after Lil Wade was stabbed, no one was hungry.

The second thing that made Dog and me tight was a fight that I had in the Dungeon. I'm assuming because I was little and I looked so young, it was time to get tested. A girl named Debbie tried to put my "new booty" status to the test. In the hood, there was always some-one that undercover didn't like you. But, because they were afraid that they couldn't whip you themselves, they would find some unsuspecting victim to take you on. That was Brenda, she had the bark of a dog and a bite of a fish. At the time, I thought Brenda was cool, after all she was the one that introduced me to Dog. Brenda bluffed many girls, but she knew I wasn't scared of her. I was coming up in my hood and what I didn't know at the time was Brenda didn't like my reputation. She also didn't like the fact that me and Lil Dog were now tight. One Saturday Brenda came by to kick it in the Dungeon and she brought, Debbie. While we were in the Dungeon, I noticed Brenda and Debbie kept going into the bathroom. Debbie was a thin girl, but taller and bigger than me. I wasn't stupid, I knew something wasn't right. I just hadn't figured out what. So after about three or more trips to the bathroom, Brenda called me in. I walked in; Debbie was leaning against the sink smirking. Brenda told me Debbie had a problem with me. I was confused. I didn't know this chick. I saw her come through a few times. *What did she have against me? I didn't care.* I gave Debbie a look that let her know that my "Ghetto Fight Policy" was ready to go. As Brenda was instigating, oops, I mean explaining, Debbie walked up on me. Before she could explain what she had against me, I hit her and the fight was on.

The fight started in the bathroom. We ended up in the living room. Debbie was surprised; she could not overpower me as I flipped her on the couch punching her in the face. Dog came running from the kitchen yelling, "Now that's my homegirl!" I got so beside myself that in the middle of punching her I started throwing up my gang signs to let her know she was in my hood. She was embarrassed for a couple of reasons. One, someone smaller had her pinned to the couch and she couldn't get me off her. Two, Brenda had suckered her into getting beat up in front of everybody. Once Dog saw that Debbie couldn't get me off of her, and I wouldn't stop hitting her in her face, he broke the fight up. It was confirmed --Debbie had lost. As Debbie got up trying to fix her hair, she looked at Brenda and walked out without saying a word. Dog was sold; we were homies for LIFE!

Brenda instantly tried to explain that she had no idea why Debbie had tripped out on me. Dog didn't want to hear shit; he knew Brenda had tried to set me up. He yelled out, "What up Brenda?" That was my cue that he had my back, and I could get Brenda, too. I walked up and asked her if she wanted to see me, meaning fight. She let me know that she didn't. This was the beginning of our "frenemy" relationship.

Upon the completion of this book Dog died of an overdose. RIP 10/2016

Although I was staying in the Dungeon, money was hard to come by, and I didn't have much. When I left home, I did not have clothes or anything. When my brother finally met up with me and gave me some of my clothes, I didn't even have a place to put them. In the Dungeon, there wasn't a lot of room. There was only one small bedroom. We all slept either on the floor or the couch. It went like this; whoever got in early had the best spot on the floor. When it was time to shower I went to Bone's house. Big Bone was in jail, but his brother Lamont looked out for me. I went during the times I knew my father wasn't home. By Lamont letting me shower on a regular basis, it started rumors that I was sleeping with him. I didn't care. I needed somewhere to shower, plus he knew I had slept with his brother Big Bone. Not long after, Lamont started hanging in the hood. He took his brother's name; he was called Lil Bone.

While at the Dungeon I sent word to my teacher Ms. Hoover that I ran away, and I was ok. She started sending me books and letters to the dope spot. I never told Ms. Hoover the truth; I told her I was at a friend's house. In between selling dope I was reading "Roll of Thunder Hear My Cry" and "Let the Circle Be Unbroken." In the spot, my homie Big Houn was tutoring me in math. *Yes, in between dope sales, he was a math whiz. FYI gang members are some of the smartest people you'll encounter. It's sad that a lack of resources limits their opportunities.*

Petrie was tutoring us "youngins" on how to sell heroin and how the dope game was about to change. Stealing from ABC market could only last so long, besides, stealing was never my hustle. Petrie explained that they bagged the heroin up in balloons, and when customers come never open the door, so they won't see your face. The problem with selling heroin was that it was not that profitable at the small street level. Once a dope fiend got high, he could go for days before he would come back for his next fix or worst yet if he OD'd, which happened all the time, you were out of a customer. Petrie also introduced me to selling Sherm or Butt Naked. It was PCP/ formaldehyde. We would buy cheap black cigarettes; dip just the tip into the Sherm, so the cigarette would absorb the chemical. The problem with PCP was just like heroin, users stayed high for long periods of time. Not to mention, those who got high became dangerous and crazy. Some hallucinated and got stuck in London or got butt naked. As the drug suggested, they took off their clothes right there on the spot and some were so out of it, they were somewhere else. *Oh, yes London.*

PCP was also not criminal-friendly. If the police came, you could not hide it like you could hide the balloons. It smelled like burnt rubber. You could smell it from a mile away. Weed was the drug of choice for many, but Sherm was a favorite for many of the homies. *They went to London all the time.* On many nights, it was a zombie convention. The homies were stuck and all you could do was avoid them because depending on the disposition of the person you never knew how the drug affected them. Years later, Lil Dog became addicted to Sherm. He often walked through the hood high; unaware of his surroundings. He had lost his mind a few times; he never recovered from the mental damage of the drug.

Selling balloons was getting complicated. The sales were slow and dope fiends were OD'ing on the regular. On a usual day in the Dungeon, I was waiting for the next customer to come through when a man came and bought a balloon. Lil Bone had already sold him one earlier. The man asked for Petrie. I guess they were friends. Petrie stepped out of the house and went into the back of the duplexes to shoot up with him. Not even an hour later Petrie came banging on the door screaming for ice. We hurried up and opened the door. *Ice for what?* Petrie was really nervous. He ran into the kitchen and grabbed the little amount of ice that was there then ran out of the door. He banged on another door and screamed for ice. A man came to the door with ice and they ran around the back of the duplex. At this time, Lil Bone and I wanted to know what was happening. Why were they screaming for ice? We ran out behind the duplex and as we came around the corner of the building, we saw four dope fiends shaking a man that was on the ground. As we got closer, we could see it was Lil Bone's customer and he was unconscious. Petrie was still screaming for more ice. Another dope fiend came running with more ice. Petrie poured the ice down the front of the man's pants. It did nothing. The man was still unconscious. After a few more attempts to get the man up, Petrie yelled, "Get out of here!" Lil Bone and I looked up. He was talking to us. In our naivety, when we looked up the crowd of dope fiends were already gone. Lil Bone and I ran back into Petrie's spot not sure about what was going to happen. Lil Bone looked at me, "Do you think the man is dead?" I shrugged my shoulders. It was 20 minutes before the paramedics came. I'm not sure if they took long because no one called immediately or just because it was the ghetto and they always took their time to respond to our so-called emergencies. They rushed to the back of the duplex. No one was there to tell them what happened. Not one person was out. It was so quiet we could hear the paramedic working on the man. When they finally rolled him away on the gurney, you could hear a pin drop. It was the busiest time of the afternoon and yet it was utterly silent. Lil Bone sat in silence for hours. No other customers came that day because they all knew the police would be looking for who sold that fatal balloon. A few days later, the word on the street was "it was too late." The man died of an overdose. This would not be the first time that I would witness the desperate acts of those addicted. In fact, as I was walking through an alley I saw a heroin addict shooting dope between his toes. I thought I was going to throw up. Usually, when heroin addicts have shot out all their veins in their arms or legs, they will shoot in other parts of their bodies including veins in their penis or vagina. They did anything to catch that high. After they shoot up, they had that dope fiend nod. This nod happens because of the drugs hitting the blood stream. As I said before, the drug game was changing.

Chapter 11

Stepped Up My Hood Game

While hanging in the Dungeon one day, Twin came in looking fresh. We never called her by her name. She was an identical twin, so we just called her Twin. Twin didn't live in the neighborhood usually she just came by to kick it. But this day she had on new clothes and expensive tennis shoes. I had to ask.

"Where'd you get your clothes from?"

She smiled "The swap meet."

It was rare for a 14-year-old to be fly like that; nobody's family was rich. While she was bragging, she reached into her bra and pulled out a zip lock bag with white rocks in it. *She bought her clothes by selling crack.* I had seen crack before. I held it for my friend, Kaos who had moved to Cali from Louisiana. He was from the 9. He asked me to hold it for him because he couldn't sell it in my hood. People from the 9 were enemies with the Hoovers. I knew it was drugs, but I hadn't gotten the true concept of what crack cocaine was, what it did, or how it would change the drug game. Twin went on to explain how she spent fifty dollars and doubled up her money in as little as an hour. *It took us all day to make that kind of money.* I sat there in amazement because with balloons I would have them for days. I was determined to get my hands on some crack.

I stayed at Petrie's for as long as I could, until he informed all of us that he was moving back to Chicago to be with his family. I had nowhere else to go. But I wasn't mad at him for leaving death and despair. I was hoping that he did well and saw his son Starchild that he talked about so much. A few years after he moved, I heard that he had OD'd on heroin. Over the years, I have always thought about him and wondered what happened. I guess it was at this point that I realized that when I was 15, a dope fiend named Ronald Petrie from Chicago took me in off the streets. He showed me how to take care of myself. He wanted me even when my own family didn't. He never made sexual advances or disrespected me. I guess I'm crying because it took me over 30 years to see what he did for me. Over 30 years to grieve over my friend. *I know what you're thinking, what kind of friend would take a 15-year-old girl and teach her how to sell hard drugs? Well, dear readers, one who knew the streets all too well and knew the chances of that 15-year-old girl surviving without it were low to none.* Without the hard knock instructions, my chances of becoming a prostitute, strung out on drugs, in jail for the rest of my life or somewhere raped or dead were high. Petrie knew the rules and hustle of the streets. He knew the streets waited for young runaways to come and get caught up. Out of all the runaways that came to his spot, he took the time to school me because Petrie saw something in me. He knew all too well that the streets didn't care about your age, ethnic background, looks, or intellect.

With Petrie gone, I got some crack from Kaos. I began hanging on 82nd selling. I would stay up all night. The homies thought I had a bunch of dope to sell, but I didn't. I had no place to go. I sold my crack until it ran out and then slept on the apartment stairs until I could go to Lil Bone's to shower. A group of kids ages 12-18 took turns "serving" to users on 82nd. So many people were getting high on crack that the customers never ran out. Crack was a booming business and a dangerous one. People were so desperate they would do anything. Unlike balloons or Sherm, the crack high didn't last at all. The customers were awake all night trying to get their hands on money for more. You would see packs of people at all times walking through the neighborhood looking for what they could steal to get high. They stole from family and sold all their possessions. They sold their baby's diapers, Bibles (*yes, I said Bibles*) and their children's toys. You name it, they sold it. Many of the women sprung on crack prostituted themselves. This was known as being a Strawberry because they didn't want money, they wanted crack. They would give the homies head (oral sex) for crack.

Many were injured and, even more, lost their lives as a result of the crack epidemic. Let me give you one simple example of what crack did. Let's take this woman named Tammy as a prime example. Tammy stole from her family and she was a Strawberry. Tammy had stolen so much from her family that her brother Greg snapped on her. Tammy had taken her kids' Christmas toys and clothes. She even stole meat from the freezer. Whenever we saw Tammy's mother drive slowly down the street, we knew, this time, she took something important. Tammy's brother Greg was mentally ill. Tammy took his tapes to sell for crack. In Tammy's own words, she was sleep on the couch and all of a sudden, she felt a sharp pain. Tammy said she tried to get up and when she opened her eyes, her brother Greg had stabbed her in her eye. Tammy said she put her hand up to cover her face, and Greg stabbed her in her hand. He stabbed her a few more times before he stopped. Tammy said that Greg had just missed a main artery. The doctor told her she was lucky to be alive. After the attack, Greg went to jail and Tammy got a glass eye. Greg did less than a year in jail. *Was it because he pleaded mental insanity at the time? Who knows?* That did not stop Tammy from smoking crack. It only stopped her from stealing from Greg. As she was telling me the story, she was buying crack from me. Many of the homies were murdered over selling crack. Some were jacked which meant they were robbed and some killed over drug territory.

Slanging was going well for me. When Cassey was finally put out of her place, she came on 82nd and started selling drugs with me. We claimed we were cousins to give the appearance that we had numbers. We didn't want people to know it was just us. I saw we were going to have problems. Her green eyes and light skin gave her a pass and a lot of the homies wanted to get with her. But Cassey's hoodrat tendencies were about to get us into trouble. While hanging in the hood, I learned quickly. The Big Homie Houn saw Cassey and instantly she started flirting with him. I told Cassey she couldn't sleep with Houn he had a wife. She didn't care, she was used to getting all the attention she demanded. In the hood, when a homie slept with you, his women weren't mad at him, they were mad at you. You were the enemy. Just ask poor Cookie. Cookie was about 14 years old and Houn had his eyes on her. Cookie knew about Houn's wife Crystal and his girlfriend Zenay. When Cookie decided to sleep with Houn someone snitched to Zenay. Cookie came around to the dope spot just to kick it and someone set her up. Before we knew it, Zenay came through the door. We all knew what that meant. We were sitting in the living room and Cookie was in the bedroom. Zenay stormed in the bedroom and started punching and kicking Cookie. As we looked on, Cookie was screaming telling Zenay she never slept with Houn. After a while Cookie managed to get up off the bed and ran for the door. Zenay grabbed Cookies shirt, ripping it completely. Cookie ran out the spot screaming at the top of her lungs as Zenay chased behind her. We all jumped up and ran behind them to see what else was going to happen. As Cookie ran screaming, she hit the corner of 82nd street trying to get to her apartment. Houn was standing in front of her apartment building and Cookie ran right past him topless and he didn't say a word. When Houn looked up and saw Zenay chasing Cookie he just laughed.

I told Cassey she couldn't sleep with the homies because they had wives and girlfriends, in that order. We couldn't whip them all.

So this is how it goes. The men cheat, the other women fight or get beat up, all while the wife stays at home with his kids. In hood order the wife had rank over all the others. I was trying to get Cassey to see the order of the hood, so we didn't have any problems.

It was around this time that I met three people that would change my life forever - Gwen, Nannie, and Sneak. Cassey and I were drifting apart. *She didn't get it, STOP sleeping with the all the homies! I didn't want no trouble.* At first, Cassey and I were getting motel rooms with the money we made. Then, she started inviting all the homies to the room. I wasn't feeling that. I've seen certain homies run trains on girls and I wasn't going to be a victim. I knew better. I guess she didn't care. When she invited the homies to our room, I wouldn't go. It was then that a woman named Gwen noticed that I began sitting on the stairs of her apartment building. I sat there every day and night until we started speaking. I was 15 and Gwen was 30. One day I was sitting on her car when she came out to take her kids to school. I slid off her hood hoping she didn't notice. She said, "Hey, I'm not trippin, what's your name?" I believe she knew that I had slept outside that night.

As we were talking, Cassey walked up, "Why didn't you come to the room?"

"I just didn't." Pausing I said, "Gwen, this is my cousin Cassey."

Before leaving, Gwen told me that if I was ever out late I could come hang in her apartment. Cassey had a funny look on her face. She knew I was not feeling her because of how she acted with the homies. I thanked Gwen and told her that I would come up and hang out with her sometime.

One freezing, late night I took Gwen up on her offer. I knocked on her apartment door. She let me in, and introduced me to her kids Netra, Tasha, and Michael. Michael was three, still in diapers, and on the bottle. I asked Gwen, "Ain't he too big for a bottle?" She just laughed. We instantly became good friends. I also met a new friend.

The homie Houn introduced me to his best friend, Sneak. They called themselves The Youngsters. Sneak was a homie who just had got out of jail. His name implied just that, he was Sneaky. He would walk up behind you, and you would never hear him coming. He actually ran on his tiptoes. Sneak was a killer and everybody knew it. Sneak kept a gun with him at all times. He trusted no one—homies, women and all.

Sneak kinda liked me. He started to hang out late with Cassey and me while we sold drugs. He was amazed at how young and dangerous we appeared to be. He had no idea how I had been misused and abused and that bred a murderer. There were times that I sat outside with him until two in the morning talking about all the people I wanted to get. He would just laugh. I'm not sure if he laughed because he didn't think I was capable or because of my age. Sneak came by every day to see if I was hanging on the stairs. Of course, I was. I didn't have a place to go.

May 22nd was one night that would change my life forever. As I was sitting on my couch, I mean the apartment steps; Sneak came and sat next to me. He asked me if I wanted to kick it with him for his birthday. After all, he was turning 23 and in hood years that meant he was turning 40. I really liked him. "Yes," came flying out of my mouth without a thought. The next day May 23, 1986, I went to the motel with him for his birthday. I was nervous and didn't know what to expect. Even though I had slept with other men, I still didn't know what to do. As we were having sex, I felt something under his pillow. *What was it?* I slid my hand under the pillow. It was his gun. I didn't know what to think. This was a first. He saw the look on my face and knew I felt the gun. He slid his hand under the pillow and put the gun on top of my hand.

Unapologetically, he said, "I don't trust nobody." His tone implied I was included. He told me I had to always watch myself and never allow anyone to walk up on me. He kept telling me that I was to watch my back at all times. *So let's recap: I'm in the motel with this man having a sexual experience that I clearly didn't understand, and he's giving SWAT training, on his birthday.* Something else happened that night, I got pregnant for the first time. That morning when I got back to the hood it was late and as I was going to post on the stairs when Cassey came up and angrily said, "I was looking for you all night."

"Looking for me, for what?" I replied.

She kept talking as if I didn't say a word. She was mad that I didn't tell her I wasn't coming to the room. *Did she not know that I didn't have a Mama? I guess she didn't.*

"I was with somebody."

She turned her nose up and asked, "Who? Sneak?"

With a smirk on my face, "Uh yes. I didn't know you were my Mama."

Was she surprised that Sneak had taken her place as the number one person in my life? I had slept with other guys, but I didn't feel anything for them like I felt for him. *Mind you, I didn't get anything out of us sleeping together. My body never reacted.* I think I can say I loved him. *Why?* Because, before we even slept with one another he would spend hours making sure I was ok. He schooled me on who was who in the hood. And who and what to look out for. He fed me and he loved the thug in me. He loved Alicia bad and all; he embraced that fire that was in me. I believe that's why he was attracted to me. *Don't get me wrong, he had other girls on the side that I didn't know about until later. I thought I was the only one, ha! I guess I was still naive in certain areas and this was certainly one.* I learned from Petrie on a dope selling level and from Sneak on an overall hood level.

Another important person that came on the scene was Nannie Blue. I met her on a hot summer day while I waited in front of the apartments to see if I would see Sneak. As I was standing there, I heard a bunch of loud popping noise. *Was someone shooting?* I looked up to see a girl lighting firecrackers. As I watched her light the next one she looked at me with a sly laugh because she knew she scared everyone, including me.

From that day, we became friends. Nannie lived on 82nd with her grandmother. Her grandmother had a rule if you didn't get in by a certain time you were locked out of the house. One night, Nannie didn't go in, so now she was a runaway, too. The hood was tough, but so was Nannie Blue. She came from a large family. In her family you had to know how to throw them, meaning she also had the "Ghetto Fight Policy" instilled in her at a young age. Nannie started hanging at Gwen's and we began getting into trouble and selling drugs together. I thought Nannie was 15, until her mother showed up at Gwen's house threatening to put my homeboy TK in jail for statutory rape. Nannie's mother Gene found out where Nannie was. She stormed up to Gwen's and banged on the door. Gwen answered.

Gene demanded, "Tell me where my daughter is! Where is Chanelle?"

"Who is Chanelle?"

Gene interrupted, "I know Chanelle has been hanging with you. Sleeping with a grown man! She is only 12 years old!"

We were still confused. Finally, Gene yelled, "Don't play dumb. You know Nannie."

Our Nannie?

Gene yelled again, "Nannie is only 12!"

Stunned I blurted out, "Nannie's only 12?"

Gene did not answer. She stormed off threatening to send the police to Gwen's house. We couldn't afford that. We were all selling drugs out of her apartment.

Gwen was angry, "Nannie can't hang here. I don't want the police at my house."

We waited all day hoping to see Nannie, but she heard her mother came. We didn't see her for a few days. When she returned, Gwen allowed her to come back.

The tension with Cassey was on the rise. I refused to go to the room with her. I had new friends, Nannie and Gwen. I was cool on her and she knew it. She kept trying to get me to stop hanging with Gwen. She even hinted that Gwen and I had a big age difference. *Really? Wasn't she an adult herself?*

One hot summer night it was getting late and as usual, when Cassey saw Sneak and me sitting on Gwen's stairs she walked up. "Are you coming to the room?"

"No, I'm cool."

She kept bugging me until Sneak interjected, "I'll walk you to your room. Reluctantly I went with her because I wanted to be with him. We all walked down Figueroa, the hoe capitol, to our room. Sneak walked with his baseball bat over his shoulder and his gun in his waist. I was mad but, glad to be in his company.

When we got to the room Cassey did something trifling, she invited him in. I looked at her like, "What are you doing? My plans were to sit outside with him. He gladly came in. She began to tell him how I helped deliver her baby, Andre, and all the things we had been through. He was impressed, but at that point, I wasn't sure with who, her or me? She knew he liked me. She also knew she could control me with him. Because I just wanted to be around him. After all, I was 15, and he was 23, a grown thug. She talked with him all night. Angrily I eventually went to sleep refusing to join in on the conversation that she kept trying to include me in. I woke up early that morning but he was gone. I got my stuff. I knew I was done with her.

Later that day, she found me sitting on Gwen's steps with Nannie. She walked up and asked, "Why did you leave without waking me up?"

Being nasty, "Because I wanted to."

She apparently noticed that I had taken all my clothes, but left a pink Sweatshirt with a bunny rabbit on it. It was the sweatshirt she had given me. She was wearing it. Nannie saw that this was clearly a family matter going bad so she excused herself.

Cassey then asked, "Are you coming back to the room with me?

"No."

"Why?"

"I have more Yay(crack) to sell." *But in my head, I was saying because you're a trifling ass hoe.*

As we were going back and forth, Sneak came up. She lit up like Christmas lights. She turned to Sneak and started telling him how I would normally walk to the room with her. *Really? Hello, I can hear you! Was she throwing me under the bus?* I gave her the meanest look I could possibly give without it being obvious to Sneak. She was used to getting her way. I guess she thought she would use Sneak to control me. She then said she would be right back; she was going to the corner to the liquor store.

As soon as she was out of sight Sneak asked me, "What was wrong with you and your cousin?"

"You mean my fake cousin."

He said, "Cassey seems cool. Why are you mad at her?"

"I'm not mad, I'm just not with it."

"With what?"

"Nothing."

As we were talking Cassey walked back up. *Liquor store my ass; she came back too quick.* She wanted to see if her game of divide and conquer had worked, and it did. The first thing that came out of her mouth was, "Licia, it's late come to the room with me."

Did she not hear the word NO? I guess not.

Sneak was like, "Come on Licia cuzz, I'll walk y'all home."

I looked at her and answered him, "No thank you, I have work (crack) to sell."

Cassey said she was leaving. Sneak looked at me and said, "You can't let your cousin walk by herself."

I gave him a look that said *watch me.* Sneak then said he was going to walk Cassey to the room and asked me to come and I refused. He said he was going to walk her home and he would be right back. I sat outside all night. You know he never came back. That was the end of our cousinhood, friendship, sisterhood, because if I knew Cassey, she slept with him.

That morning Gwen saw that I stayed out all night on the stairs. I actually fell asleep there. Gwen asked me why I didn't want to go with Cassey. I told her the whole I'm not down with screwing everybody in the hood scenario. I also told her that Sneak walked Cassey to the room and never came back. Gwen gave me a look. I already knew what that meant, *you know he fucked her last night.* Gwen told me to come up to her house and get some sleep.

Later that afternoon I was at Gwen's house when Sneak came through. He was trying to feel me out to see what I thought about his disappearing act. As I sat on the couch listening to music, my heart was hurt, I knew what happened. I knew Cassey was scandalous. I was just hoping that he wasn't. He approached me with the "I went home" story after he went to the room. I knew he was lying.

"You mean the cleanup woman didn't give you none?"

He laughed. "You're crazy. Who is the cleanup woman?"

I gave him a lot of attitude. "You know Cassey?"

He kept laughing, "The cleanup woman?"

I looked him dead in his eyes and said, "Yes. The Betty Wright song, you don't know it? Well, let me sing it for you." I began to sing fighting back tears,

"A clean-up woman is a woman who gets all the love we girls leave behind, the reason I know so much about her is because she picked up a man of mine, etc…

Cause I found out all I was doin' was makin' it easy for the clean-up woman to get my man's love, uh-huh, yeah, that's what I did. I made it easy for the clean-up woman to steal my baby's love, oh, yeah.

The clean-up woman will wipe his blues away, She'll give him penny lovin', 24 hours a day, the clean-up woman, She'll sweep him off his feet, She's the one to take him in, When you dump him in the street, So take a tip You better get hip To the clean-up woman, 'cause she's tough I mean she really cleans up."

After I had sung the song he was no longer laughing. He looked me in my eyes and he knew I was hurt. *Is this one of the reasons he told me never trust anyone?*

Then he looked at me and said, "Your cousin loves you. We didn't do anything."

I knew in my heart that he was lying. But what could I say? I was a 15-year-old that loved a 23-year-old. Before iTunes and YouTube my song went viral. I had everyone in the hood calling Cassey the cleanup woman. In the hood you could be scandalous, don't get me wrong, but to be blatantly sleeping with your cousin's boyfriend was a no-no. After that mysterious walk home, I didn't see Cassey for days.

When Cassey came back around I clearly made it plain she was a hoe, and we weren't cousins anymore. She stopped coming around because the hood was calling her the cleanup woman. She knew the girls in the hood didn't want her around, because I had put it out there that she slept with her "cousin's" man a.k.a. my man.

Around this time, Cassey started living with Chris and Diane. Chris was the neighborhood drunk that lived on my father's street. Diane was his girlfriend; she was also a drunk, so anything went at that house. The hood knew there was a war between Cassey and I. It was just a matter of time before other causalities would get involved. One neutral territory that everyone went to was the corner liquor store on 83rd and Hoover. One day while I was there with Nannie and Gwen I ran into Karen, Cassey's former roommate, she was with Rhoda, Diana's daughter. I could tell Cassey had been talking about me by the tension with Rhoda and Karen. Rhoda was my age, and she gave me a nasty look. After they stared, I purposefully bumped into Rhoda. I did this to let her know I wasn't scared of her crew. As Rhoda turned around to say something, I socked her in the mouth. Rhoda and Karen were in shock because they weren't expecting this. Rhoda grabbed her mouth. It was bleeding and I was ready to fight. Rhoda ran out the store holding her mouth. Gwen and Nannie stood there. They were ready for whatever went on. Karen left the liquor store, she had nothing to say.

Later that day I got some good news: I found out Sandi was down from the foster home, despite my day, I was excited. I went on my father's street to Tina's house. Her older sister Jeannie gave us all a ride to the store. I was happy to see my sister, I began to tell her about Sneak, Cassey, and all that was happening to me. As we drove down 85th with Jeannie, Rhoda's mother, Diane, came out the house and yelled out, "You bitch! You jumped my daughter." *What was drunk Diane talking about?* Nobody jumped Rhoda; she got in the middle of the war and got socked in her mouth, period. I immediately told Jeannie to stop her car. She asked me if I was sure and I said yes. Jeannie stopped in the middle of 85th street. I got out the car. Diane was yelling that I jumped Rhoda, and she wanted a fair fight. I looked at Sandi and surprisingly she had no, "Stop it, Alicia" lecture for me. *Had she recognized that something had morphed within me?* I was now just evil. I told Diane to send Rhoda out so we could go head up, meaning a one-on-one fight because she really thought I jumped Rhoda. As Diane stood on her porch cussing, she had Rhoda put a scarf on her head. In ghetto fights, this was done so that the hair wouldn't get pulled out. As Diane was getting Rhoda ready for the fight of her life, my sister said, "Licia, be careful. Diane just gave Rhoda a knife." *You ask, what mother would give her daughter a knife? Hood mamas - that's who*! I looked up Rhoda was coming off her porch with her hair tied up in a scarf and a knife in her hand. I told Sandi, "I got her."

Rhoda, an inexperienced fighter, came in the middle of the street. She was actually what the hood would consider a pretty girl. Rhoda had a rep like Cassey; she only slept with men with the intent to be taken care of. On those facts alone she was already outmatched and didn't have a clue. I'm assuming she thought having her mother and the knife would help. She was dead wrong. Before she could get a swing, I was already punching her and took the knife out of her hand. I threw the knife to my sister and continued to beat her up. The fight got so bad that her mother came off the porch to jump in. Chris grabbed her and said, "Let the girls fight." Rhoda probably had no clue that I was channeling anger about being betrayed by Cassey or that I was now her pregnant ex-cousin. Poor Rhoda! This was not her war, she was an innocent victim.

That day I had three fights. *Yes, I said three fights.* The last one I was jumped. After the fight with Rhoda, I went to my father's house with my sister. My father had not seen me since I ran away. When he saw me, he had nothing to say to me except "Hi." Just as I was talking with my sister before heading back to 82nd, I heard someone calling my name. It was, Rowland, a childhood friend. I knew it meant trouble because Rhoda was sleeping with him. *Mind you, his wife was Sonya.* I went to the door and Rowland was standing outside with five girls telling me to come out. Now these were no ordinary girls they were called the Towne Girls. They were a group of about six that consisted of three sisters and the other three were friends. Rowland's wife Sonya was one of them. They called themselves the Towne girls because they lived on Towne, a street around the corner from my father. They had a reputation for jumping girls and many of the girls in my neighborhood were scared of them. During this gathering, ironically, Sonya was not with them.

I came out. The oldest and the biggest of the group Dee said she came because of the fight I had with Rhoda. Dee wanted me to fight her sister NeNe. I knew NeNe from Bethune Middle School. We didn't get along, because she hung with the enemy gang. I was thinking a couple of things. One, you're about to fight me over a girl that is sleeping with your friend's husband and two, what was NeNe doing here? She wasn't hangin' with the homies when we were at Bethune, but that wasn't the issue at that time. *So before we go further, let me explain something: Rowland was angry that I beat up his girlfriend Rhoda, and he went and got his wife's homegirls to fight me. At that time, the Towne girls had no clue Rhoda was Rowland's side chick, haha I'm sorry I had to laugh...*

As I began to walk in the middle of my father's yard, my sister cautioned me that there were six of them, and she didn't know what they would do. All the Towne girls were bigger than me. NeNe was the only one that was my age. *Looking back, they were all adults. I was 15 they were 18 and older.* I reassured my sister that I wasn't worried. I guess I was still flaming mad over Cassey and Sneak. NeNe was just going to be another causality. I was not scared of her. In fact, I already hated her. So, I turned my back and had my sister help me take off my gold chains. Sandi said, "don't turn your back on them." I replied, "I am not worried." She helped me take off my chains.

Rowland instructed NeNe to get me. He said it as if he was telling a dog to bite someone. The fight began and NeNe was trying to pull me to the ground and I grabbed my father's gate so she wouldn't get me on the ground. I was tired, pregnant and already had two fights that day. As I was holding on to the gate, Dee came up slapped my hand and said, "Oh no little Mama, let the gate go."

NeNe and I went at it for a while. I'm assuming the Towne girls were happy with NeNe's progress and then something happened, I got my second wind. We ended up brawling one-on-one in the middle of the street. That ghetto policy was double or nothing. *I wasn't going to let this punk ass chick beat me.* I had space and now a second wind. I backed her up from the street into my father's yard where it started. We ended up in my father's driveway and NeNe was now getting beat up. She was outmatched. I didn't see it coming and before I knew it, the other four girls rushed me and began hitting me. It didn't matter, I kept fighting anyway. I was still socking NeNe, and for me, that was all that mattered. I could feel the punches coming from everywhere, so as they punched me I punched her. I pinned NeNe to my father's car. She was under me, while the others were on me hitting me and trying to pull me off her. It felt as if we were on that car forever. I couldn't give up. I was mad, these big bitches are jumping me because Rhoda and their scary ass sister can't fight?

This was the first time I had been jumped. I was not about to let NeNe go. As my sister and Tina watched, finally, my brother came and tried to get them off me. As my brother was pulling them off, NeNe was pinned under everybody. He got them off and started to argue with Rowland. I dragged NeNe to the front porch. I wasn't done, Edwin had bought me some more one-on-one fight time. I had NeNe on the porch kicking and punching her. In the midst of my brother arguing with Rowland, someone hollered, "Who's going to get NeNe?" While arguing with Edwin they didn't realize, I had dragged her to the front porch.

Dee looked up past my brother and yelled, "I'm going to get her." Dee had to be 23 and 180 pounds compared to my 98 pounds.

I started kicking and hitting NeNe even more. NeNe was done she could not get up. My mind was racing. This big chick is about to kill me so I had better stomp NeNe while I can. As Dee ran up to hit me, something crazy happened. *ARE YOU READY FOR THIS?*

My father came running out the house jumped from the porch and yelled "You bitches ain't going to jump my daughter!" *IS YOUR MOUTH OPEN? Mine was.* I was so surprised, I let NeNe go. She got off the porch and ran. My father with all his might tried to knock Dee out. She barely ducked the punch. I don't know who was more in shock her or me. When she ducked that punch, she almost fell to the ground. She looked up with nothing to say.

Rowland yelled, "Edwin your daddy is in trouble."

My father then yelled at Rowland, "Come on!"

Rowland had nothing to say. They all ran and jumped in their cars and left. My father looked at me and went back into the house as if nothing happened. I was still standing there in the middle of the yard; in shock. *Did my father just defend me?* During this battle, I had a sister, a friend, and brother and out of everyone that watched me get jumped, the one that I thought least likely to help came out to fight that day. *MY FATHER.*

I wasn't angry that they didn't help me, after all, this was my life, hood life, my war. I could not get over what happened, not the fact that I had three fights and was jumped; I couldn't get over the fact that my father helped me. Later that day, I was exhausted, so Jeannie gave me a ride around the corner. As she drove me, she said, "Alicia just because your father hurt you in the past, does not mean he will allow others to hurt you now." *Wow!!*

The war wasn't over yet, I was determined that I was going to get them back, plus this wouldn't be the last battle. The next unexpected battle would be a game changer, and it would determine who would be the victor once and for all.

Chapter 12

Survive or Die Period!

When I got back to Gwen's, I told her and Nannie what had happened. *Fueling the war.* In the midst of all these fights, where was Cassey? I sat with Nannie and Gwen plotting who I was going to get first. Sneak tried to ask me what happened.

"I have nothing to say. If you hadn't screwed Cassey I wouldn't be fighting."

Sneak stuck to his story, "I never slept with her."

Later that day Gwen explained to Sneak that I was not just angry over Cassey but pregnant. Over the next couple of weeks, I had little to say to him, but I still loved him. Eventually I was sleeping with him again. When we were kicking it at Gwen's house, once again he reinforced his mantra about not trusting anyone. Gwen's house had now become the hang out spot. All the homies were in and out. I tried to do everything I could to stay at Gwen's because I was homeless and because Sneak was there. Gwen allowed us to stay in her room. She was in and out selling her dope. Once after I slept with Sneak, he asked me about being pregnant. I told him maybe I was. He then asked me if I took care of myself. I lied and said yes. I had not been to a doctor since I left foster care. Later that night Gwen came to me and she explained that Sneak wanted me to take care of myself, especially, since I was pregnant with his baby.

Hood life was on and crackin'. I had not forgotten about being jumped or Cassey betraying me. I was waiting for my opportunity. The one thing that was right in my life was the fact that my sister had graduated from high school. She was back from the foster home for good. She had moved back in with my father. I started going by my father's more often to see her. I was glad she was back. Sandi told me stories of how Mama took her money and how she continued to work in the beauty shop for free. Basically, what she was saying was, *Licia you were right.* It didn't matter that she obeyed and was the good sister, Mama was not only a liar but a thief too.

One day as I left my father's house, Jeannie saw me walking and offered me a ride. She was going on 83rd. She was now dating one of the homies' brother, 'Tyrone". She had moved in with him. Jeannie's 6-year-old son Derrick was sitting in the back seat with me. I looked down to see him playing with an army knife.

I yelled, "Boy that's a real knife, where did you get it?" Scared, he did not answer. I took the knife and put it in my pocket. I never thought twice about it. I got out at T-man's house, and began to walk around the corner. As I crossed at the light on 83rd and Hoover, I saw two people kissing. When I got closer, it looked like Sneak. As I got closer, I realized it was Sneak! He was kissing some girl with braids in her hair. I didn't get a close look because I wanted to get past them without being seen. Damn it. I caught him now. I immediately went to Gwen's. I was hurt, but tried to play it off and pretend I wasn't bothered. I told Gwen what I saw. Gwen just stared at me, she wasn't laughing. She asked me to describe the girl. I really couldn't. I just knew the chick had braids and was wearing a pink sweatshirt. Gwen had a look as if she wanted to cry.

"Alicia that was Cassey."

My laugh now turned into serious hurt. "What? Cassey who?" Still trying to laugh it off.

Gwen said, "I saw Cassey earlier today. She had on a pink sweatshirt with a bunny on it."

What was up with that damn sweatshirt? I knew Cassey was scandalous, but would she go that far to get me back and hurt me? She never liked Sneak as a person let alone a boyfriend. My fake laugh immediately turned into tears. As the tears began to flow hard, my heart raced as I went for the door.

Gwen asked, "Where are you going?"

"To confront them!"

Gwen jumped up and ran after me. I didn't see, but Nannie followed suit. I ran to the corner but when I turned the corner, Sneak was gone. Cassey was walking towards me. I ran up in her face and confronted her. "You fucking Sneak?"

She looked at me with a smirk, "What are you talking about?"

"Are you fucking Sneak? You dirty bitch! I want the truth"

She looked me dead in my eyes and said, "Yes, I'm fucking him."

I hit her in the face as hard as I could. We started fighting in a small driveway space between the Dungeon and a church. She was not like Debbie, NeNe, or Rhoda; I was having a hard time. I couldn't beat her. She was older, bigger and I guess she was just as mad at me as I was at her. As the fight progressed, she kept slamming me into the gate that separated the Dungeon and the church. I would bounce off the gate and run up on her again; she would grab me and slam me into the gate again. The last time she slammed me into the gate I felt the knife in my pocket. She didn't even see me take it out of my pocket. I ran up on her again this time when she went to grab me I stabbed her. She did not understand what was going on because as she was trying to slam me back into the gate, she was getting weak. I remember as I stabbed her it was unreal. It felt like I was moving in slow motion. Her sweatshirt was just puffing up with each jab. Eventually, we ended up in a deadlock position. We were both exhausted. We had one another by the hair, but her hand was on the knife. She did not have enough strength to take it from me, only to hold it so I would not stab her anymore. As we stood there, both tired, you could hear the sound of water hitting the ground. *Or was it blood?*

Gwen yelled out, "Somebody's bleeding!"

I said, "I'm bleeding!"

Gwen said, "No Alicia, Cassey is the one bleeding."

Cassey looked me in my eyes and said, "You were supposed to be my cousin."

I looked her back in her eyes and replied, "I was until you fucked Sneak, knowing I'm pregnant."

With that, she let go of the knife and I let her go. Cassey staggered on 82nd and collapsed. I went around the corner to Jeannie and asked for a ride. When Jeannie saw me, she was shocked I had blood all over my clothes and in my hair.

"I need a ride to my father's house."

Jeannie kept asking me, "Are you ok?"

"Just take me home." As I got in her car, I said, "I had a fight with Cassey." Jeannie didn't ask me another word.

When I got home Sandi was there and when I came up with blood on my clothes, she started panicking. She thought I was hurt. I wouldn't tell her what happened. She kept yelling for me to tell her what happened.

I told her, "I'm ok. I need to get out of these clothes."

Sandi started pulling my shirt off. My shirt and bra were soaked with blood. During the commotion my brother, Edwin came in, "What the fuck happened to you?"

I started crying and told him I had a fight. It was rare for me to cry over a fight. They knew something bad had happened.

Edwin kept asking, "Whose blood is this Alicia?"

With tears rolling down my eyes, I said, "Cassey's."

They both stopped and looked at me. My sister could no longer move. Edwin took over. He started taking my shoes off. They were soaked with blood, too. When he took my shoes off, I started crying even more.

He yelled, "Why in the hell are you crying over those bloody shoes?"

"Because they're my shoes!" I bought those shoes with my money. He ran into the kitchen and came back with a plastic bag for me to put my clothes in it.

When I started wrapping my clothes to dispose of them I forgot an important thing; I still had the knife. I had put it back in my pocket. I was in tears, angry, hurt and scared that I was going to jail. I put my clothes, shoes, and that knife in the bag. My brother left with it. I had not been at my father's long, before someone came and knocked on the door. I hid in the bedroom thinking it might be the police looking for me. It was someone from the hood, they came to tell my brother that the police had put up yellow tape on 82nd and Cassey had died. My sister looked at me. I started to cry again. She held me and cried too. *I guess maybe she was crying because for years she had tried to save me from destroying myself and the reality was it didn't work.*

Chapter 13

Tennis Shoes

I didn't stay at my father's house that night because I knew the police would be looking for me. I went to my aunt's house. My Aunt Letty lived in Hawthorne. I didn't tell her what happened, only that I had been in a fight. I stayed there for a few days. I was uncomfortable. One night I sat on her couch as she was teaching her two daughters the books of The Bible. Genesis, Exodus, Leviticus… I sat on the couch listening, I couldn't help but wonder what was going to happen to me. To my baby? My family didn't know I was pregnant.

After my aunt put my cousins to bed, she sat at the table and asked, "What happened?"

Did she know I was lying to her? I couldn't tell her what I did or that I was pregnant.

"When you are ready, you can tell me." She then asked, "Do you know Jesus?"

I shook my head no.

"He is the way, truth and, the light. If you want to be saved, all you have to do is accept him. When you're ready, Alicia, God is waiting for you." She then got up and went into her room.

I could hear her and my uncle Jerome praying for me. I don't know if I felt guilty for lying to her, but I went to her room door and said, "I want to be saved."

Instantly she jumped up from her knees. She and my uncle continued to pray for me. I stayed a few more days, but I felt so guilty because I was pregnant that I finally told her I was going home. I didn't go back to my father's. I went to my Aunt Darlene's house. That is when I heard from my cousin that one of the homies said Sneak was looking for me. *Looking for me?*

I told my cousin, "Nigga please, looking for me for what?"

In those days, I had no cell phone, so I called Gwen's house. She was happy to hear from me. She said she wasn't sure if I was ok. I assured her that I was ok and she told me Cassey was alive. Gwen said after the fight Cassey walked on 82nd and collapsed. They put yellow tape up because she stopped breathing. Gwen also let me know that Sneak had been at the hospital everyday with her. Once she told me that any remorse that I had went out the window.

"Where are you?" Gwen kept asking.

I would not tell her.

"You need to talk with Sneak."

"No I don't. I have to go now, I don't want my aunt to know what I did."

"Promise you will call me back tonight," Gwen said.

"I promise."

That night when I called back she purposefully said my name so that Sneak would know I was on the phone. I could hear him, asking her where I was. I didn't want to talk to him. She told him she didn't know where I was, because I wouldn't tell her.

Finally, she got tired of Sneak asking, so she just gave him the phone. "Hello, hello." At first I wouldn't say a word. "Hello, are you there?"

Finally, I said, "I'm here."

He asked me, "Are you okay?"

I snarled, "As if you give a fuck. You've been at the hospital with that bitch."

Sneak said, "I was there to make sure she was ok. I've been worried about you. Where are you?"

"None of your business! I don't trust nobody and I don't trust you."
He started laughing.

"You and your hoe won't be sending me to jail."

"I told Cassey not to press charges against you. Where are you?"

"None of your damn business."

"Man, you're dangerous."

"Well teacher, never teach what you don't want to be learned." After that he didn't have a word to say. I hung up the phone in his face.

During my time of hiding out, the tension in the hood was still brewing because of what I did to Cassey. Zenay, Houn's girlfriend, thought she would confront Nannie because rumor had it Nannie gave me the knife. What Zenay didn't know was Nannie packed a helluva "Ghetto Fight Policy" and because of that she was not the one to mess with unless you really wanted a fight on your hands. I'm assuming Zenay thought it was her public duty to investigate what happened when she ran up on Nannie to question her. She got beat up by a 12-year-old. They had to stop the fight because Nannie was beating and dragging Zenay up and down the sidewalk. After hearing about Nannie and Zenay, I could no longer bear it. The hood was calling my name. I had to go back. I was no punk, plus I had been calling Gwen every day. She convinced me that it was safe to come back. I trusted her, but I didn't trust Sneak, after all, he lied about everything. *The number one hood rule was no snitching. Would he set me up for Cassey?*

I called Gwen and told her I was coming back. My sister Annette dropped me off a few blocks away. I wanted to see my surroundings before I just walked up on 82nd. When I got to Gwen's, Nannie was there. She was as happy to see me, as I was to see her. Just as she walked me in the door, Sneak came banging on the screen door yelling for Gwen to let him in. Gwen looked at me and without hesitation she opened the door. I continued talking to Nannie. Sneak came, took me by the arm and said, "We need to talk." He took me to Gwen's bedroom. We exchanged words. The more aggressive I was, the more he laughed. *I didn't think it was funny.* He simply told me, "I'll never betray you. I would never let her send you to jail." *Wouldn't you know it? In no time, I was sleeping with him again.*

I continued to stay at Gwen's. When Cassey was released from the hospital, she continued to live with Rhoda and her mother so they could take care of her. I heard that Sneak went to see her, but I never asked him. He knew how I felt. Cassey being on my father's street did not deter me from going over there. I was hoping to catch him there. *Why? I'm not really sure.* On one of my visits with my sister we decided to go to the store. While walking back to my father's house, we saw what looked like Cassey in the front yard with my father. My heart began to race. This appeared to be round two. Mentally I was ready. The closer we got to the yard I started taking off my chains. Of course, Sandi helped. Once we got right in front of the yard, I heard Cassey tell my father, "I'm not satisfied."

My father told her, "Leave it up to God."

She said "No!"

"Call the police."

She said, "No."

What was my father's last offer? "Whoop her ass if you can. Here she comes."

I immediately knew it was time to fight especially since this was the first time that we met face to face since I stabbed her. I walked up on her. It was just like two fighters squaring off the night before a pay-per-view fight. We both stared each other in the face without blinking.

Finally, Cassey broke the silence. She said, "I just came to let you see what you did to me." Without warning, she unzipped her jacket exposing her bare chest. I looked down and all I saw were stab wounds everywhere. I had no idea I had stabbed her so many times and in so many places. Speechless, I held back tears. Somewhere I began to feel remorse, until she said a few magic words. "You were supposed to love me." Cold-heartedly I said, "I did until you fucked Sneak." *What changed my heart? Well, it was the fact that she had stabbed me in the back with Sneak and even after our altercation she continued to see him as if I didn't know.*

Clearly, we were both hurt and tears were now streaming from both our eyes. She zipped up her jacket and walked off. I stood there for a moment not knowing exactly what happened and why. I didn't realize we had gained an audience. The neighbors had come to see the showdown. As I walked into the house, I heard the neighbor Johnnie Hat tell my sister, "Your little sister is too dangerous to be just 15."

I heard later through rumors that Sneak had told her to leave the situation alone. *Was she plotting to get me back?* Not long after our confrontation Cassey moved to Ohio with her family. I kept hanging on 82nd and sleeping with Sneak. Every day I felt closer to him and acted as if Cassey never existed.

Cassey wasn't his only side detour. I wasn't wifey. I wasn't a side chick. He put me in the category of "the baby," meaning I was his youngest, and he didn't expect me to be sleeping with anyone else. I didn't, because he was all I wanted. *Sad, but the older homegirls knew better. I was the only one in the dark.*

The hood was getting hot, meaning the police were raiding houses and taking people to jail left and right. One afternoon I left and went to hang out with Sandi. When I made my way back to Gwen's house, they had raided her house and were taking her to jail. I stood in silence not knowing what to expect.

The homie, Pokey, came and stood next to me. He said, "I hid my dope. I can't get it because of the police. I told my girl Crae." He didn't know if she got it. Pokey asked "Can you get it?"

"Yea I'll get it." It wasn't 20 minutes later that the police had Pokey, too.

After the raid, I went up to Gwen's house. The police left her apartment open on purpose hoping when she got out of jail nothing would be left. The neighbor Sharon had Gwen's kids when the police raided. After the police left Sharon brought the kids to me. I called Gwen's father, he and her brother came and got them. Gwen's brother knew that we were close. He allowed me to stay in her apartment. Maybe he was more worried that an empty apartment would be just as disastrous as leaving a 15-year-old there. When Gwen called her father, he let her know that I was there. In all the commotion, I never went to get Pokey's dope. I was too concerned about what was happening with Gwen. That night I had an opportunity to be in Gwen's house alone with Sneak. I wasn't thinking about Pokey or his dope. Plus, when I saw Crae earlier that night, she said she would get it.

The next morning Crae came to Gwen's apartment and said Pokey's dope was gone. *Gone?* Only three people knew it was there and one was in jail. Clearly this only meant trouble for me. Later that day when she spoke with Pokey he was flaming mad. He thought I took it. Crae came back the next day and she said Pokey was insisting that when he got out of jail I better have his money or else. *You ask what else?* Pokey was a woman beater. I witnessed first-hand him beat and drag Crae. This just meant that was my fate too. I didn't tell Sneak what Pokey was saying, because I didn't tell him that I agreed to get Pokey's dope. Over the next couple of days, Pokey had sent various people to me to give me the message that he wanted his dope or he was going to get me. *What was I supposed to do?* I didn't steal his dope. I wasn't a thief plus, I knew better.

Pokey sent Crae back to Gwen's because he knew I was there. This time, when Crae came to Gwen's door Sneak answered. Crae told Sneak what Pokey said.

Sneak told Crae, "She didn't take that dope. Tell cuz she ain't giving him shit. He has to take a loss."

Sneak came to me and I explained what happened. Sneak knew I was a thug, but I wasn't a thief. Gwen eventually made bail. When she got home she saw how well I took care of her house, she let me move in. I also told Gwen the problem I had with Pokey. I knew it wasn't the end of it. Not even a day after Gwen was released, I was outside the apartment and I saw Pokey. *My heart froze, what was I going to do?*

I refused to run. I also knew I couldn't whip this man. As he got closer, he began to ball his fist up. Pokey was mumbling he wanted his money. It was no longer about dope; he was mad that I didn't comply when he sent messages through Crae. When Pokey walked up on me, Sneak came out of nowhere and confronted him. Pokey explained that

Crae went to get the dope and she said the dope wasn't there. Sneak told Pokey, "I sent you a message, Cuz. You have to take a loss." Pokey kept trying to tell Sneak that I took his dope. Finally, Sneak walked up on Pokey and said "This is the last time I'm going to say it, Cuz. You takin a loss, she didn't take your dope. She was with me." Sneak called it and the situation went exactly how Sneak said it would go. Pokey took a loss. He never approached me again about it.

After this, he hated my guts because he couldn't get me. Sneak was that nigga in the hood, they knew he was a ride or die, a killa and if you came to him, you better come correct. Everybody knew Sneak was down and crazy.

How crazy was Wilford Jones a.k.a. Sneak? I'll tell you. Once I was mad at him because I saw him talking to another girl. I asked Gwen to take me to the store.

When he saw us leaving, he asked "Where you going?"

I wanted to make him mad so I said, "None of your business."

He laughed at me as always. When we left for the store, we weren't paying attention, so we didn't realize Sneak had followed us. I guess he didn't think we would see him because he hardly drove his car. As Gwen and I were driving down my father's street, we saw someone driving crazy. They were coming straight at us. We started to panic. "Wait, it's Sneak in his chocolate brown glasshouse." I guessed when he spotted us he decided to play chicken. To scare us, he came head on with his car. When he got close enough to hit us he swerved his car. He lost control and ran into a light pole. In horror, I watched as the light pole fell on top of his car and smashed the top completely in. I just knew he was dead. I jumped out of Gwen's car. Before I could even get to him he jumped out of his car laughing. He got out, pushed the light pole off his car, and said "I'll meet you on 82nd." *Yeah. That's how crazy Sneak was... A light pole just fell on his car and he was calm.*

Sneak parked his car at his mother's house and then came right over to Gwen's. Both of us were still shaking. He just laughed. *This was the nigga that everybody knew not to fuck with.*

Everything was starting to change. The homies had a new spot that they were hanging at, some apartments on 79th and Figueroa. I heard that Sneak was messing with some girl named Ashley; Gwen told me she heard it too, but she didn't want to get in the middle. Maybe she knew I wasn't going to leave him alone no way. Pregnant and emotional I actually started sleeping at my father's house at night. *So you know it was bad for me.* If he was messing with a hoodrat I didn't want to be around him. *Remember, I had nothing say so. I was the baby out of the line of his women.* Although he didn't claim to have any other women. The next morning I decided to go see my sister Annette because I never spent time with her anyway.

Chapter 14

Hood Loss

When I came back to the hood, things were crazy. The police were everywhere. I hit the corner of 82nd and saw the street surrounded with police. They had raided the apartments, again. I saw Sneak being chased by a police officer. She was frustrated because she could not catch him. He just kept running in circles to make her angry. Eventually, another officer helped her out. I watched them rough him up before they took him to jail. I was nervous; he was still on parole. Any contact with the police meant a parole violation. Usually a parole officer gave a year off the top even without a crime being committed.

It was a Friday; Sneak called Gwen's house late that night asking her to bail him out. I was still angry with him over the cheating and told her not to do it. Sneak stressed the importance of getting out before his PO returned to work on Monday. It would be an automatic parole violation for coming in contact with the police. So what did Gwen do? She bailed him out.

I continued to sleep at my father's house. On August 2nd, I had a hard time sleeping due to an earache. *Was it this baby? What was wrong?* Early that morning there was banging on the door. My brother Curtis answered. It was Gwen. I rolled over on the couch.

She was screaming to the top of her lungs, "Alicia get up! Sneak is dead!"

Half asleep and still in pain, I looked at her in the doorway and asked, "What are you talking about?"

Gwen then pushed past my brother at the door. She came to the couch insisting that I get up now and come with her. She was screaming, "Sneak is DEAD! We have to go."

"SNEAK is..." I instantly jumped up. My heart was racing maybe it was a mistake. I ran outside in my pajamas. We jumped in her car. As we drove to where his body was supposed to be, Gwen kept saying, "I didn't know who to tell and then I thought oh my God, what about Alicia?"

Gwen and I pulled up on 82nd. I got out the car. The homie Bear was standing in front of Gwen's apartment building. Without saying a word, he immediately came over and took my hand. At this point, I knew in my heart that it was true. Bear walked me through the cut from 82nd to 81st, holding my hand. When we got to a certain set of apartments, the police were out front. Bear walked me up to a gate; the police officers were inside the gate still wrapping up the crime scene.

You could smell death with your eyes. Things were not the same. It was silent and none of the old men that hung out early in the morning were around. It was like a desert.

I saw a half covered body with the legs exposed from under the sheet. I recognized those cutoff shorts and socks, it was SNEAK. At that point, all I could do was slide down to the ground. I held onto the gate trying not to pass out. An officer came up from behind the gate and kicked it. He said, "This is a crime scene, you have to go." Bear came and helped me up off the ground. As my mind was racing, a car pulled up in front of us.

It was Sneak's mother. She opened her car door. Bear approached her car. She asked, "Kevin, is it him?" Bear replied, "Yes, Mrs. Jones, it's him." Without another word, she closed her car door and drove off.

Bear, Gwen, and I went back to her apartment. As soon as Gwen opened her door we both walked in and fell to the floor. I can't tell you how long I was on the floor crying, but I couldn't get up. It was so bad that Bear said he couldn't take it. He left Gwen and me to weep bitterly. He could hear us crying outside the door.

Later that day Nannie came to the house, all we did was cry; death was in the air. There was an emptiness that could not be described. *Someone had killed Sneak. What do we do now? Who would want him dead? The most asked question was which homie did it?* Sneak didn't trust anyone. Who could have killed him in our alley? An enemy didn't know the cuts in our hood. Later on, we found out that Sneak had all his money and his gun on him. Someone had shot him in the head multiple times. They executed him. *I wept even more!*

The hood shootings and killings continued. Shortly after Sneak was killed, my homeboy Jackie was shot on 82ⁿᵈ. They brought him up to Gwen's apartment and cut off his clothes. He was going into shock. I sat and cried, not because I had not seen someone shot before, but I had a flashback of that covered body with the legs exposed from under a white sheet. *Was this what Sneak had gone through? No one was there to help him, he died alone. I wept!*

There was another shooting, this time, it was Big Wade. I was in Stacy's apartment, and I heard about 30 shots. The homies came in through the door scrambling for a phone to call the ambulance.

"Big Wade was just shot!"

I froze. Another homie came in 10 minutes later and said, "We lost cuz."

I couldn't move I sat on the floor paralyzed. *Was this what happened to Sneak? Someone hated him that much that they would shoot him multiple times? I wept some more!*

Big Crane was shot at the phone booth on Hoover Street; someone tried to take Big D-Rock's car, Big Link was murdered at the gas station on Imperial and Vermont. The list went on and on in such a small time frame. So many others not mentioned lost their lives and they were young. *Hood Life, the dope game, gang bangin,' the eighties, so many girlfriends, mothers, sisters, aunts, wives, grandmothers WEPT!*

After Sneak's death, the homies started hanging back at Gwen's. It was time to plan his funeral. Sneak's mother made it clear that there was not going to be a funeral. We were shocked. We wanted a funeral, but we didn't know what we could do to change her mind.

It was then that Gwen said, "We are going to ask her for a funeral."

"Why would she change her mind?

Gwen said, "You're going with me and you're going to tell her you're pregnant."

"Tell her I'm pregnant? I'm the backup plan?"

So Gwen, Bear, and I went to his mother's house. When she opened the door, she knew Bear, but she didn't know us. Bear started talking, but it didn't seem as if she was going to agree so Gwen interjected, "We want a funeral because Alicia is pregnant." Gwen nudged me in front of the door. I was 15, I didn't know what to say, so I didn't say a word, I just stood speechless with tears rolling down my face.

Mrs. Jones looked me in my face and turned to Bear, "If you want a funeral you have to pay for it." He agreed. Mrs. Jones closed her door leaving us standing on her porch. Although we had gotten our funeral, we were still sad.

Over the course of a week, we were collecting money. We were still short when MW, a big time dope dealer at that time, stepped in and covered the difference. I knew MW from around the hood. He had a special relationship with Sneak. Sneak had two daughters and he believed that one belonged to MW. Sneak told me he had caught MW coming from his girl's house, so he was never sure that the baby was his. Sneak said he wasn't mad at MW it was just how the game went. And, now MW had come through for Sneak because we did not have the money to pay for a funeral.

Sneak was buried in a gray Fila sweat jacket and some Levi jeans. It was some funeral. Everyone was sad and in shock while also trying to figure out which one of the killers in the room did it. We knew that person was there. Mrs. Jones kept her word. She never came to service, as a matter of fact, she went to Las Vegas. Sneak's brothers didn't come either. At a certain part of the funeral the homies were taking pictures. Someone asked if I wanted one. Horrified, my immediate response was no. At the funeral, I finally met that Ashley chick. She was telling the homies she was pregnant too. I was ready to fight. Nannie and I walked up on her. I wanted answers and a fight. As I walked up on Ashley, she didn't know what to do. I didn't care that it was a funeral. I was mad at Ashley, and Cassey, for being themselves, hoodrats. I was also angry with Sneak for trusting someone.

While I was in Ashley's face, Gwen politely came over and reminded me I was pregnant. I told the homies Ashley wasn't pregnant by Sneak. A couple of weeks after the funeral Ashley said she had an abortion. I told the homies, "Abortion my ass. Like I said she was never pregnant." As I was accusing Ashley of not being pregnant, some of the homies were saying the same thing about me. They said Sneak wasn't the father and that he didn't get me pregnant. Only the ones that were close to him said I was. I didn't care, I was alone and pregnant. *What could I get out of lying? Nothing.* I was already behind in the game with a baby on the way without a father.

After Sneak's death, everybody and their Mama had the nerve to tell me who he was sleeping with. *My response, what good is it now?* My homie Charles came to me and told me that he and Sneak had bumped heads going over a girl's house. When he mentioned me, Sneak told him that I was the one he would not share. Charles never said the name of the girl they were both sleeping with, but once again I couldn't do anything about it. Yet and still the stories kept coming. I even had someone tell me that when Cassey heard that Sneak was dead, she was crying on the phone. *Was I supposed to give a damn?* I was actually sick of everyone snitching on a dead man. Some nights, I just walked around the neighborhood late, hoping to see Sneak. I would walk through allies at two in the morning because it was still unreal to me. *Would I see him again? In my mind, I was hoping so.*

CERTIFICATE OF DEATH
STATE OF CALIFORNIA

STATE FILE NUMBER			LOCAL REGISTRATION DISTRICT AND CERTIFICATE NUMBER
1A. NAME OF DECEDENT—First	1B. MIDDLE	1C. LAST	2A. DATE OF DEATH (MONTH, DAY, YEAR) 2B. HOUR
WILFORD	D.	JONES	Found August 2, 1986 1040
3. SEX	4. RACE/ETHNICITY	5. SPANISH/HISPANIC 6. DATE OF BIRTH	7. AGE IF UNDER 1 YEAR IF UNDER 24 HOURS
Male	Black/Amer.	No May 20, 1963	23 YEARS MONTHS DAYS HOURS MINUTES

DECEDENT PERSONAL DATA

8. BIRTHPLACE OF DECEDENT (STATE OR FOREIGN COUNTRY)	9. NAME AND BIRTHPLACE OF FATHER	10. BIRTH NAME AND BIRTHPLACE OF MOTHER
CA	Wilford Jones, Sr. - MS	Ora Calvin - MS

11A. CITIZEN OF WHAT COUNTRY	11B. IF DECEASED WAS EVER IN MILITARY GIVE DATES OF SERVICE	12. SOCIAL SECURITY NUMBER	13. MARITAL STATUS	14. NAME OF SURVIVING SPOUSE (IF WIFE, ENTER BIRTH NAME)
U.S.A.	19 TO 19	Unknown	Never married	

15. PRIMARY OCCUPATION	16. NUMBER OF YEARS THIS OCCUPATION	17. EMPLOYER (IF SELF-EMPLOYED, SO STATE)	18. KIND OF INDUSTRY OR BUSINESS
Laborer	5	Various	Various

USUAL RESIDENCE

19A. USUAL RESIDENCE—STREET ADDRESS (STREET AND NUMBER OR LOCATION)	19B.	19C. CITY OR TOWN
613 W. 82nd Street		Los Angeles

19D. COUNTY	19E. STATE	20. NAME AND ADDRESS OF INFORMANT—RELATIONSHIP
Los Angeles	California	Child of Minor

PLACE OF DEATH

21A. PLACE OF DEATH	21B. COUNTY	1431 W. 104th #4
Alley	Los Angeles	Los Angeles, Ca. 90047

21C. STREET ADDRESS (STREET AND NUMBER OR LOCATION)	21D. CITY OR TOWN
629 West 81st St	Los Angeles

CAUSE OF DEATH

22. DEATH WAS CAUSED BY: (ENTER ONLY ONE CAUSE PER LINE FOR A, B, AND C)		24. WAS DEATH REPORTED TO CORONER? 86-10018
IMMEDIATE CAUSE (A) MULTIPLE GUNSHOT WOUNDS	APPROXIMATE INTERVAL BETWEEN ONSET AND DEATH	25. WAS BIOPSY PERFORMED? No
CONDITIONS, IF ANY, WHICH GAVE RISE TO THE IMMEDIATE CAUSE, (B) DUE TO, OR AS A CONSEQUENCE OF		26. WAS AUTOPSY PERFORMED? Yes
STATING THE UNDERLYING CAUSE LAST. (C) DUE TO, OR AS A CONSEQUENCE OF		

23. OTHER SIGNIFICANT CONDITIONS—CONTRIBUTING TO DEATH BUT NOT RELATED TO CAUSE GIVEN IN 22A	27. WAS OPERATION PERFORMED FOR ANY CONDITION IN ITEMS 22 OR 23? TYPE OF OPERATION DATE No

PHYSICIAN'S CERTIFICATION

28A. I CERTIFY THAT DEATH OCCURRED AT THE HOUR, DATE AND PLACE STATED FROM THE CAUSES STATED. I ATTENDED DECEDENT SINCE (ENTER MO. DA. YR.) I LAST SAW DECEDENT ALIVE (ENTER MO. DA. YR.)	28B. PHYSICIAN—SIGNATURE AND DEGREE OR TITLE	28C. DATE SIGNED	28D. PHYSICIAN'S LICENSE NUMBER
	28E. TYPE PHYSICIAN'S NAME AND ADDRESS		

INJURY INFORMATION

29. SPECIFY ACCIDENT, SUICIDE, ETC.	30. PLACE OF INJURY	31. INJURY AT WORK	32A. DATE OF INJURY—MONTH, DAY, YEAR	32B. HOUR
Homicide	Alley	No	Unknown	Unk.

33. LOCATION (STREET AND NUMBER OR LOCATION AND CITY OR TOWN)	34. DESCRIBE HOW INJURY OCCURRED (EVENTS WHICH RESULTED IN INJURY)
629 West 81st St - Los Angeles	Shot

CORONER'S USE ONLY

35A. I CERTIFY THAT DEATH OCCURRED AT THE HOUR, DATE AND PLACE STATED FROM THE CAUSES STATED. AS REQUIRED BY LAW I HAVE HELD AN INVESTIGATION	35B. CORONER—SIGNATURE AND DEGREE OR TITLE	35C. DATE SIGNED
	Deputy Coroner [signature]	8-7-86

36. DISPOSITION	37. DATE—MONTH, DAY, YEAR	38. NAME AND ADDRESS OF CEMETERY OR CREMATORY	39. EMBALMER'S LICENSE NUMBER AND SIGNATURE
Cremation	8-11-86	Rosedale 1831 W. Washington Blvd L.A. CA	6316 Debbi Green

40A. NAME OF FUNERAL DIRECTOR (OR PERSON ACTING AS SUCH)	40B. LICENSE NO.	41. LOCAL REGISTRAR—SIGNATURE	42. DATE ACCEPTED BY LOCAL REGISTRAR
House of Winston Mortuary	639	Robert Fits L-W	AUG 11 1986

STATE REGISTRAR

A.	B.	C.	D.	E.	F.
96cu					4-9-4-2001

This is a true and certified copy of the record if it bears the seal, imprinted in purple ink, of the Registrar-Recorder.

MAR 20 1989

[signature] REGISTRAR-RECORDER
LOS ANGELES COUNTY, CALIFORNIA

I was pregnant, still selling dope and soon I'd be feeding another person, *what was I supposed to do?* I didn't have a clue about being a mother, hell I didn't have a mother. The good thing about being pregnant with Sneak's baby was that the real homies helped me out and gave me money. Don't get me wrong, there were those that said my baby wasn't Sneak's. *Please note: Some didn't claim their own children. So I couldn't exactly take it personally.*

I had my baby shower at my great aunt's house and my teacher, Ms. Hoover came. The last letter I sent her said I stabbed some girl and was on the run; it was now time to catch up. Ms. Hoover was excited to see me; she had quilted a blanket for my baby. Ms. Hoover always told me how smart I was. She asked me if I was going back to school. I told her I couldn't go back any time soon because of the baby. Ms. Hoover said she did not want that to deter me, but it already did. I was a 15-year-old pregnant girl, a criminal, and homeless; whose baby's father was murdered. *Why would I care about school? I had nothing...*

When I was around six months pregnant I started hanging with the homie Lil Beetle, we developed a bond. *What did we have in common that brought us together? Loss!* Lil Beetle had lost the most important person in his life, his older brother Big Beetle. His brother was found murdered in his car that was parked in front of his baby mama's house. Word in the hood was a female set him up. We also shared the hurt of not knowing what happened to our loved ones. Many nights we sat at Gwen's place talking about Sneak and Big Bro, as he affectionately called his brother. I was crying less because Lil Beetle said he didn't want to be around me when I cried. That said, I had to hold it together because I needed him to be around at this time.

One day Sharon, a lady in our neighborhood, got the autopsy report for Sneak. She brought it to Gwen's. Sharon gave me the report to read and it stated multiple gunshot wounds. Rigor mortis had set in, and ants were on his body. I held back my tears because Lil Beetle was there, so I waited until after he left. That night I cried myself to sleep.

After hanging with Lil Beetle for a while, we eventually slept together. The sex was not the most important aspect of this new relationship, it was the bond of great loss. The last night I was with Lil Beetle he said he had my back and I would see him later that day. That morning, the police picked him up and took him to jail for murder. A murder he did not commit. I lost him too. I tried writing him a few times but when I wasn't consistent, he told his sister to tell me to be consistent or don't write him at all. Beetle did 17 years and I never heard from him again.

At the time, I was looking for something. I was looking for that person that looked out for me. I was looking for my friend, the good, the bad, and the ugly. I was looking for love. I was looking for Sneak. I never found him again.

Readers, please listen: Women will love one man and in an attempt to recreate him they'll sleep with multiple men. Please note, that I never said it was right or that the behavior made sense. IT's JUST THE WAY IT IS…and so it was for me.

Chapter 15

The Homeless is Homeless

Shortly after Sneak's death and Beetle's incarceration, Gwen moved off of 82nd after a fall out with some girls in the neighborhood. I went back to my father's for a brief time. I was now 16 and on February 23, 1987, I had my daughter Whitney Latiss Jones. Whitney was absolutely beautiful, but it was a sad and depressing time for me. All I did was cry. Annette came to the hospital with me, but I was still lonely. I was alone in the delivery room and didn't know what I was going to do. This was now real. It was raining when Gwen picked me up from the hospital. I cried all the way home; she cried too. There was nothing that needed to be said, Sneak wasn't there. Gwen came by my father's to check on me and brought clothes for Whitney.

Whitney was not a week old when I got a surprise visit, it was Sneak's mother. I didn't know who told her where I lived, but she came to see the baby. Mrs. Jones asked me if she could come in and hold Whitney. Just think a couple of months before I was on her porch asking for something. Of course, I said yes. Mrs. Jones held Whitney and she instantly became a part of her life. After I had Whitney, I didn't go on 82nd for some time. Sneak was dead, Gwen moved, Beetle was in jail and MY HEART was BROKEN.

From time to time Nannie stayed at my father's house. I snuck her in because she did not have anywhere to go. My brother was slanging out of dope spots with his friends, so sometimes that freed up the room. We slept between my father's house and motels.

Whenever I did stay at my father's, it was brief. He would come home from work, see the house was nasty and ask, "Why didn't you clean?"

My reply, "Because I ain't your sons' damn maid. You never say anything to them."

"Well if you don't like it, you can get the fuck out my house,"

"I'll get the fuck out your house."

As I packed up Whitney's things my brother Edwin asked, "Why are you leaving? Just fuckin' ignore him."

"He ain't gonna talk to me like that." By the end of the night, I had walked around for hours with Whitney until I finally went to one of the homies dope spots and slept there for the night.

The first time he put me out with Whitney, she was a month old and it was two in the morning. I never had a real home, I just stayed at my father's in between finding other places to sleep. There was never security or stability for me. 525 was Robert White's house, always has been, always will be.

In between being homeless, Nannie and I were partners in crime. I was older, but she knew how to drive. After Whitney was born, she came by to see me in her grandmother's car. She knew I wasn't hanging out and she asked me to go for a ride with her. My brother Curtis watched the baby so I could go. What she forgot to mention was that she stole the car. As we pulled up on 82nd where her grandmother lived, her Aunt Peggy came running out the house fussing. I never thought a 13-year old would steal her grandmother's car, but that was Nannie Blue.

After I had Whitney, an old boyfriend Dean, from junior high school, came back around. I got into some trouble because of him. I was 16 and what I didn't know was Dean had gotten a 23-year-old girl pregnant. Her name was Vanessa. Dean started telling his family that Whitney was his daughter. I asked him why he lied to his family? He said he had never stopped liking me since junior high school.

Dean invited me to a family get-together. While there, his aunt asked me my daughter's name. I told her. She then asked about her last name. I said, "Jones." Dean was a Perry. His aunt immediately went on her drunk tirade, about how Whitney could not be Dean's because of her last name. I was uncomfortable, so I walked outside. The drunk auntie went around trying to get the rest of the family to agree. Dean's brother Tiger followed me. He liked me. He remembered when Dean and I were in the 7th grade and would fall asleep on the phone.

Tiger told me, "You know she's drunk don't pay her no attention."

"She's right. Whitney doesn't belong to Dean." I told him about Sneak.

Tiger asked, "Does Dean know?"

"Of course. Dean didn't come back around until after Whitney was born."

Tiger went back into the house to do damage control. I stood outside for a while. Eventually, Dean came out of the house looking for me. When he saw me, I had tears in my eyes. Dean looked at me. He didn't understand why I was crying. As far as he was concerned Whitney was his. I think he was also confused because he knew I had been through some bad situations, and I was tough. However, that night it wasn't about Dean or his aunt. It was about a cold slap in the face. A reminder that my daughter didn't have a father. *So I wept!*

Not long after the dysfunctional family gathering, someone told Vanessa about me. *I wondered who.* Dean didn't care. He wanted to prove that Whitney and I meant something to him, so he took me to Long Beach to meet his homies. Dean was only 16, but he had a lot of money from selling dope. When we went to Long Beach, we stayed in his apartment, and he took me shopping every day.

While I was there, Vanessa called, and she wanted me to know she was pregnant. I politely gave Dean the phone and he cussed her out. After he had hung up on her, I asked Dean why a 23-year-old was sleeping with a 16-year-old? He laughed and assured me he was done with her. On the last day I was there Vanessa called again. *Was she stalking us?* This time I hung up in her face.

That evening, as we were loading the car with my new clothes, three grown women approached me.

The first one walked up to me, "You Alicia?"

I knew she was Vanessa. I said, "Yea, why?"

"Dean is my man."

"Well if Dean is your man, tell me why is it that he is fucking and taking care of me?"

Dean heard the two of us and he came out of the apartment. Dean told me to get in the car. I refused. The rest is history, the fight was on. Vanessa and her two friends jumped me. The fight went from the side of the car into the middle of the street, Dean included. While I was fighting three grown women, I heard a loud snap. I could no longer move my arm. Once Dean saw I could not move my arm, he turned up. He gave one of the girls a black eye and she left the fight. When the second girl saw he was not playing, she stopped fighting too. The fight was now between Vanessa, Dean, and me. My arm was injured; this had never happened before. Dean did what he thought was best, he held Vanessa and told me to punch her. I couldn't move my arm at all, so Dean wrapped up the fight for me. He beat Vanessa down in the middle of the street. It was sad, two teenagers fighting three grown women.

After the fight, he took me to the hospital. I had a dislocated shoulder. They put it back in place. I was released from the hospital at three in the morning. Dean drove me back to LA. Dean didn't want to leave me with my arm in a sling and a baby, so he stayed a few days with me. After about the third day his brother Tiger starting paging him. Dean had to go back to Long Beach to answer for giving two grown women black eyes. Tiger told Dean one of the girl's brother wanted to fight. So Dean went back to take care of business. When I didn't hear from Dean for a few days, I was concerned. I called Tiger, he told me Vanessa set Dean up. When he went back to Long Beach, Vanessa had him sent to jail.

I knew my arm was not in fighting condition, but I didn't care. I told Nannie I wanted to go to Long Beach and get the girls that jumped me. I got my 38-hand gun, and we took the bus to Long Beach. *How did we think we were going to get away with shooting someone with no ride home? I have no idea, but it sounded good at the time.* When we got to Long Beach, Tiger met us and he told me to leave Vanessa alone or else she wouldn't drop the charges against Dean. *Was Tiger crazy?* They jumped me and plus we had already caught the bus all the way from LA for this mission.

Nannie anxiously waited for the verdict of what we were going to do. After talking with Tiger for a while, I decided I wanted Dean out of jail more than I wanted to get Vanessa, so we headed back to LA on the bus. Once we got on Manchester Blvd, we were stuck. The buses had stopped running. We were worried because we were stuck at the bus stop with a gun. As we sat on the bus stop, we came up with a brilliant idea, we were going to get a ride from someone and take their car. I don't think that we invented the term car jack, but that's what was about to go down.

Nannie was with the program. While we sat on the bus stop, we gave sensual looks to the men and sad looks to the women to get picked up. I guess we were playing on lust and or sympathy. Every car that came by we tried to make eye contact but no one would pick us up. That was until an older man in a truck pulled up at the light and asked if we wanted a ride. We said yes and jumped into the truck. The first question he asked, was if we wanted to party? *Party meant prostitute. Prostitute? Do we look like prostitutes?* I guess he was wondering why we were on the corner late at night trying to get someone's attention. I said yes. Nannie looked at me. I leaned over and whispered in her ear that we were going to kill him and take his truck. Nannie looked at me and nodded her head ok. The man looked over and asked us if we were okay. I'm assuming he wanted to make sure we didn't change our minds about paying for this ride with sex. He suggested we get a room. I quickly declined and suggested that we could go on Figueroa, off Flower to park. He agreed. Everybody knew Fig was the hoe stroll. On Fig, you could find prostitutes turning tricks in cars all night long.

As we drove toward Fig, all I could think about was how we were going to have this truck by the end of the night. But then the ride started to go differently. This man began to talk about his personal life. The closer we got to Fig the more he talked about his grandchild. I was unmoved, in my mind our first mission failed, but not this one. *My thought on the issue was old man tonight is your last night alive PERIOD!* I noticed out of the side of my eye that Nannie kept looking at me. I leaned over to her. She whispered in my ear, "Alicia don't do it." *Was she crazy?* The old man asked if we were all right. I said, "We're cool and ready to party." He smiled.

Nannie leaned over and whispered in my ear "Alicia don't do it he has a grandchild."

I was angry. Was she punk'n out on me? "Are you serious Nannie?" She read the look on my face. She gave me a look. I knew what it meant. Although Nannie was a thug, she had mercy in certain situations. Nannie knew about God. Her family was saved. Not me the heathen, I had no mercy. *I guess you ask why kill him for the truck and why not just take it? Because murder was in my heart and I wanted to kill him.* I had no mercy for him; no one had mercy for me. Where was the mercy for a beaten, molested four-year-old? He picked up two underage girls to sell their bodies. I angrily told the old man to take us somewhere different. He agreed, believing the party location changed. He had no idea that a 13-year-old had just diverted my mission and allowed him to live. I had him drop us off in front of my father's house.

He was confused; he asked me, "So, we're not partying?"

Angrily I said, "No." I nudged Nannie to hurry up and get out of the truck.

That night, Nannie saved three lives. My life as a murderer, her life as an accomplice and his life as a victim. Nannie and I would have been in jail for the rest of our lives or a good apart of it. *This would not be the last time she would SAVE US FROM ME.* Dean did jail time for hitting Vanessa. Once he got out we talked a few times but never got back together. I didn't have time to be fighting over a man.

There were days that Nannie and I just sat up and thought about how we could kill the people we didn't like. We were so crazy; we tried to figure out how to put battery acid in needles and inject people. Fortunately, we had no luck with how to do it. However, my luck was changing and I had the privilege to catch up with some old enemies. My first break came when I finally caught up with NeNe. *Remember the girl that I was fighting and her sisters jumped me in my father's front yard? Well, get ready! Let me tell you what happened.*

Nannie and I were walking down Hoover Street, coming from the store when I thought I saw NeNe. I said to Nannie, "Hey I think I just saw NeNe." When I looked again, two girls went into the pool hall. Nannie said, "Let's go see if it was her." We picked up the pace. When we went into the pool hall, NeNe was standing there looking nervous. She must have seen me as well. The look on her face told me she thought she had ditched me because when I came through the door her face turned red. NeNe was standing in the middle of the pool hall with another young girl.

I walked up on her and asked that magical question, "What's up now?

She quickly began explaining that she didn't have a problem with me and she did not know about the beef between Cassey and me. It was too late, because before she could finish her sentence I slapped her in the face. After I slapped her in the face, she turned a new shade of red. She tried to explain that she was a woman now and she didn't fight. I told her I didn't want to hear that shit. I knew she had come into womanhood because she was now by herself. I slapped her again. Each time she tried to explain I slapped her, hoping she would fight. I can't tell you how many times I slapped her. After a while my arm got tired and my hand heavy. My hand was throbbing, so I stopped to listen to her excuses to rest it. When I stopped Nannie jumped in, not to fight, but to make sure I finished her up. She jumped in by reminding me that NeNe and her homegirls jumped me. Nannie didn't want me to let NeNe off the hook by not fighting me.

The slap fest was taking a toll on me. Finally, the young girl that was with her yelled, "If you don't stop, I'm going to call my big sister Dee." *This was NeNe's little sister.*

I looked at her, "Call her."

Nannie walked up on her, "Shut up before you get slapped too."

I'm not sure how old she was, but we knew she was young, so we let her slide. We weren't dirty fighters. We didn't go around jumping girls. I was also not the same girl they jumped before. Yes, I was a fighter then, but I had turned into something else. *Deadly.* Afterward, we went to my father's house expecting the Towne girls to show up, they never did. This time, if they came back to my father's house, it would be a different outcome. I had something for them.

Chapter 16

Longing for the Hood

Although Nannie and I were still hanging together, I had not re-turned to 82nd Street. A couple of homies from different sets had come together as dope partners and started what was known as The Connection. It was a group of different homies connecting together to sew up the dope game. These Hoovers were all about money. They hung out in an apartment building on 81st Street. They had at least four of the apartments units in that building. I ended up hanging with The Connection because my cousin Christine wanted to be grown. *You ask what Christine had to do with introducing me to The Connection?*

My cousin was homey, meaning my aunt would not let her go no-where and I literally mean nowhere. One fine day, Christine called me and asked me to lie to her mother because she wanted to hang out with her friend Missy. I agreed to lie to my aunt because Christine said she wanted to get out the house and to go to the mall. I called my aunt and told her Gwen and I were going to the mall and I wanted Christine to go with us. My aunt had no idea that I barely saw Gwen, but she trusted me, so she said yes. My aunt gave me a time that Christine had to be back. I told Christine what time to get back and she agreed. She got her freedom pass from the plantation. The problem started when it was getting late and my aunt started calling my father's house looking for us. I was mad at Christine, she knew she couldn't breathe without her mama being there with oxygen. I had my brother lie to my aunt every time she called and after about the fifth time I knew I had to go and find her. I also knew Missy from junior high school. I knew her sister Tanya stayed in The Connection apartments, so I walked over there.

When I got to the apartments, I met Tanya, she told me Christine, and Missy were out with boys. *Boys? That tramp lied to me? I mean, I was clearly no angel, but if you gonna ask me to cover for you at least tell me the truth.* I waited at Tanya's for a few hours. Christine never came back. I went back home, and I accepted my aunt's call. I told her Christine wasn't with me. She cussed me out and said, "Alicia you're so mannish. You're always starting mess." *Did she say mannish? Did she say I was always starting mess?* I told her, "Your daughter is the one that asked me to lie because she's a slave." As I began to cuss too, my aunt hung up the phone on me. I wasn't scared of her she wasn't my Mama.

The next day my cousin Tee called me and told me that my aunt went Muhammad Ali on Christine. That night when Christine walked into her house after midnight she got the beat down of her life. Later that week, I ran into Missy, she told me they were at some boy's house. *Information I already knew.* She said she also wanted to ask me a question. She asked me why my sister tripped on Christine. Missy said she thought my sister Annette was cool at least from the times she had seen her. *Are you confused? Me too, what was Missy talking about? My sister Annette was a grown woman she never hit us.* Apparently, when Missy saw Christine the next day, Christine had marks and scratches as if she was in a brawl. So, instead of telling her friends her Mama beat her up, she said she had a fight with her older cousin.

And so, I did what any red-blooded American would do, I threw Christine under the bus. I told Missy the truth. I told Missy that Christine was homey and couldn't go nowhere. That day I had lied for her and because Christine decided to take advantage of her get out jail free card; she got her ass whooped. Missy fell out laughing. We must have laughed for hours. After that day, I started hanging with Missy in The Connection apartments. I had a taste of hanging with the homies again, and it felt good.

So back to me staying in The Connection apartments, it became a problem because I had Whitney. I didn't want Whitney in the dope spot because it was no place for a little baby. My sister Annette heard I got into some more trouble and the police were looking for me. Annette called and said my aunt wanted to help me. *Help me after we fussed over her daughter?* Annette assured me it was best for Whitney. Besides, Annette lived in the house behind my aunt so she said she could keep Whitney while my aunt worked. Christine was happy Whitney was there, maybe for the company.

Nannie came by my father's house a few times, when I wasn't there. She hadn't heard that I was hanging on 81st with The Connection. When Nannie got the word, she came by the apartments. She realized I wasn't going back to my father's house, so she came and kicked it with me. While at The Connection I sold dope, but that apartment complex was no small time nickel-and-dime crack rock gig. They were moving chickens, birds, keys of cocaine. Money was tight because it was dried up. Dried up meant a drug shortage. When this happened I wasn't selling rocks like before, so I did something crazy, I went to the welfare office on King and Vermont and applied for money and food stamps. When they gave me a big stack of forms that asked every question known to man, I skimmed through them and walked out.

In between the madness I did try to get a job. *Yes, I said job.* I had no real money to give my aunt, and I wasn't going back to the County building. They were crazy. *I'm so glad you asked me what kind of job a 16-year-old with no high school diploma could get.* My friend Yvonne told me she could get me a job at the place where she worked and she did. Yvonne got me a job at Omni phone located on 1st in downtown LA. Omni phone was the party line, chat room, and sex talk. They taught you how to talk nasty to men that called in. I worked for about two weeks. *Why?* I lied about my age to get the job.

Omni phone was full of underage girls working the sex lines. I didn't look 18, heck I didn't look 16, and so they took me off the sex lines and put me just on the party line for teenagers. It didn't last long because one of the worker's mama got mad and called the company to snitch us out. Management wanted a California ID that proved we were 18. I didn't have one. On my last night there I worked as late as I could trying to get more hours because I knew the next day I was out of a job.

I had never worked that late before. When I caught the bus, I got off on Vermont and King Blvd and all the buses had stopped running. I sat on that bus stop for over two hours. I didn't have anyone I could call. It was too far and late to walk. As I sat there not knowing what I was going to do two men in a Cutlass with rims and loud music pulled up. They asked me if I wanted a ride. I had never hitched hiked before. I said yes and got in the car. The passenger let me sit in the front between him and the driver. The driver said his name was Angel. He was cute with long, pretty hair. Angel had a tattoo of a cross in between his eyes. I could tell Angel was from a gang, but I didn't know which one. I wasn't stupid enough to ask. I asked Angel to drop me off at my father's house. I didn't want him to drop me to The Connection apartments. When we pulled up, I got out the car and thanked Angel, and walked in the yard. I walked slowly to the door hoping he would pull off so I could head for the apartments. That's when he called me back to the car.

I knew it, he wanted my number, after all, I thought I was cute because he sure was. I went back to the car and leaned in the window waiting to get his number. He politely said, "The next time you out by yourself, never get in the car with two men you don't know. We could have raped and killed you, you don't know us."

I was shocked not just at the fact that he didn't want my number, but this thug was letting me know that, once again, my life was spared. The next day when I went to The Connection apartment Tanya told me that one of my big homies Whitey said he saw me out late on King and Vermont. He wanted to know if I was prostituting. Tanya said she told him I had a job. I told her, "Hell he wanted to know if I was selling pussy, but he didn't give me a ride?" *I was hot but what can I say, that's the homies.*

The next day I couldn't go back to work because I didn't have an ID. I was desperate for money. I was unwilling to go back to the Welfare office, so I started going by a dope spot that my brother was working. I was hoping that he would give me a little yay to sell, didn't happen. But, what did happen was one day when I went to the spot looking for my brother I met a young boy named Karon that worked in the spot. I told him Edwin was my brother, and he let me in. I sat on the couch and listened to him bragging about the guns, money, and dope he had. I looked around and I saw just what he was bragging about. In my head, I was about to come up. I went by the spot a couple of more times knowing my brother wasn't there just to get Karon to trust me. Whitney was with my aunt, I was homeless and on the run from the police, it was time for me to come up.

I went to Nannie and told her I knew about a lick. A lick meant an opportunity to commit robbery. We would need more than the one gun we had because Karon had guns in the spot. Nannie agreed. She was ready to come up too. I went to the homie Q who I knew had a few guns a.k.a. straps. I told him I needed one. Q asked me for what? When I told him, he laughed at me. He asked, "How you gettin there?" I didn't find it funny. *Fuck what you think if you ain't gone help us come up.* I never answered him. I went to my homeboy Bear. I told him about the lick, he was in. He also told the homie Big Cee, he was in, too. The deal was they were giving the extra strap and the ride all I had to do was get us in. That same night, me, Nannie, Bear, and Cee rode to the spot. They parked down the street. Nannie and I went to the door. When I knocked Karon came to the door acting funny because Nannie was with me. I had never brought anybody to the spot with me.

We stood at the door. He asked me who Nannie was. I told him she's cool and just when he was about to open the door, Bear walked up too early. We hadn't got in, Karon didn't open the door. Bear came to the door and said he was looking for B Dog. Karon said he had the wrong spot. Karon was suspicious. Talking to me through the door, he told me to come back. Nannie suggested that we should try another night. I told her I was cold and hungry and I wasn't going nowhere until he let us in. Then, a magical phrase got us in. Someone from inside the spot yelled, "I hope they giving up some pussy." Karon had company.

Karon started laughing and said, "Nigga, that's what I'm talking about." All I could think was, *I got your pussy all right, this mutha fuckin 9 in my pocket.* Although I was mad that they were making pussy comments, it got us in. I guess Karon thought about it and opened the door. I walked up the stairs in the loft. When I got to the top of the steps, I saw two men. I calmly pulled out my gun. Karon didn't see that he was getting jacked. I looked down; he had already locked the door. The two guys in the spot hadn't noticed the gun, either, they were still making jokes. As soon as they saw the gun, they started saying they had nothing to do with what was going on. I yelled, "Shut the fuck up I don't want to hear that shit. Y'all muthafuckas got my brother!" *You ask what was I talking about? I don't know I had just come up with an excuse for jacking them.*

Karon looked up. He was scared. I could see he was shaking as Nannie pointed her gun at him. Nannie told him to open the door, but he was panicking. Nannie told him again, but he could not find the key to get the lock off. Mad, I looked at Nannie and said, "Shoot him." Nannie gave him another chance. She told him to open the door. I was through with her asking. I told her again, "Shoot him!" She looked up at me and said, "Shoot him?" I was done with bullshit. I said, "I'll do it." As I walked down the steps to shoot Karon, Nannie came up the steps to watch the other two. Just as I squeezed past her on the steps never taking the gun off the other two, Karon got the door open and ran out screaming. On his way out Bear was running up. Bear yelled, "Boo!" Karon screamed more. Cee was right behind Bear. They came in the spot and started grabbing the dope and straps, but because Karon got away the plans had now changed. We needed to get in and get out. We grabbed what we saw as the two guys stood there with their hands in the air. After we had grabbed what we could, we instructed the two guys to go down the stairs. The first one started walking down the stairs; he stopped, looked back, and asked if his homie could get help because he was on crutches. Cee said yes. As his homie got to the steps, Cee kicked him down the stairs. We made our way to the car cracking up laughing at how he tumbled down the stairs crutches and all. I bet he'll think twice before wanting strange pussy.

When we got back to the hood, we went to the homies apartment to split up the guns, money, and dope. We got a shotgun and a 38. What could I do with a shotgun? Bear took it and I got the 38. We didn't get much money, but we got a bunch of dope. We were mad because it was blow up. *You asked me what is blow up? Blow up is cocaine that has been cut with too much baking soda, and so the strength of the cocaine is weak.* We had to keep it in the refrigerator, so it wouldn't melt. Oh, by the way, Q was there when we came back; he stood there looking stupid as hell as we divided the stuff. *What did we do with the money? What every responsible 16 and 14-year-old kids did.* We bought matching outfits every day until the money ran out.

I also bought my baby Whitney shoes and clothes. She was still staying with my aunt. I went by there almost every day. I watched my back because I didn't want those niggas whose dope spot I hit to catch me slippin'. They had an advantage; I didn't know what they looked like, but they knew my brother, so they knew where I lived. The hole I was in was about to get deeper. With the little money I had left over, I went to my aunt's and took Whitney out with me. After a few outings with Whitney, Nannie and I showed up again to my sister's to pick her up for the day. My sister said she had something to tell me.

She said, "You can't take Whitney."

I asked, "And why not?"

Annette said, "Aunt Darlene said that every time you take Whitney out you feed her nothing but junk." *I wasn't having it. I wanted my baby.*

Chapter 17

Time was Running Out

By the way, did I tell you I was dying and I only had a limited amount of time with Whitney? Was I dying from a rare disease? No. I was dying from suicide and murder. I had given myself a date with death. I had already rationalized that by the time Whitney was five years old, I would be dead. I told everyone that would listen that I would not live to see my daughter past the age of five. I lived like it in all the decisions I made. I was committing suicide by sleeping with grown men that I didn't really know. I was being murdered by all the decisions I was making, like robbing dope spots and walking through alleys at two in the morning waiting for someone to shoot me. I wasn't sure which one would be it, but best believe I already had my mind made up, it was going to happen. In fact, some of our enemies were putting in straight work. They were shooting and killing everybody that wasn't from their hood. A shooting happened in our hood on 84th and right after the shooting, a News team interviewed my homegirl and me. The cameraman asked me where I planned to be in some years. Confidently I told him, "Dead."

Because I knew my time was running out, I wanted my baby. I told my sister I didn't give a damn what she thought, I wanted my baby. Annette told me again that I couldn't take Whitney. I never disrespected my sister, but it was coming. She called my aunt as I gathered Whitney's' stuff.

Annette shouted, "Darlene is on the phone and she said if you take Whitney you can't bring her back."

It was then I had to make a choice. I had nowhere to go, people were looking to kill me, but I still wanted my precious time with my daughter as dysfunctional as it was. I did something that shocked my sister and aunt. I yelled, "No damn problem!"

Nannie and I began walking out the door with Whitney. I shocked the hell out of them both. As Nannie and I got to the front gate, my sister came running behind me. I looked at Nannie and asked, "What is the fuckin problem? They ain't getting my baby."

Annette was yelling that I was an unfit mother and we started to argue. "I'm not giving Whitney up. You're a traitor. I'm your sister. Aunt Darlene isn't your sister, and quiet as kept, she don't like you either, Annette." I went in for the kill. *Remember, Ma taught me well.* I continued, "You just her house slave whose mother is dead. All she needs you for is to clean her house and watch her kids." My words did as I wanted them to, they hit a major artery, and she began to bleed with emotion.

Good old Christian Annette went on and called me a broke hoe.

I told her, "I'd rather be a broke hoe, than a rich bitch." Then I thought about it and told her, "You ain't even a rich bitch; you're just a bitch."

That was the first time I had ever called my sister out of her name. At that point I told her I didn't give a fuck, she was trying to help my aunt take my baby. The argument got louder, then Renie, Annette's sister in law, came running out of the house and jumped into the argument. I was ready to fight them both and so was Nannie. *I didn't get it. What were they so mad about? Oh, yea Annette and my aunt had been telling the family how unfit I was as a mother, and they never thought I wanted my baby.* When they gave me a choice I said, "Fuck all y'all, I choose to keep my baby unfit and all." My self-declared death sentence was in effect, and I didn't have time for their bullshit. I had recurring dreams about being shot. My dreams ended the same way; violently with a man shooting and killing me. So with that, time wasn't on my side. I put the diaper bag on my

shoulder and Whitney on my hip. We were about to leave and in the
middle of the argument; Sandi came up. She jumped in front of me as I
was still cussing Renie out. Sandi jumped right in Renie's face and told
her to mind her business. Sandi came to my rescue as always. She had
always encouraged me to take care of Whitney no matter what my family
said about me.

After the family feud, Nannie and I left walking down Hoover Street.
I had Whitney on one hip with her diaper bag on the other. Nannie had
the swing on her shoulder. I didn't know what I was going to do and at
that point I didn't care. They weren't getting my baby; even if I was a bad
parent for feeding her chili cheese fries and taking her to the Hoover
hood picnics, my gang was my family.

Nannie and I went back to the spot, but that night I stayed at Tanya's.
Although I was on the run and homeless, I had a few homegirls that had
my back even when I wasn't doing right. I stayed in and out of Tanya's
apartment and my homegirl Voss kept Whitney. She called Whitney,
"Ms. Jones." Big Angie was another homegirl that kept Whitney for me.
As for my aunt we had a big argument on the phone and I let her know
not to worry about Whitney because her precious daughter was about to
give birth soon. Yes, as a result of her outing with Missy, Christine was
pregnant and as always my aunt had no clue. How she had no clue, I
don't know seeing as it was summer, and Christine walked around with a
trench coat on. Aunt Darlene was still in denial so she took my cousin to
the doctor and he confirmed, Christine was due the next month.

*So let's do a small recap, I'm homeless, on the run from the police, and now
some dope dealers are looking to kill me because I jacked their dope spot. I fell out
with my aunt, my sister, and my brother, and I'm just 16. Some life.*

While in and out of Tanya's and motels, I befriended some Jamaicans.
In the hood, there were plenty of Jamaicans that came and set up shop,
meaning sold drugs out of our hood. Almost every Jamaican I knew
had an alias. The two we dealt with were Dover and Tony. Tony had an
unusual look for a Jamaican. He was very light skinned with green eyes.
Nannie and I kicked it in their spot. We ate and hung out. Tony liked

me, but I didn't date Jamaicans cute and all. Dover liked Nannie; he let her wear his gold chain. Jamaicans had an unspoken rule, they loved to sleep with American women, but they weren't going to marry us. If you found one that did, it was rare because if you were black you were a foreigner to Jamaicans. My thought on dating Jamaicans, if they killed you they could go back home. Blacks had nowhere to go, but jail. I was cool on Jamaicans. I stuck to my usual American thugs.

We started to kick it so tough that Dover introduced us to his brother. Of course, we didn't know his real name. He went by Ricky. He was slanging a lot of dope. He supplied Dover, Tony, and other Jamaicans. Our friendship ended with the Jamaicans because the homies were tired of the Jamaicans making money in our hood and decided to do something about it. One night Dover paged Nannie, he wanted his gold chain back, so we went to see him. As we left the spot, three homies that were hanging in front of the apartment building approached us.

One homie asked, "Why y'all hang with the Jamaicans?"

I told him, "Uhh because our asses are grown and they are cool."

The homie Tee Loc said, "The Jamaicans have to get out of our hood."

Nannie and I both said, "Whatever."

We knew the Jamaican's had a rep for putting in work on your ass, so we weren't trippin on what he said. If he ran into their spot, he'd better be prepared to kill them because they didn't do no talkin'. Just as another one of the homies was saying our Jamaican friends needed to go, we heard shooting. We ducked behind a car. As we were outside giving an FBI report, one of the homies ran up in the Jamaicans' spot.

The homie came running out; Tee Loc grabbed me by the arm and said, "Let's go!"

I looked up to make sure Nannie was with me. Dover came out to the front of the apartment building. He was still shooting holding his shoulder; he was hit. Shaking, I ran behind Tee Loc, who, by the way, had a messed up leg so he wasn't moving fast. We ran through the cut and made it on 82nd street. Nannie and I took a few more cuts, separated from the homies, and went to The Connection apartment. We both stood by the window and wondered if Dover had made it, after all, he was our friend. After the shootout, the hood was silent for a while. We couldn't take it anymore.

Nannie said, "Let's go back and see what happened."

I said, "Okay."

We walked to the corner of 81st Street, where we heard a loud car zooming. It suddenly stopped. We didn't know what to expect. When we looked closer, it was Ricky, Dover's brother. He was driving his 280 Z with an Uzi hanging out his window. We both froze. My life flashed before me. I knew he was going to kill us for what the homies did. I had my gun on me. I was so scared that I forgot it was in my jacket. I wouldn't have pulled it out anyway. *A 38 against an Uzi* I couldn't stand a chance. Besides, he had a right to be mad. My death sentence had come for me. *Funny, I knew it was coming and still in the face of death nothing could prepare me for being shot, my dream was about to unfold as truth.*

Chapter 18

Grim Reaper: Death Came

Ricky looked at me and Nannie and said, "You know them bumbaclots shoot me, brother?" *It was a rhetorical question so let me translate— Y'all know them muthafuckas shot my brother, and I'm gon' get their ass.*

We were still frozen with fear. I couldn't say a word, afraid he was about to shoot me. We were both caught like two deer in headlights as he was talking. Ricky didn't wait for a response he floored his 280 Z. All we saw was fire coming out of his window. He shot up the entire street from 81st and Hoover to 81st and Fig.

Nannie and I took off running. We didn't know if he was coming back for us. We ran to the apartments. When we were inside I told her, "Why did I listen to you?" *I already know what you're thinking, the nerve of me.* After that, we never saw our Jamaican friends again.

This wouldn't be the last time I was caught in a bad spot. Those dope dealers that I robbed came for me. Once again standing on a corner, I got caught slippin'. I was at the light on 82nd and Hoover and a car with two guys in it pulled to the light. They looked at me. I knew it wasn't a, "What's up, baby?" look. I looked back. I didn't recognize them as my enemies. Then they did something strange. They sped off. Just as they sped off another car came to the light, it was the homie TK.

TK asked, "You knew them niggas?"

I said, "No."

TK said, "You got caught slippin', them the niggas you jacked."

I looked at TK and told a bold-faced lie; I had them mutherfucka's and flashed my gun. I was too embarrassed to let TK know that they did catch me slippin'. I had no idea who they were. They sped off because TK was behind them. He saved me that day. Mad and embarrassed that night, I told Bear what happened. I told him I was worried about my sister because they knew where she lived. Sandi had moved into her friend Gina's house and shared it with my brother, Edwin. I didn't care about my brother, he was talking behind my back saying that I was scandalous for what I did. I was concerned for my sister. I didn't want them to get her. So, that night Bear told me he would meet me at Sandi's house. When I got there, my sister cautiously came to the door. She looked relieved when she realized it was me.

I knew she was worried about her life. She was pregnant and my brother kept putting salt on me by telling her that I was going to get killed. When I came in the house Edwin gave me a dirty look, and I returned the favor. After the stare down, he told me he didn't want me in his house. I told him, "I don't give a fuck about you or the niggas I jacked." It was a part of the game. They got caught slippin'. I told him I wasn't giving nothing back to him or his bitch ass homeboys. This was Hoover! He must have forgot for a small moment that I was no longer that little girl he tormented. I told him I was there for my sister. As the exchange went on there was another knock on the door, everybody stopped. He didn't say another word. Sandi went to the door. I went behind her. I had my gun; I was ready. It was Bear. I was happy to see him. Bear had mad respect in our hood, nigga's knew not to cross him.

I introduced Bear to my sister. My brother stood in silence because if he gave Bear any bad talk about me it was on. Bear pulled out a sawed off shot gun and a case of bullets out of his coat to give to my sister. Sandi, who was about eight months pregnant, took the gun. She looked at me as her boyfriend came out of the room to listen to Bear's instructions.

Bear told her, "When some niggas come to your door if you don't recognize them, don't open the door just shoot their asses through the door."

Bear took the gun and pointed it at the door, then he showed her how to load it. I felt much better because my sister agreed to shoot, and, more importantly, Bear, just like TK, had my back. The Hoover's were feared. Bear sent the word that if the niggas we jacked fucked with my family or me; they were in for some shit. After that, they dropped it and took the loss.

Thank God Bear saved me, but I wasn't done getting caught slippin.' I kept running into bad situations, some were my fault and some weren't. As you may know, getting high and being a gang member/criminal never turns out well. Once when the homie Lil Genie from The Foe, came through, we had some weed and Gin. As I said, I didn't get high or drink. *Please don't ask me why I did it. Remember the last time I got high and drunk; I ended up homeless.* That night we all got a little drunk, for me, it didn't take much. We decided to go get something to eat. We went to the hamburger stand on Main and Manchester. We pulled in the drive-thru buzzed. We saw a suspicious looking nigga walking in front of the drive-thru. Even though I was high, I knew it was a problem. There was no way to get out of the drive-thru. One way in, one way out. We couldn't back up. We were trapped, unless we ran him over.

We were all sitting in the front seat of Lil Genie's Cutlass. He was driving, Nannie was in the passenger seat and I was in the middle. Lil Genie didn't flinch at the guy that kept staring. Until finally the guy flashed a white plastic grocery bag with an Uzi in it. "Who the hell is this bastard?" Then it hit us. Pipestreet Sheperd was killed in gang rivalry. *What did that have to do with us?* Well, we were in their hood looking suspicious, and they were ready to take niggas off the map. We realized they probably thought we had something to do with it. Genie slowly took his gun out of his pants.

Nannie at this point started screaming across us to the men in the drive-thru, "Where's the food? We ready to go!"

Once again, my life went before me. My high came down, instantly. Talking between my teeth, "Shoot him, shoot him."

The nigga just stood there in front of Genie's car waiting for us to move. As calmly as I could, I said, "Shoot his ass."

Lil Genie wouldn't look at me. He kept his eyes ahead. I said it again, "Shoot his ass."

Genie replied, "I got him Licia."

Got him? This fool was standing in front of the drive-thru with an Uzi in a plastic bag. There were only two options in my mind. Option A was to run his ass over. Option B was to shoot his ass through the windshield. I chose Option B.

Genie calmly said, "Don't worry; I got him."

At this point, Nannie was hysterical she was still screaming at the men in the drive-thru window, "Where is our food?"

They were watching the stare down, so they were stuck too. I just knew my death sentence had come to claim me. I guess the guy realized we weren't enemies or we didn't want it and he walked passed the drive-thru. It wasn't just the fact that we didn't want it, Genie wouldn't serve his ass. If it had been up to me, we would probably all be dead since my thought was still Option B. That night Lil Genie probably saved our lives. As we drove home, Genie was good, my high was gone, and Nannie was quiet. When we got back to the hood, I went inside the house and fell out on the couch.

I told Genie. "I'm done. Fuck that getting high shit. That's why I don't get high"

He looked at me and smiled, never saying a word to my "Just Say No" drug campaign. He was just as calm and quiet as he was in the drive-thru.

After the drive-thru standoff, I did get caught slippin' once again. My old enemy had come back around. Pokey was out of jail. He still hated my guts because Sneak checked him. He was still the same, a woman beater. Around this time, my friend Keisha went with Pokey's girlfriend Donna to the county jail to put money on his books. Pokey claimed he never got it. He let it be known that he was going to beat Donna and Keisha when he got out. Keisha said she took the money Donna gave her and put it on his books. This time, he was after Keisha. It was a Saturday when I went on 82nd with Keisha, we were hanging out when Pokey walked up on me. It was déjà vu. I froze. This was the same exact spot where he had confronted me before. Keisha just stood there too. He had a mean look in his eyes. He took out his brownies (brown gloves) and put them on his hand. He gave a gesture to say, "I'm about to fuck y'all up." My heart was racing, but I wasn't going to let him punk me.

He turned toward Keisha and said, "Bitch I want my money."

She told him she put the money on his books. Just as I thought he was going to hit her, I stepped in front. *What the hell was wrong with me? I knew I couldn't whip him.*

He put his hand on my chest pushing me back. "Get the fuck out the way or I'll fuck you up."

Sneak must have still been watching over me. As I reached to push his hand off my chest, my homeboy Meek came out of nowhere.

Meek told Pokey, "This one, you can't mess with." He nodded his head toward me. Pokey was beyond mad because this was the second time that someone told him to leave me alone. Pokey looked at me, then looked at Keisha and spit in her face. "I'll see you later." He walked off.

I asked, "You ok?"

Shaken, she said, "Yes."

When I turned around Meek was gone. I didn't have to tell him thank you, he knew Sneak had me. He was looking out for the homie, dead and all.

Best believe this situation with Pokey wasn't over. Later that night, Keisha and I went to a house party on 81st Street. *Guess who was there? Yea, you got it, Pokey.* This time, he was in Keisha's face saying her folks were Bloods. Anything to beat her up. The house was so crowded I couldn't get in. Some folks outside were repeating what Pokey was saying.

I said out loud, "Who gives a fuck where her people are from? He's a bitch; he just wants to beat up a girl."

Before I knew it, a guy walked up on me. It was Naunie from The Foe'. He asked me what I said. I looked him in his face, because I was thinking, "nigga you ain't from the tray." And before I could finish repeating my statement, he snatched me by my jacket and threw me up against the flowerbed in front of the apartment. He grabbed me by my jacket again, but before he could hit me, I bounced up and hit him in the eye. He grabbed his eye. Someone yelled, "Here comes the police, here comes one time," Everybody ran including me. I ran through the apartment and went to The Connection to get a gun from Bone. When I got to the door a homie named Big Body answered. Body told me Bone wasn't there. I asked if I could wait on Bone. He let me in and I went to sleep. The next day the homie JJ came up to me and asked what happened. He told me he was going to check that nigga, Naunie. That night we went to the liquor store in 7-4 hood and guess who we saw, Naunie with a black eye. When he saw JJ he jumped in his car and took off.

JJ looked at me and said, "Bitch ass nigga. Did you know you gave him a black eye?"

I shook my head no and we laughed. I wasn't trying to give him a black eye, I just had that Ghetto Fight Policy that said hit a nigga back. Come to find out another angel saved me that night. It was Lil Genie. He was the one that yelled that one time was coming. There were no police that night.

Chapter 19

The Connection

After that night, I started hanging with Big Body. He was 26 and I was 16. After some time, I started sleeping with him. This was normal in the hood. Big Body was just that, he was big and buff. That's where he got his name from. He drove an old school Chevy called a glass house. The color was Lakers gold with a rag top. I wasn't his girlfriend, just a fuck buddy as the hood called it. The more I hung with The Connection, the more some of the homies didn't like me. This was because, although The Connection was made up of different Hoovers, they were only about the money. Everywhere you went there were punks and G's (original gangsters), but The Connection had a majority of G's a.k.a. ridas, so some of the homies couldn't come and jack or shoot up The Connection like they did the Jamaicans.

I didn't realize that I would get caught in the middle of that underlying feud until one night walking home Tee Loc saw me. "What's up Licia where you going?"

I replied, "Home." It wasn't strange for me to be walking around at one in the morning.

Tee Loc said, "I'll give you a ride." This was the homie that looked out for me during the Jamaican shoot out.

I got in the car. As soon as I got in, I knew I was in trouble. Tee Loc looked at me and said, "Yo' ass hanging tough with The Connection niggas, ain't you?"

I sat there and didn't say a word. I knew he was looking to do something, I just didn't know what.

He looked at me, "You over there fuckin' them niggas." Before I could respond he grabbed me by my shirt and began to tear it as he was driving. "You gon' give me some pussy too, since you only fuck Connection niggas."

I began swinging on him to make him let my shirt go. He was trying to guide the car, and then slapped me in my face. *Was this nigga serious? I started crying and couldn't stop. All the time I had been down for the hood and this nigga is gonna rape me?* I began to scream. He looked at me; still holding onto my shirt yelled, "Shut the fuck up!"

That only made me scream louder. This went on until I opened the door. He slammed on the car brakes. We both went forward toward the windshield. He yelled, "Shut the fuckin door right now!"

I yelled with everything in me, "Hell no!"

When he saw I was willing to jump out of a moving car to avoid to being raped, he told me to get out his car. He shoved me out the door. *Guess what y'all? I went Gladly.*

I jumped out of the car with my shirt torn and tears still running down my face. I went toward Figueroa. I went to the New Bay Motel where I knew Bone was. I asked a smoker what room he was in. He pointed me to the door. I tried to knock lightly so he wouldn't think I was the FBI, after all, he was slangin out of the room. Bone peeped out the window to make sure it wasn't the police before he opened the door. He was surprised to see me. I started crying. I told him I needed to come in.

He looked me and asked calmly, "What the hell is goin' on?"

I could barely talk, "Tee Loc tried to rape me. Tee Loc tried to rape me."

Bone said, "WHAT?"

"Tee Loc just tried to rape me. He offered me a ride. When I got in the car, he began to tell me that I only fucked with The Connection and that I was going to give him some pussy too." I tried jumping out the car, forcing him to let me go.

The more I told Bone; the more he got mad. He knew what Tee Loc did wasn't about me. It was about the fact that some of the homies couldn't get at The Connection. It was about money and power.

Tee Loc was sending a message to The Connection, but especially to Body. We'll take what the hell we want from y'all Connection niggas including your bitches.

Bone kept telling me I had to tell Body. If I did I knew this could start a war between some of the homies and The Connection, so I told Bone I couldn't.

He said, "Licia you have to tell Bro." That's what they called each other.

I told Bone, "Maybe later, but not now."

Bone knew I wasn't going to tell, so he let me get in the bed to go to sleep. As I laid there, I couldn't believe it was just a year earlier when Tee Loc had saved me from being raped in his house by Jo. Now he turns around and tries to do the very same thing. Some of the homies saw me as a trader for being with The Connection. *I know what you're asking. Weren't all Hoovers on the same team? The answer was no. Not all Hoovers were on the same team, especially when money was involved. That's everywhere just look on your job.*

The next morning, I walked home and Nannie came by. We were supposed to get tattoos with the little money we had left from the lick we pulled. I told her what happened.

She said the same thing as Bone, "Tell Body."

My response didn't change. "I don't want to start a war. Plus, aren't we supposed to get tattoos? Why ruin the day?"

I got dressed. We walked around the corner. Body pulled up, "Where y'all going?"

Nannie said, "To the tattoo shop."

Body had a look on his face. He looked at me and said, "Licia, you cool?"

I knew then, Bone told. "I'm cool Body."

Body said, "So what's up with you?"

Nannie looked at me. She knew it wasn't over. I told him, "I'm good. On the way to get tats."

He told us, "Hop in I'll take you."

We both got in the front seat and told him the place was downtown. As he was driving he took a detour. He went on 82nd, which, we weren't expecting. He parked the car. With death on his face he said, "I'll be right back."

We were nervous because we didn't know what he was going to do. Why did he stop on 82nd? *That's where some of the homies hung out.* Body got out of the car and approached the apartments. The gate was locked. He called for someone to open it. It was no secret he was mad. The homegirl Penny said something through the gate. As she opened it, we couldn't hear what she said. When he walked through the gate he started slapping her.

Nannie yelled, "Oh damn, Penny is getting slapped down by Body."

The more he slapped her, the more she tried to cover her face. We heard him yell, "If you gon' act like a man, I'm gon' treat you like a damn man. Now go get bro. (meaning her boyfriend) so, I can deal with cuz if he has any issues!"

Penny held her face and ran up the apartment stairs. It was as if a bull had come into the arena and everyone was trying to get out the way because they didn't know who the bull was going to get next. We knew her boyfriend wasn't going to say a thing because she disrespected him and because he was Big Body, a straight G.

Body went into the apartment and came out. We were on silent status. He got into the car, looked at us with a devious smile, and said, "Where to?"

I couldn't say a thing. Hell, I was in shock. He was just grinning away. Finally, Nannie broke the silence and said, "To the tattoo shop."

We pulled off and drove downtown to get our tattoos. I never discussed the issue with Body and I never had any problems from that day on with Tee Loc or anybody about hangin' with The Connection.

Nannie and I were still homeless until we met a lady named Belle. Belle let us move into her apartment. She lived on 81st. I believe she thought like everyone else in the hood. She thought we still had money from the lick we pulled. What Belle didn't know was the money was spent on matching outfits, tattoos, and eating out every day. The dope we had was hard to sell, so Nannie gave the majority of hers to the homie, Linky. He took it out of town to move it. He disappeared for three weeks. When he came back, he gave her a couple of dollars claiming the police caught him and he lost the dope. *Yeah right, we were young, not dumb.* Nannie never saw the rest of her money or dope. *I guess the jacker, got jacked.*

Even though I lived with Belle I still kept hangin with The Connection, but something was happening between me and Body. I was getting a little jealous. Although I never saw him hug or kiss anyone, I wasn't stupid. One day I said something that changed the game. *You ask, what did I say?* I said I was pregnant. You don't say those magical words in hood life. Of course, Body asked me if I was sure the baby was his, because he couldn't have kids. That is another famous line meaning, "I ain't taking care of no baby." I was mad. That night, I went home and I was talking to Belle and Nannie about my thoughts on the matter. I said, "I'm going to fix his ass." I couldn't sleep that night, so I got into smoker gear to go pull a mission. I didn't tell Nannie about my mission because I didn't want her caught in the middle, this was personal. Later that night, I put on my black hoodie, jeans and tennis shoes and got my equipment. I pulled sticks from the broom, eggs, and a candy bar. My mission was about to be possible. I went to The Connection apartment at about 4 a.m., when I knew things weren't moving. I walked up on Body's car that was parked in front. It was sweet. I knew I had to be careful. I didn't want someone to come out and catch me messing with that car because I would be shot for real. I put the candy bar in his tank and the small sticks in his tire stems. The air started to go down immediately. I threw eggs on the paint and ran off. I went back home and laid down. I was happy in my heart. *You ain't got to take care of no baby, but you'll have to pay for that car. How bout that with yo bitch ass.* I rolled over and laughed until I finally went to sleep.

Later that morning, I heard beating on the door. I heard Body calling my name. Oh shit. *I know what you're thinking, what did I expect?* Not sure, but this wasn't a part of the plan. I normally slept in the room with Belle and Whitney, but because I pulled a mission I crashed on the couch. I slid under the covers as Nannie opened the door. She didn't know what happened.

Body was at the door, and he asked Nannie, "Where's your friend?"

Nannie said, "She's not here."

"Your friend touched my car. Tell her I'm looking for her."

As soon as Nannie closed the door, I came from under the covers. Nannie looked at me, "What happened?"

I told her, I went on a mission. I didn't have to explain why I didn't take her because she knew it was personal. I began to get up and get dressed because I knew he would be back for me. My crazy self went and walked to the corner of 81st to look down the street to see if I could see his car from there. I wanted to see the damage. To my surprise, he was standing out in front of the apartments. Just when I thought he didn't see me, he did. I took off running because he was coming. I was a hundred pounds; a runner and I had a head start. I thought that was in my favor. It wasn't. I ran down Hoover street. I could feel him getting closer and closer. I looked back occasionally. Then boom, he grabbed me by my shirt. He chased me down and caught up with me on 83rd just two blocks away.

He asked me why I touched his car. I told him, "I don't know what the hell you're talking about. I wasn't in the hood yesterday." He politely held me by my shirt and walked me back on 81st to show me his car. The minute he let go of my shirt I took off running. I forgot I was pregnant, so I was not the best track-star. He caught me again. He hemmed me up against the wall. I thought I was about to get slapped like Penny. After all, I touched his prized possession. I tried to brace myself for the beat down of my life. He was a big man compared to my 100 pounds. Then, Body did something I never expected, he let me go. *Did he let me*

go because he felt guilty for not claiming this baby? I never knew why he let me go that morning.

After that, Body and I were no more. I saw him all the time, but it was clearly over. There was an underlying agreement that we weren't even friends. The last major encounter I had with Body was when Nannie and I were slangin' on 82nd, and he said he wanted to talk with me. We had an argument. Before I knew it, he picked me up and gave me a bear hug. Nannie saw it and yelled out, "Hey Body! What you trying to do; kill your baby?"

Whether that was his intention or not, that what's eventually happened. A few days later, I was slangin' on 82nd I had been up all night when I started to cramp. I had no idea what was wrong. The homie Solo was driving down the street. Holding my stomach, I walked toward the street, and I flagged him down. I didn't know what was exactly happening, but I knew it wasn't good because I felt myself bleeding. Solo drove like crazy telling me to hold on he was going to get me to the hospital. He dropped me off at Martin Luther King Hospital a.k.a. Killa King because everybody died there, and so did my baby. I had a miscarriage. They told me it was a girl. I named her LaTeira Smalls. I gave her his name even though he never believed she was his. I never slept with Body again. At 17, I had never experienced such pain in my body. Once again, I was filled with such sadness. *I wept again.*

Chapter 20

Gate Hopping

After losing my baby, I was done hanging with The Connection. I was kind of cool on the hood. Belle started hitting the pipe and lost her apartment. We had to move out. I went back to my father's house. I started hitting the clubs again using my friend Angie's ID. One day, I was on my way to the Broadway Swap Meet because I needed some Daisy Dukes for the club. As I was walking, some church people were out in front of a church asking people to come in and get to know Christ. *I was hoping they didn't stop me. You know they did.* The lady that stopped me was very nice. For some reason, I couldn't tell her no, just like Pastor Papa. She began to tell me about Jesus and asked me to come in to get baptized. As much as I would like to say I was thinking about not going to hell, at that moment, something else was on my mind. What am I going to do with this dope in my bra? *Was I willing to take a loss and throw my rocks away? I know you are probably thinking why did I have dope in my bra going to a swap meet?* Well in hood life you never knew when you were going to run into a customer and make that sale. I took my dope everywhere I went. Never thinking I'd take it into the house of the Lord.

The lady took me to her Pastor and he began to explain what getting saved meant. He said after I was baptized, I was going to be filled with the Holy Spirit and speak in tongues. I had no idea what he was talking about; I was still looking for a place to hide my dope. *Yes, I wanted to hide my dope in the church.* I was led to a room to put on a white gown. As I stood there, I had a decision to make. I decided not to take my dope out my bra; after all, it was in a plastic baggie so it wouldn't contaminate the water. The lady came back and took me to the baptismal pool. The Pastor met me there. He started talking and asked that I repeat his words. Then he walked me into the water. He explained to me that I was now saved, and he dunked me in the water. When I came up gasping for air, he told me to speak in my heavenly language. He began to speak in tongues and to my surprise so did I. At that moment, I had forgotten about the dope. I was experiencing something I had never experienced. I tell you it didn't last long. After I went to the swap meet, and on my way home I saw my friend Missy having a fight with a girl named Phyllis. *What did I do with my good ole baptized self? I jumped in the fight...*

The club life was getting a little boring since you can only meet so many new people. I wasn't hangin with Nannie anymore. I started going to my cousin's house in Blood hood. My cousin had a friend named Timmie. They called him Chimp. He could fix anything. His specialty was putting sounds into cars. One day when I was visiting Timmie, I ran into an old friend Shawn. We both went to Bethune Middle School together. The last time that I saw Shawn was the year before when he heard that I was at my Aunt Mae's house. He came by and knocked on the door. I went outside. My cousin Ronnie looked out the kitchen window and saw us. Ronnie came out of the door, grabbed me by the shirt and told me to get my fas ass in the house. He told Shawn to get the hell on and locked me in the house. I was kicking, cursing, and screaming, "You ain't my daddy!" Ronnie arguing back told me, "You ain't messing with the homies."

So this day when I ran into Shawn I was still embarrassed. That was the first thing he brought up. We laughed. Shawn was also a gang member. Eventually we started going out. This was a no no for a Crip to be hooked up with a Blood. But I didn't care. I loved hopping gates.

Hanging with the Bloods became a problem for me, some of the homies were mad, saying, "How can Licia hang with Bloods?" I didn't give a damn. One night I made the mistake and allowed Shawn and Timmie to come pick me up in my hood and take me bowling. I didn't think anything about it. I didn't think anyone would know or care.

The next day I was on my father's front porch on the phone when Big Bone came out of his house and yelled, "I don't have shit to say to you Licia."

I was sitting on the porch wondering if he touched that butt naked because who was he talking to? It was at that moment I realized he was talking to me. He didn't see me on the phone. I stood up and yelled, "I aint talking to your ass."

He yelled back, "You be messing with them Blood niggas and I ain't fucking with you."

I yelled back, "When you on pussy I'm not in your business, and I know you mess with girls that's not from around here."

He replied, "Like I said. I ain't fucking with your ass Licia." I sat down and kept talking on the phone. I didn't give a damn what he thought or anyone else.

I stopped hanging in the hood while I was messing with Shawn. I was trying to make this Crip Blood thing work. The one thing about Shawn was he was fine and he knew it. He had slept with women who didn't even know his real name. So our flame was starting to burn out fast because my attitude was "Nigga please, I'm not the one." You can take your cute ass somewhere else. Cute doesn't move me, I love thug.

After a few months of off and on, me cussin him out, I was through. I was sick, weak, and I couldn't figure out why. I went to take a pregnancy test. It came back positive. I cried all the way home. What was I going to do with another baby? I was 17. I told Timmie I was pregnant. He told me I had to tell Shawn. I told Timmie I didn't want to have anything to do with his broke ass. So, Timmie told him. That night Shawn called me and asked if I was pregnant. When I told him that I was, he said he couldn't have any kids. My response was, "What the hell you calling me for if you shooting blanks?"

You may want to cover your ears because my baby mama anthem went like this. "Fuck you, fuck you and fuck you, with yo' broke ass, you ain't got shit no way, living with yo mama driving the homies car." *I know you think I'm the crazy one, but think about it... he was the one that sat on the phone and listened to me.*

Throughout my pregnancy, I only saw Shawn a few times, but that didn't stop me from doing my thing. I turned 18 and was clubbing at five months pregnant, dating, and selling dope. *Yes, I said clubbing and dating.* For some strange reason the men in my hood loved pregnant women. *Was it the thought that they couldn't knock a girl up twice?*

When I finally went into labor, I went to the hospital by myself. After all, Shawn said it wasn't his baby. After I had my son Tyshawn, I got a call while I was there. I thought it was my sister, but to my surprise, it was someone on the phone saying she was Shawn's sister. She asked if the baby was her brother's.

And so, I had to give her my baby mama anthem. "Bitch why in the hell are you calling me about your sorry ass brother? He ain't got shit I want. I didn't ask you to call." I hung up in her face.

About an hour later, Shawn called and asked about the baby. I tried to be nice, seeing I wasted my energy cussing his sister out. He told me he was coming to the hospital. My thought, "Whatever nigga." I never waited on Shawn and he never showed up.

I went back to my father's house, because I couldn't run the streets with my new baby and one-year-old. I was at my father's house for about a week when someone knocked on the door. My brother came and got me, "Some strange people want you."

Who wanted me? When I went to the door it was the homegirl Shonie from Bethune middle school. I hadn't seen her since the eight grade. As Shonie began to explain why she was at my house a really pretty lady came to the door. Shonie said it was her aunt. *OK, I'm still confused.* Shonie was Shawn's cousin. She helped her family track me down.

Shawn's mother introduced herself as Pat and asked if she could see the baby. She came in with about three other people. Once I gave her my son, she instantly fell in love with him. She called him Mann. This would be her Mann. She invited me to her house. I told her that Shawn and I didn't get along. She said it didn't matter; she wanted Mann to be part of her family.

Pat told me she wanted me to come to her house right away. I took Tyshawn about a week later. When I went to her house with Mann, I was uncomfortable. I was in Blood hood, in a man's house with a baby he didn't want or claim. As I sat on the couch, Shawn came through the door. *You should've been there to see the look on his face when he saw his Hoover baby Mama on his couch.* He didn't know his family had found me. He gave me a dirty look, and I returned the favor. His mother took him in her room. He came back out and spoke. His Aunt Lynnette was there. She told me "Don't pay him no mind." I gave her a smile. *I thought in my head: that nigga can go to hell.* She thought her words brought me comfort; when actually it was the thought of his ass being hit by a bus that was soothing. He sat next to me on the couch. Both of us loathing each other. His mother took pictures as we tried not to get close to one another. I can say at least, he put on a fake smile for his mother. I didn't, I couldn't.

This would be our ongoing relationship. His mother would help with the baby and I would cuss him out. There were many days in the middle of me telling him to go screw himself that he would give his mother the phone and say, "See, I told you she's crazy."

And, when Pat got on the phone I tried to hold my tirade back because I respected her for helping with Mann. She was the best grandmother ever.

Shawn's sister once asked me, "How did you two get along long enough to make a baby?" I looked at her and said, "That's a good question." I didn't have an answer.

His entire family helped with Mann. His sister Tracy was willing to be the referee because she knew I was cussing Shawn out at least twice a week. When Tyshawn was 8 Shawn went to jail for selling dope. They gave him 3 strikes, 25 years to life. It's been over 20 years. He's still locked up.

I stayed at my father's house for about a month when I moved in with my brother's baby mama, Tina. We moved in Rollin hood and Tina started to date a guy that was in prison. *Yes, women really do this.* His name was Markie. He started having his cousin Dale come by to bring Tina money.

One day as Dale dropped off the money he asked me if I knew what Markie was down for? I said, "Yes, dope."

Dale looked at me and said, "You mean rape?"

I yelled, "Rape? Who the hell rapes people with all these hoes screwing niggas for free?" Dale responded, "My cousin, Markie."

I thought it was my job to tell Tina. Maybe she didn't know. When I told her she had the nerve to be mad at me. *Hold up! You're dating a rapist and you're mad at me?* I told Tina it was foul. I also told her I would no longer watch my niece for her to visit a rapist in jail. After that, our roommate situation didn't work out that well. Not long after our disagreement, I moved in my grandmother's back house on 76th. This was my first official place outside of living in motels and being homeless. I hooked up with Dale. He was different from the other guys I kicked it with. Dale was a square with a job that worked at Amtrak. He had also been in the military. I thought I'd give this square a chance.

One thing I can say about Dale is that he was down for me, even though he wasn't a gangster. He did prove that he was willing to fight over me. *How, you ask?* One night my sister invited us to her house for dinner. When we got there something didn't feel right. For some strange reason, I called my own house and the phone was busy. Busy how could that be? I didn't leave my phone off the hook. I told my sister I had to leave, something was wrong. Dale thought I was crazy for calling my own house, but he took me home anyway. When I walked up to the front gate of my house, I saw all my lights on. I literally dropped my son out of my hands. I knew it! I ran to my house. I had got, got. Someone had robbed me. The burglary was strange because the robbers left me a lot of items. It was like a courtesy robbery. Instantly I knew who it was, it was my crack head cousin, Earl. He was on his mother's front porch when I left.

The first thing I did was go to the front house where my Aunt Darlene lived. I beat on the door and asked for Earl. My cousin Christine came to the door and said he wasn't there. I told her I figured as much cause he was out selling my shit. I told her what happened. As I was cussing, my cousin Earl came up on the porch high as a kite. I knew he sold my stuff for crack. I ran up in his face and we started arguing. When I was done talking, I socked him in the face. The fight was on. We both fell off the porch into the flowerbed. That's when Dale jumped off the porch right into the fight. Dale pushed me out of the way and began to beat my cousin up. Earl wasn't expecting to get his ass whooped by a square, but that's what was going down. My dear aunt came out to break up the fight. As my aunt and cousin were trying to get Dale off of Earl I ran to my house and got my gun from my stash.

When I came back to the front house my brother Edwin was there pulling Dale off Earl. I figured my brother was in the area because he sold the crack to my cousin never knowing Earl got the money from robbing me. While my brother was pushing Dale back, Earl started talking shit and I started shooting.

My brother yelled, "What the hell are you doing?"

"Um trying to shoot this fool. If you move out the way."

My cousin took off running down the street. My aunt was threatening to have her sister put me out. *So let's recap, Aunt Darlene your son is a thief and a crackhead who has robbed everybody including you and you are going to try and get me and my kids put out on the street? Don't you just love dysfunctional families?*

The next day there was someone at my door. It was a white man in plain clothes. I asked through my screen door, "Can I help you?"

He said he was there to investigate a crime. I never called the police on Earl, but he called them on me. The detective told me he was there because I shot at my cousin. I opened my door in rage and told him,

"I live behind a crackhead that had robbed everybody from my grand-daddy to his Mama and you're at my door."

I think the detective was in shock because he had nothing to say except he would leave me his card. He told me I could call when I calmed down. I told him when my shit comes back, I'll calm down. He politely put his business card in my screen door, laughed, and walked off my porch. He never came back.

As the detective was walking off, the next-door neighbor called me to her gate. I was surprised because she didn't like my family, or me. *Why?* A few short months after she moved into her house, Earl broke in and robbed her. She wanted to know if it was true. Did I shoot at Earl? And did he rob me?

"Yes," I said with a snarl.

Well, her face lit up. We were no longer enemies. She was now just Earl's enemy. I didn't go to jail for shooting at Earl, but not long after, Earl went to jail for rape. *Please note a crack head will take anything and I do mean anything.*

Now I would like to be clear, my cousin was a fair crack head, he robbed everybody including his Mama. One day my daughter was playing in the backyard and all you could hear was, "Stop, stop forget that Mama I'm tired." It was my cousin Christine and my aunt chasing my cousin. He had grabbed the TV out of their house and was running through the back yard. They gave chase and ran right past Whitney. *Can you believe it? They couldn't catch him with a 19-inch TV in his hands?* He jumped the back gate with the TV. My cousin Christine was holding the cord in her hand and my aunt was screaming for her to let it go. Well, that didn't last long, as they were playing tug of war he snatched the cord from the back of the TV and took off running down the alley. *Yea that's what happens when you have smokers in your family.*

As I stayed in my house, I still went back in Blood hood and sold my dope. It was starting to be a problem because I wasn't from Rollin's and I no longer lived in the apartments. That changed when I met Melvin a.k.a. Big Ren from Rollin. Ren was a big man with a big heart. When I met Ren I was still with Dale. *So what did I do?* After I dropped Dale off at work in his car, I went and picked up Ren and we kicked it. I thought having a square was going to be cool, but it wasn't. Dale could only understand so much hood life. I wanted someone like me who thought like I did and understood me. I just loved thugs, period. So, at night while Dale was at my house with the kids I went in Rollin's hood with Ren and sold my dope. Ren asked me when I was going to get rid of Dale. I didn't have an answer for him. My sister loved Ren. He was a respectful gangster that wanted a family. I didn't want anymore kids, plus everybody in Ren's family was smoked out or had smoked at one time.

I continued this routine until my gig was up. Tina had asked if she could stay a few weeks with me. She had lost the apartment and her rapist jail love affair didn't work out. She and my niece needed a place to go. I let her sleep on my couch. During the two weeks she stayed with me Dale began to ask me questions about the Rollin's. Finally, he asked me if I knew Ren, because word on the street was I was messing with him. I told Dale I didn't give a damn what the word on the street was he could get on. He didn't want to do that, so he stayed. *I know Dale was related to Markie but who was snitching me out?*

Chapter 21

Loss is the New Normal

D
ale, Ren, and I finally ended when one morning I was dropping
Dale off at work as usual and I went and did my thing and picked up
Ren. No sooner than I got home Dale called and said he wanted his car.
I told him, "Fine not a problem homie." I drove to Amtrak and picked
him up.

When we pulled up in my driveway he said he needed to use the
bathroom. I told him to go piss outside. As I got out the car he did too.
Did this fool hear me? I said it again, "Go piss outside or at your job." I
walked fast to get to my front door. Dale started walking behind me. I
knew I had to get to my door first because Ren was there. Before I could
pick up the pace, Dale took off running and so did I. He beat me to the
door and walked in my house. Tina was sitting on the couch looking
clueless. Dale peeked his head in my room. Ren was sleeping in my bed.

He looked at me and said, "Choose."

"Choose what? Nigga this is my house."

Angrily Dale looked at me and left. Ren never knew Dale saw him
in my bed. Later that day, Ren's homie came and got him. I told him I
might not be in his hood. He asked me why. I told him I had some business to take care of. Dale kept calling me wanting to talk. *I told him to go*

to hell as if he was in the wrong. In my mind he was. He was wrong for all the right reasons, wrong for wanting me to love him and myself.

Finally, I spoke with Dale. He wanted to know what Ren had that he didn't have. After all, he had never been to jail and had worked all his life. His father owned a liquor store, which meant they had a little money. He had been in the military, he said he loved me and accepted my kids.

What he didn't know was I had never experienced a normal life or relationship, he was asking too much from me. *What could Ren offer me?* Ren, on the other hand, had no family support, no job, felonies, was a drug dealer, a gang member, but the sad thing was—he actually LOVED me, and so I chose. I chose the familiar and that was to function in my dysfunction.

After my break up with Dale, I lost someone else, Gwen. Before I moved on 76th I would go over to Gwen's house. Her father had bought her a house on the eastside. Right before I had Tyshawn we had an argument over a skirt. A skirt I would not give her, because I got it for my sister Sandi. We had stopped talking for months. One day I ran into her old boyfriend. I asked how she was doing?

He said, "I'm not with her anymore, you haven't heard?"

"Heard what?"

"Her baby daddy got out of jail and got her on crack. She smoked out."

"Smoked out?"

That day I got a ride to Gwen's and at first, she wouldn't let me in. I yelled on her front porch that I was not going anywhere. She finally came to the door looking like all the people we had sold crack too. *She was smoked out.* All her long pretty black hair had fallen out. She let me in. We sat and cried for hours. I told her I had a son and my own place and that I wanted to be close again. Just as quick as I found her, she was gone. She was driving her car and tried to beat a train. Her car stalled on the train tracks. When she finally got it started, she panicked and took off the tracks. She didn't see the truck coming. She ran head on and died instantly. *I wept.*

Loss appeared to be the new normal in my life. After a few months with Ren, he went to jail. I was pregnant. *What was I going to do with 3 kids at 18?* My brother Edwin suggested the abortion clinic. I asked him, "The abortion clinic?" I told him I had never had an abortion in my life. *I know what you're thinking, I was only 18. But, let me school you.* I had friends that had more than ten abortions before they were 20. So, for me this was new. My brother kept bugging me with his rationale, his church-going girlfriend had many abortions and she was fine, plus Ren was locked up. During this time, Ren called. He begged me not to have an abortion and to wait until he got out. Ren and his mother called me, pleading with me not to do it. On the other hand, I had my brother telling me that the abortion was best for me. I had waited so long before making my decision that I was five months pregnant when I finally let my brother and his girlfriend take me to the clinic.

I had never been to an abortion clinic before. I sat in that room filling out the papers. I was scared, nervous and unsure, but my brother was there to make sure I didn't change my mind. *How you ask?* He kept reminding me that Ren was going to be in jail for a long time and this would be baby number three without a father. So, I signed the paper agreeing with my lips. However, my heart was unsure. As I sat there still looking at the papers I signed, I didn't fully understand what I was agreeing to. That's when I heard them call me, "Alicia White."

My brother urged me to go in the back with the nurse. I got up belly showing and went to the back with the nurse. I got undressed and got on the table. They put seaweed sticks in my cervix to make me dilate. I had to come back the next day for the second part of the abortion. They had to do a two-day procedure because I was so far along in trimesters. Once they put the seaweed sticks in, I cried because I knew I couldn't change my mind. I came back the next day and murdered my child.

When I went home I had on my, "I don't give a fuck face." On the inside I was hurt, sad, and ashamed of myself. I was angry that I had listened to my brother and his girlfriend, not that I wanted a baby by Ren, but because it was my baby I murdered.

After Ren got out of jail, I believe he still loved me, but what I did broke his heart. *How do I know this?* Because of the sound he made when I cold-heartedly told him over the phone that I had the abortion. It was the sound of a gangster mourning from jail because his only child was aborted and because I allowed him to be a part of my dysfunctional life. *Ren Wept...*

With Ren gone and not being with Dale, things were getting tight. On top of that, my cousin Tee stole the rent money. Tina let him in to borrow something from the kitchen. She forgot the rent money was on top of the TV. When she came back into the living room, he was gone and so was the rent. Since I wasn't making money like before I decided to give the old welfare office a try. I went back to the office on Vermont and King and as usual, they gave me a big stack of papers. I stayed this time and finished them. The worker sent me to the district attorney's office so they could ask me about Sneak. Sandi went with me to my interrogation. When I went in the room the nasty lady asked me, "Where is your daughter's father?". I told her, "He's dead." She told me she still had to ask to see what he had.

"UMM, what part of the man was killed you didn't get?" Then I told her, "If you can get something out of a dead man, you're better than me."

She said she had to ask the usual questions. Who did you sleep with? Did he say it was his child? Did anybody see you sleep with him?

I gave her what I thought were the usual answers. "I slept with him in a truck behind a liquor store, and his friend watched."

You had to be there to see the look on her face, not to mention the look on Sandi's face. She sent me back to the rude intake worker and she said someone will contact me in 15-45 days.

I told her, "Hell, I'll be dead by then."

About two weeks later a worker named Ms. Curry contacted me and told me my application was still pending because I received Social Security money from my mother.

I yelled at her, "What in the hell are you talking about? My daddy gets that money I don't."

She kept trying to explain, and finally I said my magical words, "Fuck you, bitch." I hung up the phone in her face.

My sister called me the next day and said Ms. Curry called her house looking for me. Annette said Ms. Curry was mad and said, "Nobody cusses Ms. Curry out. Have your sister call me."

I tried to respect my sister when she told me, but I said "I know she don't think I'm scared of her ass."

I was ready for her. First thing in the morning I called her with my attitude. Somewhere between me getting smart she told me she was trying to help me.

"Help me? You're a welfare worker. Why would you help me?"

She told me again, but this time, I shut my mouth. Ms. Curry asked me about my mother's social security checks. I told her my father kept them. She asked me why. I told her I had a health condition that I had received hospital bills for. *Health condition meant fighting and getting injured.*

Ms. Curry said, "You just turned 18. He is still responsible for your care."

"What care? He don't buy me nothing."

For the first time, she was shocked. "Does he have receipts?"

"What receipts? I've been on my own since I left foster care."

After I told her this, we became friends. Ms. Curry told me that they would offset my benefits and deduct the amount that I received from Social Security, but she was going to help me get my money. She told me exactly what to say to my father.

I went to my father the next day with the very words she had told me. "I applied for welfare and they want all the receipts for my care. If you don't have any -- it's fraud."

My father looked at me with a mean look, and said, "I kept your check for hospital bills".

Once again, Ms. Curry was talking through me, and I told him, "Well the county worker said you were supposed to take care of me anyway, and hospital bills had nothing to do with my Social Security checks from my mother."

Not two months later, he started giving me my money, and because I wasn't in school it terminated. Ms. Curry was able to give me a full welfare check. Just think, all this help came from cussing someone out. My cussing did not push her away or make her terminate my application because of my nasty attitude. Ms. Curry was determined to get to the root of my issue to help me. And that's exactly what she did.

I was now 19 on the welfare with two kids. I couldn't afford my grandmother's house anymore. I was living in motels and still selling dope because the welfare check wasn't cutting it. When I went by my father's, my brother had another girlfriend named Sam. When I went with him to pick her up, I met her brother Devin. Devin was not a square or a gang-banger; he was a hustler. Devin had money. We hooked up not knowing where it would go because he had a dope case. In a few months, he had to turn himself in and do his time. Devin decided to take me to his house to pick up some of his dope. When we got there, his mother was standing in her door looking a hot mess. She had blonde hair, a large black mole on her face, and fingernails so long they wrapped around her hand. I had already heard horror stories about her from my brother, but I finally got to see this hot mess in person.

As we sat in the car he started to give me a warning, "My mother is from the pit of hell. She is Satan's lead man." At least, that was my interpretation. She came out of her door with a mean look on her face. I got out the car and stood in front of her gate. It was clear she did not want me in her house. Devin introduced me.

She walked over to me, looked me up and down like a slave at the auction block, and said, "Well her feet are little but her ass ain't."

I turned and looked at Devin. He gave me the, "Baby please don't cuss my Mama out on the first day," look. I knew then she was going to get cussed out on the regular. I guess my little feet had her fooled, because my mouth wasn't little.

After a couple of months of kickin' it with Devin, it was time for him to turn himself in. Neither of us thought we would still be together, and so when Devin turned himself in I had a surprise for him. I was pregnant. Devin asked me to hold on until he got home. I was in and out at my father's and his mother's house, 19 years old with two kids and pregnant. *How was I going to stay down for him?* I didn't do prisoners, when you go to jail-- I'm straight out. For some strange reason, I told Devin I would wait on him.

My dad's house was still crazy. Ann, my father's girlfriend, was painting the kitchen walls, ceiling, refrigerator, and porch black. *Yes, I said painted everything black.* We were all selling dope out the house and a hundred people were in and out. During this time my brother and his homeboy Jose had two guys slanging for them, Ron and Harpo. They were homeless. Ron took dope out of town for Jose and got caught; we never saw Ron again. Due to the hundred people that lived in the house, I moved in with Tina again to a place in Inglewood. *I know you're asking me why? I know, but I did anything not to live at my father's.*

While in Inglewood I wasn't slangin' anymore and it was rough. But I was cool because I bought my first bucket, a Honda Civic. I was rolling with no license. The apartment building was in Blood hood, and the dudes in the building knew I was a Crip. I wasn't trippin' because I had two kids and was pregnant. Tina moved out to live with her boyfriend Ronald. So, Harpo moved in with me.

I watched my back; I didn't trust them fools in my building. I did meet another Crip living there, Chris. My distrust was right. Ann came over one night and knocked on the door. What the hell is Ann doing at my door? She asked me to take her on 104th and Crenshaw a few blocks away. I didn't want her crazy self at my house, so I agreed. I asked Harpo to come with me because that was the bottoms where the Bloods were. I took Ann to an apartment and dropped her off but something said not to leave. I waited for her to come and give me a sign that she got in. When she didn't, I told Harpo I'd be back. I kept the car running.

He was in the back seat with my kids. I went through the apartments and I knew it was no good because too many niggas were out. One started shouting, "Hey what you need?" *Do I look like a crackhead?* I hurried up and went up the stairs. When I got to the top of the stairs

Ann was in a corner. A guy had her hemmed up asking what she need-ed. Translation—buy your dope from me. Ann kept telling him she was there for her friend. I walked in between them and told Ann lets go. I grabbed her by her arm. We started to walk down the stairs. I was that bold, pregnant and all. What I didn't know was as he followed, more Bloods joined in. When I looked back it was one of the young Bloods from my building. He walked up on me and asked what I needed. I told him I didn't need nothing. I kept watching my back, because he was so close on me. I then started to walk backward as I held Ann's arm be-cause I didn't want him to hit me from behind. Just when I got to the car another guy came and stood in front of me. I told Ann to get in the car. It was just me against them. Harpo just sat there. The other guy started asking me for my number. *Are you crazy? I thought.* As I turned to hurry up and get in the car, the Blood from my building grabbed me from behind and broke my chains. My chains fell into my shirt. I caught them. He gripped my shirt as the other guy was still asking for my number. I told him to let go of my damn shirt. I thought they were going to jump me. I was scared. I was outnumbered, outmatched, and in Blood hood. I did one good thing which was I kept my car running. As I pulled away from him, I jumped in my car and took off. As I drove home, Ann thanked me. I had no words, I was angry. I asked Harpo why didn't you help us? He said he didn't see what happened. I yelled, "You buster ass nigga. You had to be blind not to see that!" A few days later Harpo moved out. As for the young Blood that lived in my building, he never came back home because the homie Chris was waiting for him.

I knew it was time for me to move because that young Blood would be back. Devin wrote me and I told him what happened. He told me to start looking for a place because he had some money put away with his mother. Devin said he would have his brother Savage get it for me. He knew Satan's helper wasn't going to give it up. I moved back with my fa-ther and did what Devin asked. I started looking for a place and decided to look in Torrance. What I didn't know was that Torrance was where the good ole boys lived. I asked my two homies Ty and Derrick to ride with me to look at a house. When we got to Torrance we never got to see the house because the police pulled us over immediately. I had on a pink romper with a-b-c lettering on it, with a big ole belly. When the police pulled us over they asked me why was I there? *Why was I there?* I told the officer I was looking for a place. He then had us get out and he made Ty and Derrick assume the position. The officer looked at my tags and noticed they had just expired. The officer angrily told me that I could not drive my car home and to get a ride. As he was talking, it started sprinkling. The officer kept talking. He wasn't worried about getting wet; he was worried about it raining in his neighborhood with black people. He told me that my car had to stay parked and I had to have someone else drive it home. In the middle of our "Back South" interrogation, a call came over the officer's radio. They were angry because they had to take the call and leave us.

One officer walked up to me said, "If I come back and your car is moved too soon, I have your address and I'm coming to your house to get your ass."

The officers then ran and jumped in their car, probably to go beat some black people. We walked to a hamburger stand. I called my brother, but there was no answer. As we stood at the corner in front of the hamburger stand a truck was coming across the light. It had two white men in the back. Just as the truck was coming to the light one of the men shouted out, "Nigger go home, Nigger go home." *WHAT? WHO? GO HOME?*

That was the first time I had been called a nigger by a white person. He was about to shout it again and the light turned red. The truck was stuck at the corner, and he was surprised. I yelled out, "WHO GO HOME? Muthafucka I am at home."

Ty hunched me, "Licia we need to get out of here."

Ty recognized we were not in our hood. The light changed and the truck sped off. I was mad, it was raining and tears started to roll down my face. *Have you picked up that when I'm sad I cry and when I'm mad I cry?* First, the racist police makes a pregnant woman walk in the rain and then two white men yell at me, "nigger go home." I stood there as the tears and rain rolled down my face.

I looked at Ty and said, "I'm out of here."

Ty looked at me, "Out of where?"

"I'm going to my car."

Derrick was scared. He said he wasn't going because the police said they would come for us. I looked at both of them and politely said, "I don't give a damn," and started walking in the rain. I was pregnant, hurt, and angry. When Ty and Derrick saw I wasn't playing, they followed behind me. We got to my car and I drove like a bat out of hell. We sat in silence. That ride seemed like the longest ride of my life. None of us had anything to say. I had experienced gang violence, homelessness and foster care, but this was the first time I had been called a nigger by a white person and it stung my soul.

I continued looking for places but, didn't move because Devin's mother wouldn't give his brother Savage the money. She knew it was for me. She told Savage Devin had to get out and get it himself. Devin called her from jail and told her to give it to his brother. Her response was the same. I stayed at my dad's like Devin had asked and continued to visit him in Wayside Jail. At the circus a.k.a. my father's house you know there's never a dull moment. While staying there this pregnancy was different. I wasn't running the streets or clubbing, I was trying to be a real girlfriend.

One night Ann came by in one of her crazy rages. I was sleeping on the couch when I heard my father arguing with her. Seven months pregnant, I got up and wobbled to the door. Ann was in his face. It was three in the morning. *She couldn't come start a fight in the daytime like the rest of us criminals?* Ann had always showed up at my father's house crazy and out of her mind. She'd been hospitalized on "5150" a.k.a. crazy holds. My father would go sign her out. *Why? Sex, that's why, because there was no other logical reason.*

This time was different. He didn't get her out. I looked out the door and was about to go back to lay down when she yelled out something I had never heard her say before. She told my father, "You molested your perfect kids." I looked out the door at her and said, "This bitch is crazy." She yelled out some more stuff and all I heard next was, "with your dead wife, that bitch." Bingo that hit the spot.

I came out the door and asked my father, "What did she say?"

He looked at me and said, "Nothing, babe, go in the house."

My father had never called me babe or showed any kind of affection, so I knew then he was lying. I wobbled down the stairs and walked up on them. My father stood between us.

Ann looked at me, "You heard me."

My father told me again, "Go in the house."

I told my father, "You gon' let a crackhead prostitute talk about my mother like that?"

My father said it again, "She didn't say anything."

Ann yelled, "I did say something about that dead bitch!"

Her mouth wrote a check that her ass had to cash. I reached over my father and hit her dead in her mouth and the fight was on. It was the WWF combined with ultimate fighting. I was trying to kill her.

My father kept yelling, "You're pregnant!"

As I was fighting all I kept saying was, "You would let a crackhead talk about your wife?"

He had no words expect, "Stop it! Licia you're pregnant."

Eventually, all three of us fell on a rail that was on my father's porch. My father was getting a lot of the licks that were thrown because we were swinging around and over him. Ann got tired and she just stopped fighting. That freed my father up to just hold me. I cursed at the top on my lungs as he held me down on that rail. Ann walked away as if she wasn't in a fight. I was so angry I couldn't sleep. Just think, a month ago three Bloods almost jacked me for helping her; now she comes and calls my mother a dead bitch? I sat on the couch fuming. I had never cared about what my father did or didn't do, but he claimed he loved his wife so much. Why didn't he defend her? Was it because he knew Ann was just Ann? Her words cut my heart. My mother was dead, and I had been told all of my life it was my fault. *I sat on the couch at three in the morning, seven months pregnant and, I wept.*

Chapter 22

Family Life

It wasn't long after that night that Devin had done his time and came home. Devin's stompin' grounds were Lancaster/ Palmdale. It was 1990. *Where in the hell was Lancaster/Palmdale?* To keep him from driving so far we set up shop at my father's house. It was rolling on 85th. Devin was moving ounces. I didn't want Devin's money, so when my homeboy asked me to go out of town to make some money, I agreed.

Devin was mad, "Why you going out of town? I got money."

"You got money, not me"

Before I left, he asked me one more time not to go because I was pregnant and anything could happen. I didn't give a damn, I was going. The homie Lil Hog told me all I had to do was ride in the car. They were moving some birds across state lines. They needed a female in the car so they wouldn't look suspicious. The homegirl Joann came and gave me some money. I took Tyshawn to Pat and Whitney went with me. We were going to Des Moines, Iowa because the dope game had just started cracking out there. I can't remember how many days it took us, but Eddie, the one they paid to drive, was a smoker and was tweakin'.

When we finally got there, we went to a house and I saw my homeboy Mike. When I spoke to him he said, "Don't say my name." I told him, "Nigga that ain't your name." I guess when they got there and set up shop they had new gang names. Whitney and I slept at this house. The next morning, I was ready, but Eddie was gone.

I went in the living room and asked Lil Hog, "What's up? I'm ready to go."

He told me, "You have to stay until we move the product."

"I'm not staying no damn where! I want to go home."

Lil Hog said, "I gotta get on the telephone with the homie to see about that."

"See about what? You gon' take me home."

Lil Hog went into another room. When he came out I had my famous words ready. "You buster ass nigga. I trusted you. Don't you ever ask me to do shit for you again. If you don't take me home, I'm going to raise hell and this little ass town will know all y'all names when I'm done."

The next morning I was on my way home. When I finally got home, Devin was still mad because I took longer. To top it off, when Joann came to bring my money, she had an attitude. I guess they were mad they couldn't get me to stay in Iowa. She gave me the money, came back 30 minutes later talking about, she gave me too much and needed a couple hundred back.

I looked at her and said, "Hell yea y'all ass can have your money back." I was just that mad, I gave her two hundred dollars back.

Devin told her, "I told Licia don't mess with y'all you ugly bitch."

That was the last time I saw her. Lil Hog and I were never friends again. Devin kept going to Lancaster/Palmdale making money, and we moved to Lynwood. I should say, I moved to Lynwood, because it was rolling on my father's street and Devin didn't want to come home. I had to page him every night with a 911 code.

When he called I told him, "Bring yo' ass home to your family."

On November 1st, I went into labor and had my third child, Dwayne. This was the first time that I had a father at the hospital with me. Devin was in the delivery room. When Dwayne was born they laid him on my chest. My first words to Devin during that special moment were, "That's one ugly ass baby." I would love to think it was the drugs, but Dwayne was ugly, white, long and funny looking. Devin looked at me and I'll never forget his face. He was hurt over his little ugly son.

The first day after Dwayne was born I noticed he would not eat. When I told the nurse, she told me it was normal. I told her, "That's a lie. I have two kids at home."

She looked down on me because I was only 19. I stayed in the hospital for a day, and I was released drive-thru style. In the 80-90's, they kicked you out the hospital the next day. I went home with the kids and Devin went back on 85th Street. *Ain't that about nothing? I'm home alone with a newborn, and he's with my brother selling dope.* I asked him if he was getting some from my brother because he got more time than I did. Even though Devin didn't help, I was happy with my baby that we now called Baby Dee.

I had just turned 20 and Baby Dee was home for two days and he still wouldn't eat. A green chemical started shooting out his mouth like in *The Exorcist.* Something wasn't right. Devin took my car to go on 85th because his 5.0 Mustang was on a flat. I paged Devin 911, because something was wrong with Dee. I must have paged him five times. He probably thought I was going to cuss him out like I always did. He didn't answer. I was desperate. Something was wrong with my baby. I took the keys to the 5.0, loaded Baby Dee and the other kids up. I drove his car all the way to Saint Francis Hospital with a flat tire on his custom rims. I didn't care, my baby was sick.

As I was driving I could see the sparks flying from the rim. I was hoping that the rim didn't come off. When I got to the hospital that green chemical was still shooting out of Dee's mouth. They took us in the emergency room. The nurse stuck Dee at least five times.

I told her, "Bitch you got one last time."

She became nervous and called another nurse in. His veins were so small they had to put the IV in the top of his head. At this point I was crying. Devin got home and realized I was missing. He paged me. *I can't type all the cuss words I called him, his Mama, and his generations to come.* By the time he got to the hospital, they were transferring Dee to Millers Children's Hospital in Long Beach.

Once we got there, they told us Dee was very sick and he needed emergency surgery. The doctor came in and told us he had intestinal malrotation. He was three days old when they did the emergency surgery. I stayed at the hospital with my baby; he was there for two months. At this time, selling dope was last on my list. Once Dee was released, Devin went back on 85th, and I was left at home with the kids as usual. This was going to be the norm. I couldn't run the streets with Dee being sick.

One night, I watched my usual scary movies and went to bed. As I slept, I felt something come over my chest. I couldn't tell if I was sleep, but it was as if my eyes were open and I couldn't move. I tried getting up, but its presence held me to the bed. I tried to speak; I couldn't open my mouth. I could feel the tears running down my face. I yelled in my head, "Jesus, I'll die for you!" It let me up. I jumped up, got my kids, and put them in the room with me.

I looked under our mattress, pulled out the Uzi, and began to page Devin 911. He tried calling the house phone, but I wouldn't pick up. All I was thinking was, "Bring yo' ass home! There is something in this house." This time, Devin came right home. I had every light on in the house with the kids in the bed with me and the Uzi. I tried to explain what happened. He thought I was crazy.

The next morning, I called my sister and she came over. I explained to her what happened. Sandi told me it was from allowing spirits into my house.

"Sandi, I'm a Crip, what do I know about spirits?"

She immediately told me that every time I watched scary movies I allowed spirits into my house. She told me to stop letting my kids watch scary movies. Her intervention worked. I never wanted to have that experience again or invite spirits into my house. So, I stopped watching scary movies. Devin could not understand how one experience stopped me from watching my daily slash-your-throat, demon-possessed movie collection, but no gun could protect me from what I experienced. I was done. As a matter of fact, he couldn't watch them either.

After that experience, I didn't want to live in the house, but we had just moved there. I also had another problem; I was pregnant again. I was 20 and Dee was a couple of months old. Devin was not having it. He clearly told me he did not want another baby.

I told him, "Hell, you don't want the one you got now."

Something clicked in my head. Yea, he didn't want his son. He told me to get an abortion. Usually, when anyone tells me to do something I did the opposite. This time, I didn't. I made the appointment and Devin took me to the abortion clinic. He tried to comfort me, but all I could do was resent him. They called my name. *I thought, I've been here before.* They took me to the back. They prepped me. I was on the table trying to talk myself into getting up.

I had a conversation with myself. Fuck Devin. He ain't shit no way, you can take care of this baby like the rest of your kids.

Inside of my head the argument continued weighing out, the why's and why not's. *Then I told myself, he doesn't love you enough to have another baby with you.* The argument was over.

The abortion clinic was so booked that I laid on the bed in a hallway for over two hours. Finally, the nurse came for me. As she wheeled me to the room I was crying. *It was too late to change my mind.* My heart was saying, don't do it, don't do it, don't do it.

Just like all the years of being abused, I laid on my back and said nothing. I felt violated as I aborted my baby. Kind of like when someone touches you. You lose a part of yourself with it. After the abortion, Devin drove me home, and for days, I laid in my bed and cried.

One night Devin came in our bedroom and laid next to me. He wrapped his arms around me and whispered in my ear, "I wanted the baby after all."

I looked at him and asked, "Are you fuckin kidding me? You didn't want my baby."

In my mind, the baby I murdered wasn't his, only mine. *Did he think that after he got what he wanted we were cool?* After the abortion, the relationship with Devin was never the same. I had no respect for him or myself for that matter.

There was constant tension between us and to help smooth things out he picked up Harpo. I guess he thought having someone in the house would help with the chaos.

Things were still tense between us and we had another argument, and he grabbed me by my neck and began choking me. Devin was 6'4" and 280 pounds. I couldn't believe it. He had never touched me before. I grabbed his hands, but I couldn't get him to let go. I felt my body becoming limp. As he choked me, I could hear someone talking. He kept choking me until we were both on the bedroom floor. That's when Harpo came into the room and yelled for him to let me go. He finally did. I began to gasp for air. When I sat up, Devin had the Uzi to my head. Harpo kept telling him, "Don't do it man. Don't do it Devin! She has your baby."

I still hadn't came to myself when Devin went to the closet, grabbed some clothes, his dope and took off. Harpo stayed with me for a few days, then he left. Eventually, Devin came back, but we were done. It was just a matter of time.

This was around the time that Rodney King was beaten and just before that Latasha Harlins was shot in the head by an Asian storeowner. The hood was hot. For the first time, I was glad I lived in Lynwood. It was 1992 and just like everybody else I was watching the news waiting for the Rodney King Verdict. Not guilty. Disappointed I went to sleep. My house phone started blowing up. It was Christine.

She asked, "Where are you?"

"You called my house, so that would mean I'm at home."

She called to tell me that the looting had begun. I jumped up and told Devin I was going to LA. We loaded the minivan and dropped the kids off to my brother. We were ready to come up. By the time we got to LA, all of the good stuff was gone. The pawnshops and grocery stores had already been looted. Devin and I drove in our minivan jumping out where we saw people coming out, but everything was gone.

That night we did not expect to be trapped in LA. The National Guard was called out. Army tanks drove down Figueroa. Everyone in the hood had a curfew. It was said, if you were caught outside after curfew getting shot was going to be the outcome. After waiting for hours at my father's house, I couldn't take it anymore.

I told Devin, "We're going home. If we get caught, I guess we'll get shot because it was the same as staying at my father's."

My brother tried to talk Devin out of leaving, but I wanted to go home. We jumped on the 110 and took it all the way around to Lynwood. We made it home with no bullet holes.

After the riots, everyone from different neighborhoods joined the peace treaty. No more Bloods on Crips or shall I say black-on-black crime. The homies met with other gangs in the Nickerson Gardens housing projects. Everyone came to an agreement that after the way the police beat Rodney King, there would be no more killing between blacks. The police did not like the peace treaty. Now when the police stopped people they were not looking for dope, they were looking for guns. With the peace treaty going on and black-on-black crime down, there was a new enemy, the police. They were sweating people on the streets, they wanted to know where the guns were coming from.

Devin and I always had a gun and crack, so we were ready for whatever. One day while I was at my father's, I got a page. I called my cousin back and learned my grandfather died. Me, Devin and the kids went to Hawthorne to my aunt's house. My grandfather had died in her house. She was waiting for the coroner to come. Poor grandpa, he was a good man. We stayed there for a while, and on our way home the police pulled us over.

They searched the car and found Devin's gun. The police interrogated Devin as he sat on the curb. The kids and me watched from the car. I was scared not just about the gun, but Devin had a couple of cut up ounces of cocaine in the dashboard of his car. He had it in a large plastic zip lock bag rolled up in a sock. He did this so when he moved the vents from the dashboard he could stick a hanger down the vent and pull out the sock. The police kept searching the car. I was nervous. The hanger was on the floor, but they never picked it up. The police took Devin to jail and I explained that my grandfather had died, so they let me and my kids go. *I thought they were being nice, yea right.*

I went back to my father's and hours later Devin called the house for me to come and pick him up.

"Come pick you up?" I asked him.

I just knew he was going to jail for years since he had a record. I took a different car, went to the 77th police station, and parked out front. Devin came out limping. *Did they beat him?*

He jumped in the car, "Drive!"

"What happened? How the hell did you got out of jail when the police had you for a gun?"

"We need to get out of here. I'll tell you later."

Were the *police setting us up? Did they let us go to follow us?* I found out the answer a few days later. Devin was gone and the phone rang. I missed the call. It was a police officer from 77th street station.

He left a message for Devin, "Nigga you lied to us and we're going to get you."

I paged Devin 911. He came right home. I asked what happened and Devin told me when they took him to the station they wanted to know where he got the gun. They told him they weren't going to be out-gunned by a bunch of gang members. Devin said they were trying to get all the guns off the street. He gave them bunk information. He told them about Byrdie.

I looked at him and said, "You snitched on someone that didn't have guns?"

He had nothing to say. I asked him again, "You got out because you sent the police to your homie's house?"

Byrdie was a Mexican dude that sold Devin dope. They went on a bogus gun sting and they were pissed. We packed up the kids and went to a motel. That week my brother and my sister helped me pack up the house and put my stuff in storage. We never lived there again. *I knew we were through because of the abortion and choking, but this was the icing on hood cake.* We eventually moved to Hawthorne.

We were still watching our backs. I had our neighbor in Lynwood get our mail. She was a nice lady who never knew we were dope dealers. Our house in Hawthorne was different; it was expensive. Devin wasn't making money like before because he knew the police were out to get him. I wasn't selling dope at all and it was starting to take a toll. The water pump went out on my car and Devin wouldn't give me the money to get it fixed. We were still in that space after that abortion. We weren't a team anymore. I don't think we ever were. I had to go to Lynwood to pick up my mail, so I used Devin's SS Monte Carlo.

On the way, I had an accident on Century and was taken to Killa King Hospital. I was all right, but his car wasn't. I was released from the hospital and when I got home the car had beat me there. And so, the argument began. *Was I speeding?* Of course I was speeding. Devin wasn't worried about me; he was worried about his car. His mother called to make sure her son's car was fixed. I cussed her out. The tension between us was unbearable, and the arguments were happening every day. To get away, I walked to my sister, Annette's house since she lived in Hawthorne too. During one of the last arguments we had, he let me know that it was his money and he didn't give a fuck that I didn't have a car. I was hot. I looked at him holding back tears, because I wouldn't give him the satisfaction of thinking he broke me.

Walking out of the door, I looked at him and said, "I'm about to come back up."

He looked confused as if he didn't know what come back up meant. *It meant, nigga, I'm about to get me a sack, slang my dope and get my own money. So go to hell.*

I walked to my sister's house and I did something that I rarely did, I borrowed money. My sister gave me fifty dollars. She had no idea that she was contributing to the dope game. I asked her to drop me in LA, and she did. I hit LA and the homies were happy to see me. I spent my fifty on a double up. In less than a few hours, I had doubled my money. I quickly went and got another double up; it was rollin. I had to hurry up because I knew Devin wasn't going to pick up the kids from school and my sister had my youngest Dwayne. I came back home with money.

The next morning, I drove my car to LA; it was running hot. I paid a smoker to put my water pump on. *Guess what y'all? I was back in the game.* Every day I got up like clockwork, dropped my kids off at school and hit the streets. Every morning Devin was looking stupid. He knew I had money, and I didn't have a damn thing to say to him. He was used to me staying home, after all, I had left the hood when we got together. He had no idea I went back. Amateur, he should've known I was going back home. Back to what I knew, my hood.

I stopped paying rent, so we were behind. The owner said he was going to evict us. Devin told me that he couldn't pay the rent by himself and showed me the notice. It was now my turn to tell him, "I don't give a fuck." I was on my way out. I wasn't giving him or the landlord another dime. Two weeks later, I came home and packed my stuff as he stood by looking confused. He told me he was keeping everything in the house if I left. I didn't care, I was starting all over again. Just like Tina Turner, I walked out with my clothes and my name. The same damn name I came in with, cause his ass didn't marry me.

I left everything in the house, dishes and all. I moved into my father's house and was out all night, so I didn't have to be there. Things were looking up. My money was being stacked, I was clubbing and slangin'. Devin kept paging me trying to get me to come back. *Was that fool serious?*

Chapter 23

New Man, Old Enemy

One day while I was standing outside my father's house talking to a customer, I met Dae Dae. He sent his Aunt Brandy to tell me he was looking at me. My reply was, "That's nice." Dae Dae was fresh out of jail after doing seven years for murder. I wasn't tripping on the murder part, I was trippin' that he thought he could just come and I was supposed to fall out because he wanted my number. *Oh, let me explain something, in black culture, they have this thing that if you're light skinned you're beautiful, and you should be glad or honored if a light-skinned person wants to talk to you.* Needless to say, Dae Dae was light skinned with long hair. But guess what? I had my own car, my own money, and I wasn't moved. After a few attempts I started hangin' with him. *When Devin came to see my son, yes I said my son, he was mad.* The only time he would keep Baby Dee was if he thought we were getting back together. Once Devin figured out I was seeing someone else, he kept trying to get me back. *No thank you, sir.*

I kept seeing Dae Dae and clubbing. He thought his alleged cuteness was going to move me and he insisted that I stop hanging out in our hood. *Hold up, stop hanging out? Was he crazy? I'm grown. I'm 23. I know you think he was concerned about me, but the truth of the matter was he was getting at other girls and he didn't want me to know.* Dae Dae and I had an unspoken agreement that said we were together, but then again we weren't. But because we slept together, we weren't supposed to sleep with other people. I'm assuming he thought he was ahead of the game until he paged me one day and I wouldn't call him back. He came to my father's house and found me outside talking to KK from our hood.

Dae Dae walked up and asked, "Did you get my page?

"I did."

Dae Dae's Uncle Whitey walked up, "I'm trying to buy weed. That's why Dae Dae paging you."

Whitey was trying to help his nephew out, so he didn't look like he was chasing a chick. I knew better. Dae Dae was mad. I went into the house holding my laugh, got the weed, and brought it to Dae Dae and Whitey. Poor KK, he was standing there not having a clue that my fake boyfriend rolled up on us. Later that night Dae Dae came to my father's house. He wanted us to be a couple. Funny, he only wanted to make it hood official because I wasn't chasing him and someone else was chasing me, but I agreed anyway.

Little did I know I was about to get into another relationship, one I wasn't expecting. I was walking on Vermont and saw my old enemy, Kai. We were enemies because of the homie, Cee. I had dated him for a minute. It was over between us when Cee told me he was going to get a bitch that obeyed. Kai was my replacement. They had a son together. We mad dogged each other and we exchanged words. I told Kai, "Take your son home and meet me to get down." *That meant fight.* She agreed, because she didn't like me no more than I liked her. I dropped my son to my brother and went on 82nd to have this fight that had been a long time coming.

I parked my car. Kai was already there. We both walked to meet in the middle of the street. Something was happening. *You asked if a change of mind had occurred?* Had two mothers came to their senses and realized they shouldn't be fighting in the middle of the street like dogs? *No that would be wishful thinking.* Cee rolled up on us. Her face changed. She started talking low. What the hell was happening? She asked me not to tell Cee we were about to fight.

As he got out the car, he started cussing, "Bitch where's my son while your ass is over here?"

I was waiting for her to cuss him out and something amazing happened, she said nothing. I was in hood shock. *Did he just call her a bitch? Did she really just not say or do anything about it?*

Cee looked up at me, "What's up Licia?" I was still in shock. He told her, "Take your ass home and get my son." He got back into his car and left.

Talk about awkward; we were just standing there, she was embarrassed and I was still in shock. We couldn't really say anything. The fight match was just canceled. She went to her car and left.

A few weeks passed, Dae Dae was still trying to convince me to stop hanging in the hood. One night when I showed up on 81st, he got mad and left. I was standing outside minding my own business when Cee came out of a spot. Kai was behind him. He turned around, grabbed her by the coat, and was threatening to beat her ass. *I was thinking, aren't you already doing that?* He slammed her to the ground, took her car keys and threw them. It must have been about five homies outside watching, but this was Cee's business, so they had nothing to say. I didn't even like the girl, but I was thinking that's fucked up. Cee got into his car and left Kai standing there with no car keys, stuck at about two in the morning.

As I was standing there shocked as hell, Kai came up to me. She asked me if I could help her. *Help her? We were enemies, but I felt bad for her.* I asked her what she needed. Kai said she needed me to take her to a friend's house, so she could get her extra set of keys. I took her and came back. Kai got her car and left. I was waiting for the next customer when Cee returned. He jumped out of his car. Kai's car was gone.

He went into the spot where Kai was and came back out shouting, "Who helped her?" Cee yelled again, "Who helped that bitch get her car?"

I just stood there. The homies were silent. I acted as if I didn't know what he was talking about.

Finally, the homie Bruce said, "Fuck this shit man, 'Licia gave her a ride somewhere."

I looked at him. *Nigga are you serious?*

Cee walked up on me and confronted me, "You gave that bitch a ride? She don't even like you."

As Cee was talking, he noticed I had reached into my pocket.

He asked, "What you got in your pocket?"

"If your ass hit me like you hit her, you'll find out".

He started smiling, "You gon' shoot me?"

"Hit me and you'll find out just what I got in my pocket."

I had a dagger that fit between my two fingers. I was ready to go. He knew I would stab him. I wasn't taking no ass whopping from him. Cee still wanted to tell me how Kai hated me when I interrupted him.

"That's my car that I bought with my own money, I can and will put who the hell I want in it."

The next time I saw Kai, she thanked me. We were on the same team. She heard about how I stood up to Cee. We were no longer enemies, we became friends; imagine that two women who slept with the same man were now good friends. This was unheard of in the hood.

Things were still shaky with Dae Dae. He gave me one last ultimatum to stop hanging in the hood. I didn't take it, so we weren't going to be sleeping buddies anymore. I was cool with it. I told him he could get on because he wasn't going to tell me what the hell to do. That same night, I was hanging with the homie from The Foe, Lil Snake. He was cool, but he was younger. I was 23 he was 20. He came over my house; we talked until we fell asleep. It must have been about four in the morning when I heard knocking on my door. *Who the hell was at my door?* I didn't slang out of my house. I looked out my bedroom window and saw that it was Dae Dae on my porch. *Oh no he didn't.* Did he think that after he had just dissed me that he could come and sleep with me? He knew I was there because my car was in the driveway. Snake woke up and asked me if everything was ok. Before he knew it, I was giving him some. He was a little shocked because he didn't even ask for it, but I gave him some good ole sex anyway.

You may be asking why I did it? Well, because in my crazy mind I was paying Dae Dae back for trying to control me, and for dissing me. *If he wanted to sleep with the homegirls fine, I'd sleep with the homies.* In the hood, the homies got to do whatever they wanted, with whomever they wanted, but girls/women were expected to quietly accept it, but not me. I talked with Lil Snake for a while and we went back to sleep.

The next morning I felt someone tap my toe. *Was it my kids? They knew not to come into my room without knocking.* When I looked up, it was Dae Dae. One of the kids had opened the door and let him in. My first thought or should I say prayer was, "Lord let this be a dream and if it is I'm going to get Lil Snake out of here." Well, it was no dream, but it was about to turn into a nightmare. I laid there frozen. Snake was on his stomach, so Dae Dae couldn't see who it was. Dae Dae walked through my kitchen back into the living room to wait on me. I put my clothes on and went into the living room.

He asked, "So that's how we're doing it?"

"Hell yes! That's what you said."

He looked at me and started laughing, "Cool." He left without another word.

I went back into the room and woke up Lil Snake. I told him what happened.

He asked, "You ok?"

"Yea, I ain't trippn. Dae Dae ain't my man."

I went to the bathroom and started to brush my teeth when I heard a knock at my door. *What now?* I went and opened the door. It was Dae Dae. Before I could say anything, he slapped me in the face causing my toothbrush to fly out of my mouth. He started walking up on me, backing me up as he came into my house.

He asked me, "Who is cuzz in your room?"

I said, "A friend." I honestly thought he wasn't mad, after all, he was fuckin' half the neighborhood.

Dae Dae demanded, "Go get him!"

"Go get who?"

He said, "Go get cuzz right now."

I said, "Ok."

I went into my bedroom. Lil Snake was fully dressed now.

He asked me, "Everything ok?"

"Um, yes. It's Dae Dae. Can you go out the back door?"

He stood up, "If cuzz wants to see me, tell cuzz we can handle it."

I begged him not to fight Dae Dae. I went back into the living room and lied. I told Dae Dae my friend didn't want to see him. Dae Dae insisted I bring him out. I went back into the room, this time Lil Snake was mad, but he was trying to respect my house. I told him I needed him to go out the back door. Just as he was about to go into the living room, I tried to stop him. When I turned around, Dae Dae was standing in my bedroom door.

Dae Dae yelled out, "Bitch you fucking the homie?"

I ran right passed him into the bathroom and I locked myself in.

Dae Dae came behind me trying to pry the door open, but I pushed the door shut and got the latch on the door. He was at the door telling me to come out, and for the first time, that was a fight I didn't want. I didn't date men who beat women. I didn't fight back because I didn't want Snake to fight with Dae Dae.

Snake came to the bathroom door, "Licia you ok?"

"Yes, just go."

I heard Dae Dae ask, "Did you hit that?"

Lil Snake didn't respond. He asked me again, "Licia are you ok?"

This time, I answered, "Kevin I'm ok. Just go."

I heard Dae Dae ask him again if he slept with me. Out of respect for me, Lil Snake said no. Dae Dae knew he wasn't scared of him. I didn't want any problems between The Trays and Foe's. At the end of the day, if the two of them had a fight, it was my fault for doing what men do all day long, and that is sleep with two people. Dae Dae stayed at the door trying to get me to come out for about 30 minutes before he left. *One thing*

I want you to know is that during that time, no news spread faster than hood or jail news, and since I wasn't in jail, the hood news spread.

It wasn't even 10 a.m. before Dae Dae's Uncle Whitey, showed up at my house. He was beating my door like the police. I looked out before opening it.

Whitey yelled, "Hey girl, your pussy must be something else cause I hear you got niggas jumping out your windows."

He walked in my house and sat on my couch. He wanted to know everything that happened. He let me know everybody in the hood was talking about me. I stood there wanting to drop dead of embarrassment. *Who told?* Whitey wasn't mad at me. He knew his nephew was no angel; he just wanted the hood scoop. Right after he informed me that I was on the hood news, my pager started going off. *Who was paging me?* It was Kai. *Was something wrong?*

Whitey left. I called her. She was paging me to tell me she heard what happened. Cee had made a personal trip to her house to tell her not to hang out with me because I was a hoe. *Mind you, Kai was his other woman. He had a wife and two other girlfriends. Yet, I'm the hoe?* Later that day, Kai came by; we went to a hamburger stand. She kept looking over her shoulder because if Cee caught her with me, she was going to have problems.

I was pissed. Dae Dae had slept with women, probably half the hood. Why when a woman does it she's a hoe who is not to be talked to or seen with? After about two weeks, it was getting old for me. I thought the Dae Dae scenario would have died out by then, but it hadn't. People were still talking about me as if I had cheated on Prince Charles.

That wasn't the bad part either. My friend Londie came over; she had something to tell me. *What can be worse than my being on the national hood enquirer?*

Londie told me, "Dae Dae found a new girl."

Irritated I said, "So!"

"Licia, you don't understand."

"I don't understand what?"

"Dae Dae is with Brenda!"

"BRENDA? BRENDA? I know Dae Dae is mad, but he wouldn't do me like that. People just saying that because of what I did."

Brenda was my enemy from back in the day. She instigated a fight between me and her homegirl Debbie. I beat Debbie's ass as Brenda watched. We hated each other, but she was scared to fight me.

Londie looked at me. She could tell I wanted to cry.

She said, "Licia, I saw them myself."

Was this Sneak and Cassey all over again? I got on the phone and called Kai. She couldn't believe it. *What I didn't realize was when a man's pride is hurt, oh wait let me rephrase that, when a woman hurts a man's pride openly, you better believe the woman that did it will be hurt openly.*

Everywhere I went people were talking about me. Dae Dae was now sleeping with my enemy, Cee was telling Kai to stay away from me. *What's next?*

Chapter 24

Out of the Frying Pan into the Oven

The hood commotion was still underway when I saw my old homie Bugsy. He was much older than me. He was with his brother when he came on 84th where I lived to handle his business. Every time I saw him, he always had a smile on his face. Bugsy told me that he heard about me. He always encouraged me to stay out of trouble. As he was talking, his brother got out of the car. Bugsy stopped the conversation and introduced us. *Low-key, Bugsy was hooking us up.* I had known Bugsy for years, but I had never met his brother, Lee. I spoke to Lee. He was quiet, had a nice body, and seemed cool. Bugsy told me to hit him up later, so he could give me his brother's info. *Cool, I needed someone outside this madness.*

Over the next week, I saw Lee walking everywhere. He was always by himself in his wife beater shirt. One day, Lee was walking down Fig. He ended up at the local liquor store on the corner of 83rd and Fig. We spoke and it went from there. Lee came by my house and we talked for hours. He came by every day for the next week. He didn't live in the hood, he lived in Lakewood with his father. Lee had me take him to his house. While on the way he explained he didn't give a damn what niggas were saying about me. He also said that Dae Dae was wrong for trying to stop me from hanging out. *WHAT? Somebody that wasn't TEAM DAE DAE.* I was excited because Lee seemed to walk to the beat of his own drum. He didn't do what the rest of the homies did. I was thinking in my mind he's not a follower, and he does not get into hood gossip, surely making for a keeper.

When we got to Lee's house he went in to change his clothes. As I waited in the living room I got a surprise. Lee came into the living room drying his hair with nothing on. *Hold up, did I miss something?* Lee asked me if I called him? *I guess I was supposed to drop my panties because he had a bangin' body, no thank you.* As we drove back to the hood, he had a big smile on his face, just like Bugsy. *I may have come up if he is anything like his brother, because Bugsy was really sweet.*

He then proceeded to have a "special" conversation with me. *Was this because I didn't fall for the naked man with the sexy body who just walked out of the shower scenario?* I was anticipating that he was going to tell me how easy it was for men to get women. As he was explaining the number of men to women, he gave me a special fact. He told me that men can have any woman they set their mind on. Lee then went into classified info. He said if a man really wanted a woman that would do anything for him then all he had to do was get a white girl and fuck the shit out of her. *What? Wait, did this fool just tell me this?* I sat in the car mad all the way back to the hood. When we pulled up at my house he didn't understand my attitude. Lee didn't come around for about a week or two. Then he showed up as if we never had his special conversation about men and women.

Over the next week, I rode around with Lee. It felt hella good. When we went anywhere, hood and all, no one had a damn thing to say to him or me. He got out with pride that he was in my presence, unlike Dae Dae who wanted me to stay off the block. He was proud to be with me. He gave niggas the, "I dare your ass to say something look." They never did. *Ok, I think he's the one. He's down, don't give a damn about what people say, and he wants to be seen with me. It was the icing on hood cake, he wanted Alicia!!!*

I was excited about my new boyfriend. Where in the hell has he been all this time? Another plus was, I hadn't heard about him sleeping with any of the girls in the hood, so he was no hoe, at least to my knowledge. No one in the hood had kids by him so that eliminated baby mama drama. This meant I could have him all to myself. Things were looking up for me.

Lee finally told me he had a son named Lil Lee, and he wanted to spend time with him. *A family man too, wow!* But, when Lee went to pick his son up he just dropped him off to me and left. The first couple of times he did this, I didn't say anything. However, the last time he left Lil Lee when he came back Lil Lee was mad. He didn't want to sit in the house with me. He wanted to go with his father. The same day when Lee told him to do something, Lil Lee disobeyed. Lee socked Lil Lee in the chest.

I jumped up, "How are you going to sock the boy in the chest? Are you crazy?"

We argued about how he didn't spend time with his son. Up until that point, Lee was ok in my eyesight. Now the real him was showing up. That day after dropping Lil Lee off I wanted to go clubbing. Lee had something to say about it. At first, I thought, he's jealous; wow he really wants to spend time with me. That was until the next opportunity came for me to go out with my friends. He locked me in my house literally.

Ok, it was no longer cute. He didn't want to spend time with me; he was just possessive. That night we argued over me going to the club, and he hit me. We tussled for a bit. He used his weight to hold me down. The next day, it dawned on me, I was in the same situation that I told Kai she shouldn't be in.

That day my homegirl Ned had been paging me and she wanted to know why I didn't come to the club. I told her because I was around a psycho. Ned told me that it was cracking at the Name of the Game and we should go Friday. I told her come hell or high water I was going. Friday came, but this time, I didn't say a word to Lee. I got dressed. When I got into my car with Ned, he showed up at my house. He wanted to talk with me. He tried to make me get out of the car. I refused. I backed out of my driveway. When I looked in my rearview mirror Lee was running full speed.

I looked at Ned, "What the hell is he doing?"

Lee jumped on top of my car. I kept driving. He could not hold on. He slid off the top and grabbed my side mirror. I kept driving as Ned screamed for me to stop the car. I told Ned I was going. I screamed at Lee telling him to let go of my car. He wouldn't. He held on while I dragged him down the street. He kept yelling for me to stop the car. I kept telling him to let go. In between our ghetto exchange, Ned kept screaming for me to stop. I drove faster. He wasn't going to let go. Ned wouldn't stop screaming, so I honored Ned's request. I slammed on the brakes. He tumbled to the ground. I looked in my rear view mirror, laughed, and hit the gas. I was off to the club. Poor Ned, she didn't enjoy the club, she was still in shock.

I told her if he was crazy enough to hang onto the car, I was crazy enough to drag him. I danced and got my party on that night. After I dropped Ned off, I watched my back when I went home, because I knew he would be looking for me. I didn't see Lee that morning. He did something better than stalk me; he called my mother a.k.a. Sandi. She told Lee she was coming by my house the next day. When she arrived, guess who just so happened to be walking up at the same time? He came in with her and told her how I dragged him in the middle of the street. Then he had the nerve to pull out his black jeans that he had on. They had holes in them. Sandi looked at me. I was angry. Sandi told us to stop fighting. *Who's fighting?* That psycho jumped on the top of my car, that's no fight. After Sandi left, Lee and I had a big argument.

I paged Dae Dae and he called me right back. I asked if I could see him. He was happy to meet me. Dae Dae and I hadn't been friends or spoke since the Lil Snake and Brenda incident. Dae Dae met me around the corner at my father's house. We parked and talked. He said he was sorry that he had gotten with Brenda, and that he still liked me. We knew we couldn't turn back. We both realized that the situations that we were in were far worse than what we encountered with each other. Dae Dae told me I could always call on him. He would be there for me. I had already made up in my mind that I would never sleep with Dae Dae again because he had touched Brenda.

That night Dae Dae dropped me back to my father's house, my brother was on the porch waiting like a spy. He told me to watch my back because Lee had come around to my father's house with a gun looking for me. Edwin said Lee told him that he thought he saw me get into the car with Dae Dae. That night I ditched Lee. He came the next morning to apologize and say he was wrong. He said that I was all he had and he was sorry for what he did. Of course, I was feeling bad, not for dragging him, but the fact that he said I was all that he had. He had been in and out of jail since he was 19. His father didn't come into in his life until later. *So guess what I did? Yes, you got it, I took him right back.* At first, I felt needed, and soon the need became a nightmare. He went back to the same behavior. He was always trying to track where I went, and who I went with. For the most part, he liked Kai because she didn't club.

It was almost Easter, Kai and I went shopping to buy clothes for the kids since we were preparing to go to the park. I asked Lee if he wanted to go. He declined, so I left. When I got home, he was sitting on my stairs. He helped me inside. I put the kids to bed. Lee went in my room and sat on my bed. When I walked into my room to ask him about his day, he hit me. *Was I trippin, did this nigga just hit me?* He was just in the living room laughing with the kids. I never saw it coming. The fight was on. We fought until we were both tired. I cussed him out and made him leave. *You know who I called that week to help me, right?* I called Dae Dae. He had now become the go-to guy when my life was a mess with Lee.

This time, I met Dae Dae at Manchester Park to ensure Lee didn't see me get into his car. Manchester Park was the hood park where all the homies went. I thought it was a good place to go because Lee would never think to look for me there. As I sat on the grass and poured my complaints to Dae Dae, he listened attentively.

Then he said something that changed my world. Dae Dae said, "Lee is a good nigga if he didn't smoke that shit."

I yelled, "Shit? What shit?"

What is Dae Dae talking about? I asked him again, "What shit?"

Dae Dae tried to act surprised as if he didn't mean to tell. Dae Dae knew I had no clue Lee smoked Sherm.

"Are you kiddin me?"

Dae Dae said, "I thought you knew."

I sat on the grass in disbelief. We stayed for a while until Kai paged me. I told Dae Dae I had to go. I left, went straight to Kai's house, and told her what Dae Dae had told me. I couldn't believe I was hooked up with a Sherm head. This explained his calm behavior and then he would be crazy on other days. I sold Sherm before and you couldn't miss the smell. I didn't tell Lee right away that I knew he was a Sherm head, but I believed Dae Dae. I just kept selling my dope. I began to go back on my father's street to slang so Lee wouldn't find out that I became friends with Dae Dae, but things were about to get crazier.

One late night a customer paged me. She lived down the street from my father's house and she needed dope. As I was walking up the street to make the sale, some guys were sitting in a car.

They started yelling, "Hey baby," out the window.

I kept going for two reasons. One, you don't go to strange cars at night and two, you don't go to strange cars at night. On my way back, the guys were still sitting in the car. I could see their faces. I had my gun on me, so I was ok.

I was going to just walk past them when one of them yelled, "Hey, bitch, I know you heard me."

I turned and shouted back, "I got your bitch," and I put my hand on my Glock.

They didn't want to see me. They weren't expecting a chick to have a gun on her. I made it back to my father's house. I couldn't believe what just happened. When I went home, Lee told me he had gotten into an argument with one of the girls he sold dope to. The girls meant prostitutes. A larger amount of girls in my neighborhood were on drugs and that's how Lee made his money. Lee told me we were going to switch up. I would be on the corner with the girls and he would work the block, so I didn't have to deal with men.

We changed locations. I was now hanging on 83rd and Figueroa at the New Bay Motel with the girls. Lee hit the different blocks in the hood. Things were going good until I went to see my brother Edwin at my father's house. While I was there someone knocked on the door. When I answered he asked for Curtis.

"Hey wait I know you!" I told him. "You're that muthafucka that called me a bitch."

My brother Curtis came running to the door, "What happened?"

By this time, his friend was walking off the porch. I followed cussing. His friend turned around, started to argue back and I spit in his face. Edwin had come running out the house talking big and bad. My father came to the porch to see what was going on. My brother Curtis got in between us, trying to explain it was his friend Freddie, and he just moved here from Chicago.

Curtis said, "Licia that's Chloe's brother."

"I don't give a damn whose brother he is. He was calling me bitches because I wouldn't stop at his car at three o'clock in the morning. I wasn't selling pussy."

Edwin asked Freddie "what's up?" He did not have much to say considering, all three of us were in his face. Finally, I realized there wasn't going to be a fight, unless I fought and Freddie didn't want to fight.

After this mini showdown, Freddie and I became enemies. Each time he saw me we stared each other down. I always asked him an important hood question, "Nigga what you want to do?" He would never answer me. In time, that changed. He started to hang with Jose and a homie named Fish. Since Freddie started hanging with Jose and Fish he thought he was a part of the hood. I still hadn't changed.

One day as I was walking down my father's street. Freddie was mad doggin me.

I asked, "What's up nigga?"

This time, he had an answer. We started arguing and Freddie reached back to slap me. Before he could bring his hand down my gun was between his eyes.

I told him, "Your ass hit me, and it's going to be your last day alive."

I didn't know much about Freddie, but I did know he beat up his girlfriend Ley on a regular basis. Freddie and Ley lived two doors away from my father's house. We heard her screaming all the time.

I guess he thought he would do me like Ley, but that was his mistake. We both stood there, him scared out of his mind and me waiting to pull the trigger.

I kept telling him, "Do it with your bad ass."

As I had the gun to his face we attracted a crowd. Ley came and put her hand on his shoulder because he was too scared to move.

Jose came up behind me, "Licia, you don't want to do this."

I told him, "I don't what to hear that shit."

Now it was Freddie, Ley and Jose standing there while I had the gun pointed to his nose. When Lee came up and asked, "What the fuck is going on?"

I wouldn't move the gun, "Freddie was going to hit me."

Freddie then told Lee, "Tell your girl to put the strap down and her and Ley can get down."

I gave the gun to Lee. Ley and I started fighting. We fought in front of Mrs. Joy's house. When Freddie realized she couldn't whip me or get off the ground because I was sitting on her, he wanted the fight stopped. That's when Lee pulled me off her. She had scratched my face so badly, it looked like I fell on a rake. *As I got up, I was thinking this is bullshit. Why am I fighting her? Why didn't Lee and Freddie fight?* Without a word I took my gun out of Lee's hand and began shooting at Freddie. Everyone started screaming and running, Freddie included. I chased him around my car shooting. I missed him, but I put bullet holes in my car. I shot until I emptied the clip. Lee was trying to get to me, but it was too late. I had emptied the clip. Freddie ran into the house. Lee told me to leave, and I did.

Later that night I was still mad, so I went back to Freddie's house and called him out. Freddie came to the door to look. Ley stood there smiling. They wouldn't come out or say anything. The next night, I did the same thing. I went back out in front of Freddie's house calling him out. This time, Freddie had a surprise for me; he called the police. When I saw the police hit the corner, I got in my car, drove halfway down the block, put my car in park, jumped out, and ran. I ran through Mrs. Speek's yard and hit the back gate that lead to 84th. As I came down from the gate, I hurt my leg. I had to keep moving because I had my gun in my pocket. The police didn't stop for my car. They were driving toward Hoover to cut me off on 84th. One of the neighborhood smokers, Rich, saw what happened. He looked in my car and took my keys to my father's house. My brother parked my car in my father's driveway.

After that, I knew the police were going to be looking from me. Early the next morning, I took my kids to Sandi. Lee and I went to Delano where his mother lived until it cooled off. This was the first time I met Lee's mother. We were there for about a week. I was dying because the hood life was calling me. I told Lee I was ready to go. If the police were coming for me then too bad, because I didn't want to stay in Delano. When I went back home, I wasn't back two days before the police came to my house. I knew what they wanted. I stepped outside the door thinking they were going to question me. But, they were there to arrest me. One of the officers asked if I could step out to the curb because he didn't want my kids to see me getting handcuffed. I peeped my head back in the house and told Lee to take my kids to my sister. The police arrested me.

I was 22 when I went to Sybil Brand Institution a.k.a. "Silly Bitches Institution." I stayed for over 3 months waiting to go to trial. While I was in jail, I saw everybody, including all of my customers. Jail was a different beast. The smokers ran the jail; they were the shot callers. In jail they were clean and off drugs, straight OG's in there. I was housed with one of my customers Bonita. She was a trustee and she hooked me up when she could. The two women that ran our dorm were Cee Cee and Wella. Cee Cee called shots for the blacks and Wella called shots for the Mexicans. I guess Cee Cee asked Bonita why I was in. She told her that I was down and a hustler, so Cee Cee never bothered me. The whole time I was in jail I was calling home lying to my kids telling them I was at a friend's house. Every time I spoke with them they asked when was I coming home. My heart was broken because I didn't think that my kids would be hurting. I was used to hopping gates crossing boundaries and having the, "I don't give a fuck attitude." But hearing my kids ask me when was I coming to get them, hit me. *At some point, I had to care.* I thought about it, I didn't want my family to raise my kids because I was in jail.

While I was in jail I was fortunate, I got a good public defender (PD). The inmates called them public pretenders because they pretended to represent you. When we met he listened to me and asked what happened. I told him that Freddie was a woman beater, among other things. He said it's a wonder someone hadn't killed him. He looked up at me. I smiled. He knew then, I did it. My PD said we were going to fight my case. My PD asked me what I knew about Freddie. Did he commit other criminal activity? *Yes, he committed criminal activity and was an active snitch.* I told him Freddie was on parole for a gun.

After a few months in jail, I had my day in court. My PD brought it to the attention of the court that Freddie was a dope dealer on parole for a gun charge. While on the stand, my PD cross-examined Freddie.

Freddie asked, "Who told on me?"

I sat there, shaking my head. *Idiot.*

The judge called my PD and the DA to his bench. They were all laughing. The judge was talking with the both of them.

The judged stated, "Dismissed."

I was released early the next morning. I took a taxi home to my father's house. I went inside, got my gun, and went in front of Freddie's house to let him know I was out and was looking to finish it. *What kind of gangster comes from Chicago and snitches, especially on a female?* I called him all kinds of punk bitches and then I went to get my kids. I guess my thought process of not wanting to have my family raise my kids was short lived. Because there I was fresh out of jail acting a fool.

Things were not going too good at my house. My landlady wanted me to move because she heard that I had the homies at my house. It didn't help that her brother lived next door to me. I was having problems with him, too. Her brother had hunting dogs. I had a Rottweiler that I didn't tell her about. It wasn't a problem until his hunting dog came into my yard and got bit by my dog. After the incident with the dogs, she asked me to get out. I told her I wasn't going to move. She called children services on me, reported anonymously that I sold drugs and starved my kids. *I knew it was her because the social worker mentioned that my kids hung on my neighbor's gate.* I didn't have time for the club. I had to hustle up money to move. Lee was right there. He got a package from the homie; he was making money. He helped me move. Sadly, I moved directly across the street.

This time, I lived in an apartment in the back of a house. I thought it was cool because it was low key and because Lee gave me some money, I let him move in, but without a key, of course. Once we were living together, I thought I would confront him about being a Sherm head. He acted surprised. He said he smoked weed from time to time, but he didn't smoke Sherm. *Liar!*

The apartment was smaller than the house that I moved from, so the kids got the bedroom. We slept on the living room floor. It was cramped. Once again, I wanted to go out. Lee gave me a guilt trip that he had no car and if I left, he would be stranded. I went for it. We were in the apartment for about a month, when I came up on some money. I was excited I could give him some money to get his own car, so he could get out of mine.

I was telling my brother that I was going to give Lee a thousand dollars. He asked me if I was crazy.

I told him, "Hell yes, if I don't get Lee out of my car."

I went home to find Lee standing in front of the house waiting on me because I wouldn't give him a key. I was happy when I saw him. I couldn't wait to tell him I had some money to get him a car.

When I gave Lee the news he looked at me and said, "You don't have enough money to buy me out."

Buy him out? I asked him what the hell was he talking about? He went on to explain that he was not for sale and he wasn't going anywhere. He then reminded me when I was being called the hood hoe for cheating on Dae Dae that he was the only person that stuck by me. He also said he knew about my secret.

I asked, "What secret?"

He said he knew Dae Dae was coming back around. I stood there with my mouth wide open. *Who wouldn't take 1,000 dollars?* Since Lee was living with me, I couldn't call Dae Dae anymore. I was stuck.

Chapter 25

War

Now that we were living together, we weren't getting along. *As if that was something new.* He still wanted to follow me around. Now, his marching to the beat of his own drum made sense. No one wanted to hang around him because he was a fool. And, to top it all off, I finally had the pleasure of experiencing him high on Sherm. *You know the Sherm he said he never smoked, right?* He left one morning and when he came back that afternoon something was off. He was loud and stuttering. I figured out this nut was high. So, I did what any respectable girlfriend would do, I called his Mama. His mother answered the phone and told me not to let him go out the house in that condition. *Um, lady, he came in the house in this condition, but okay I was willing to listen to her advice.* She told me she was sending Lee's father, Ed, over. Ed lived two blocks away. I waited for hours. The more I tried to keep Lee in the house the crazier he acted. I called his mother again. Once again, her advice was to keep her son inside. Finally, after another hour, he was up cussing and knocking things over in my living room. *Oh hell no, Sherm and all, his ass had to go.*

He started yelling for me to let him out. I opened the front door. When he stepped out, I closed the door and locked the metal screen. No sooner than I let him out, he started beating on the door to come back in. *I don't think so.* I called his mother. She was not happy that I locked him out. I explained to her that he was destroying things in my house. I hid my kids in the room, so they wouldn't see him acting a fool. It didn't matter; she was only concerned that I locked him out of my house.

Lee stood on my porch and called me every bitch, hoe, slut, tramp and whatever else he could think of. I sat in the living room while my kids were in the bedroom. Finally, he got tired of banging on my door.

I heard him say, "Bitch, this is what I think of you." He then pulled out his "thing" and peed on my door.

I couldn't believe it. After about what seemed like forever of his ranting, he left. I told my kids to get ready we were leaving. When I went to get my car keys, I couldn't find them. *I had hidden them from myself, hiding them from him.* I looked for my keys for over an hour when he came back.

I told my kids to be quiet. I put them back in the room. He tried looking through my living room window to see if I was still there. I heard him walking back down the stairs. I got up and peeped through my curtain and I saw him talking to the little boy that lived in the front house. I heard him ask if we were in the house.

The little boy said, "No I just saw them walking down the street."

Then, someone yelled out, "Hey cuzz, that's a lie. Her ass is still in the house."

It was the homie Jr. his girlfriend lived in the apartment next door. I guess he had been watching the circus that whole day. *Now if the baby had enough sense to lie for me why would Jr. stick his nose in my business?* Furious, Lee ran back up the stairs to my apartment and started cussing all over again since he knew I was inside. I called his mother again asking where was his father? She told me to let him back in. *Was she crazy?*

I told her, "I'm not letting that Sherm head in my house."

While I was standing in the kitchen talking to her, Lee came to the kitchen window and busted it out.

I told her, "Okay, I'm done with this bullshit."

I dropped the phone and ran into the bedroom. I went through my drawer where I hid my gun. As I grabbed it, my car keys fell out of the pocket of my jeans. I told my kids, "Get your coats we're leaving!" I went back to the kitchen. Lee was reaching his hand through the bar on the window trying to pry it open. I shot through the kitchen window. I grabbed my youngest son Dee, because he walked slowly and put him on my hip. I walked out of my apartment with my gun in hand, baby on my hip, Tyshawn and Whitney behind me. I came out ready to shoot because I was tired of his ass.

I got my kids into the car and drove to the corner of 84th and Figueroa. I was about to turn the corner when Whitney yelled, "Mama, look!"

I looked to my left and Lee was running toward us, full speed with a pipe in his hand. I stopped him before he could get to my window. I rolled it down and started shooting. He started running and ducking. I shot until I emptied the clip. I rolled up my window and drove around the corner to my father's house. I had never asked my father to keep my kids, but tonight I was desperate. I was going back to find that fool.

Before I left, my father told me, "You need to be careful, because someone was shooting."

I told him, "Yea, daddy it's me."

My father gave me his famous advice, "Call PD."

I asked my father, "Who is PD?"

He said, "The police department."

I left without saying a word. My pager was being blown up. It was Lee's mother. I went down the street to my customer's house to call her. When she answered the phone, she immediately told me, if I had hurt her son, she was going to make sure I went to jail. She also told me she was going to call children's services on me because she knew I sold dope. *What?* I told her, "Your son is a Sherm head and a woman beater." She then went on to tell me what supposedly happening in my house. *Mind you, she lived four hours away.* She told me she heard that Lee had to pay me for sex before he could come into my house and that I took all his food stamps and money. *What lady?*

I told her, "If that's the case then he's behind on his pussy payments. Are you going to pay me?"

We argued for a couple of minutes when I called her a wig-wearing bitch and hung up in her face. Not long after that conversation Bugsy paged me. I knew this was coming. When I called him back, we had words about me disrespecting his mother. After the conversation, we were no longer friends. Lee ran everyone away. He wasn't sad that Bugsy and I were no longer friends. The fewer friends I had, the happier he was. We couldn't get along with each other and he couldn't get along with anybody. I was in the middle of it all. As a result of being with Lee, I lost friends and gained enemies.

A couple of weeks after I fell out with Bugsy I went to my father's house with Lee. He dropped me off and drove down the street. About 30 minutes later Lee came running through my father's door shouting, "They hit your car."

I jumped off the couch. "Who hit my car?"

He said, "Fish and Freddie."

I ran down the street. When I got to the apartment building, Fish was upstairs. When he heard Lee calling his name he came down the stairs. They started arguing.

Fish told Lee, "I told you to move that piece of shit because I wanted to get in my driveway." Fish socked Lee in the face.

Lee pulled out his gun, told Fish, "I told you I ain't the one." Then he shot Fish in the stomach.

Fish fell to the ground holding his stomach. Fish said, "I thought I was your bro?"

Fish was a heavy dude. As he held his stomach to stop the bleeding, he couldn't get up off the ground. Lee stood with the gun in his hand as Fish held his stomach.

Jose ran up and yelled, "They shot Fish!"

Fish's wife Kammie came out of the apartments screaming and ran down to help him.

Okay. I'm really going to jail this time and I'm not getting out.

Lee yelled to me, "Let's go!"

We started running down the street to my car watching our backs. As we looked back Jose was chasing us with a gun, but he didn't shoot.

By the time we passed Freddie's house, Jose yelled, "They shot Fish."

Just as we were about to get in my car Freddie busted out his door with an Uzi and started shooting at me. I had on green converse all-stars. I could see the fire from the bullets hit the ground.

I yelled, "No this nigga didn't."

I heard someone yelling for me to get out of the street. It was my friend Yvonne. She was on her apartment stairs watching the shoot-out. I ran for my father's door, while Lee covered me. He shot through Freddie's front door and backed Freddie into the house, so he couldn't shoot anymore. I ran into my father's living room. My brother was already in there; he handed me my gun. I ran back out and joined the shootout. I cocked my gun, but when I tried to fire, it wouldn't shoot. My brother had already cocked it, so it was jammed. Lee was still shooting.

When he was out of bullets he yelled, "Let's go!"

We ran through the alley and went to Lee's, father's house. I was knocking on the door like crazy. When Ed came to the door, I told him Lee just shot Fish. He knew he had to get us out of there. We jumped in the back of his van.

With tears in his eyes, Lee leaned his head on my shoulder and said, "I told that nigga I wasn't the one."

After we left, there was still shooting on 85th. My brother paged me. When I called him back, he told me Freddie shot up my car after we ran off.

"He did what?" I told Lee, "We ain't running this time." I was pissed about my car. I stayed at my sister's for a night. When we came back home we were ready for war.

Fish wouldn't tell the police who shot him even after his wife begged him to. *Fish knew the rules of the streets and gangsters, unlike snitching Freddie who sent me to jail.*

Over the next week, I was plotting on how to get Freddie for shooting up my car. This time, I was going to be smart about my criminal activity, Fish was no snitch, but Freddie was. I was coming for Freddie's car and he knew it. Freddie put his car in the auto body shop on 79th and Figueroa to get it painted. Nothing was wrong with his paint job; he did it because he knew I was coming for it. I was ready. I had my smoker outfit, my gas can, and my matches. I asked Edwin to drop me two blocks away.

All he had to say was, "Licia you don't want to do that."

"Well let's see, Freddie sent me to jail, shot at me, shot up my car that I can't drive right now, and you're telling me what I don't want to do?"

I ended up walking through alleys with a can of gas. When I got to the shop, the workers were guarding the car. *I think someone told, but who?* I went back the next night and it was gone. Freddie had got it out and began parking it in his driveway. After the shootout, Edwin and Freddie got into it over my brother giving me my gun. During their argument, Freddie hit my brother. My brother didn't fight him back. I was mad.

I asked my brother, "Why didn't you fight back?"

He said, "The pants I had on were too tight. I went in the house to change them."

I yelled, "What the hell were you doing with Michael Jackson's Billie Jean slacks on anyway?" *You scared of that fool?*

This fueled my hate for Freddie because he really thought he was the shit since he punked my brother. In the words of Lee, "I ain't the one." Freddie knew it. Fish and Lee didn't have any more issues with each other, but I still hated Freddie.

After Freddie heard I tried to set his car on fire, we had one last run in when he tried following me. I picked up Kai. Things had slowed down. She was coming around a little bit more. She was babysitting our friend's baby, Lajarie. I was on my way to take her home, when I drove down my father's street. I turned the corner and noticed Freddie behind us. I came across the light on Manchester and Figueroa. He was still following me. I pulled over and told Kai to get out of the car with the baby. Kai grabbed Lajarie, got out and started walking. I put my car in park in the middle of the street, grabbed my gun, and reached under the seat for my extra clip. *I wasn't getting caught without enough bullets like we did in the shootout.*

I got out of the car with my gun in my hand and motioned for Freddie. I yelled, "What's up, what you want to do?"

Freddie stayed in his car. We were both in the middle of Fig holding up traffic. I kept yelling that I was ready. *He wasn't going to punk me.* He stayed in his car staring me down, and pressing the gas as if he was going to run me over. Eventually, he made a U-turn and went the other way. I got in my car and drove up Fig to pick up Kai and the baby. That was the last time Freddie tried following me.

Chapter 26

Civil War

I didn't have any more war episodes with Freddie. Some months later Freddie shot someone and went to jail for murder. But the warzone in my own house was never at a ceasefire. Lee and I were fighting like crazy. The fights came from me wanting to go out. I was not around my friends and he was driving me crazy. The fights were getting more and more ridiculous. This one particular day we fought, he dislocated his knuckles socking me in my head. After the fight, he was mad that I wouldn't go to the hospital with him.

I told him, "That's what the hell you get for hitting a woman."

There was another time Lee and I had fought and I managed to get him out of the house, after which, he paged me. I called him back, and he begged me to come back.

I told him, "No,"

He said he would kill himself. *I think you know me by now.* My response was, "Oh damn well." Then I heard a gunshot and noise. I wasn't sure if he shot himself, so I asked Edwin to go with me to my apartment because I didn't want to find a dead body by myself. When we got there, Lee was alive and crazy as ever. As soon as I walked through the door, Lee reached over my brother and socked me in the head. The fight was on again. *You ask me if my brother helped me? Uh, no!*

Lee has pushed me from a moving car twice because I wouldn't do what he said. The first time I tried holding on and couldn't. After he pushed me out the car he threw my purse out the window. The second time he pushed me, he left me in the middle of the street injured. I had to go to the hospital and was there for hours. *Yes, he pushed me out of out of MY car.*

It was now 1994, I was 24. We had recently experienced the Northridge earthquake. Everyone was trying to get FEMA assistance. I qualified for temporary Section 8. I was happy because that meant no more expensive rent. I was moving out of the hood and I was not taking Lee with me. I found a beautiful condominium with three bedrooms and two bathrooms in Harbor City. We were the only black family that lived there. Of course, Lee tried to guilt me into letting him live with me. He started telling people I had used him and spent all of his money. *What money?* Every time he had money, he either got high with it or lost it.

I didn't care what he was telling people, I had already decided that he couldn't live with me. Lee offered to help me move. Once I moved in, he spent the night. We had now taken the hood drama to the suburbs. One morning after one of our fight nights, I heard a knock on the door. *Who was this?* I didn't know anyone in the complex. When I opened the door, it was a white lady with cookies. *Was she serious?*

I asked her in my hood tone, "May I help you?"

She told me she was my neighbor and she wanted to introduce herself. I stood in the door, never inviting her in.

Before she walked away she said, "If you ever want my help, just leave your window open."

What was she talking about? She carefully let me know that she used to be in an abusive relationship. She told me to leave my window open and she would call the police. *I was mad. What the hell?* I thanked her and practically closed the door in her face. *Abused? I'm not abused... I fight back!*

The fights grew more intense when Lee saw that I was serious about him not moving in. He would sleep in my garage and wait for me to come home. When I pulled in, he would jump out at me. Many nights that window offer came in handy. I was getting tired of fighting with Lee. Him calling me bitches and hoes wasn't a problem anymore. As long as he didn't touch me. But he was wearing my mind down. I started talking to myself. I would call my sister and ask crazy questions. She would ask if I was high. *Um no, I lived with a crazy person.*

We fought because I began to visit my friend Yvonne. She had moved to Harbor City too. One morning I went to her house because I felt like I was going crazy. When I came home, Lee hit me in the face. During this fight, we had locked up. He had me by the hair, and I had him by the balls when there was a knock at the door. My adrenaline was up. I knew if I let him go he would get a second wind. I wouldn't let go, so we walked to the door just like that. I opened the door. It was the police. He immediately let my hair go. I didn't and still had him by the balls.

I was breathing hard. The female officer told me, "Dear, you can let go now."

I let him go. He hit the floor in pain. I guess his adrenaline was up until the police came. Reality hit that I had him by the balls for over 20 minutes. The officer came in and said they got a call for disturbing the peace. I knew who called. The female officer pulled me to the side and said she couldn't take Lee to jail for domestic violence unless she took me too. Mainly, because Lee had scratches all over his body. I didn't have one scratch. She asked if he had warrants. At first, I wasn't going to say anything because I was raised not to snitch.

But before I could think, I said, "Yes."

She gave her partner his information. Lee's name came back as a match. They handcuffed him. He began protesting that he was the one being abused. He told the officer to look at all the scratches he had. He wanted to press charges against me.

The officer explained that she was not taking him for domestic violence, but warrants. He cussed all the way to the police car. That night, I had something I had not had in a long time, peace.

Lee stayed in jail for three weeks. While he was gone, I took advantage of my freedom. My cousin Denise spent the night. We went swimming and clubbing. I had not had that much fun in a long time. I had become isolated. I stopped going places because it was not worth fighting with Lee when I got back. While Lee was locked up I went to Denise's house and enjoyed freedom. *I could get used to this.*

Lee's time went by too fast. Before long, he was back at my house causing trouble. I didn't want to get put out, so I let him in when he got out. He said he just wanted to get his stuff and you know the story. He asked me to take him back to LA with his clothes. I was glad to do so. *Did his jail time change him?* We got into the car, and he started hitting me all over my body. We exchanged punches. I couldn't hang long. Eventually, after so many punches; I ended up leaning out of the car spitting up blood. That fight stopped.

There were many times, I had to trick him out of my house. He would come and get loud. He knew the neighbors would complain. That was his way of getting in. One night during an argument I told him I was leaving. He followed me to the garage and when he realized I tricked him out of my house he tried to get back in. He couldn't because I had locked us both out. I hid my keys in my bra. When I attempted to make a run for my door, he tried to kick me in the stomach with his steel toe boots. *You asked me what stopped his karate kick? Well the knife I hid in my pocket.* I caught his leg in mid-air. I stabbed him right in his thigh. He hit the ground. He started yelling that he had done time in the penitentiary a.k.a. pen, and he had never been shanked.

My reply was, "Well, you tried to kick the wrong one."

I ran into my house and locked the door. He left that night to get medical care. The next morning, my sister called me. Lee had called her to tell her I stabbed him. That was his MO; he was always the victim pushed into hitting me. Once he told me that he beat me with his fist because I whipped him with my mouth. That day I found out I had power in my tongue. I was glad to get this information and although I didn't always win physically, I won emotionally. My bruises went away. But, he would still be holding that emotional black eye I gave him.

After stabbing Lee, I went to Sandi's for a few days. She asked, "why don't you leave Lee"? This made me angry. I asked, "And go where? He comes to your house or calls you for everything. He goes to dad's house and everywhere I could possibly go. I've tried to leave 20 times and it never worked. He always tracks me down. You know that."

I was a mother with three kids on welfare. I wasn't selling dope. I stayed at Sandi's house for days until the fighting between her kids and my kids became unbearable, forcing me to go back home. After all, you can only sleep on someone's floor for so long. I went back home thinking he was gone. He didn't have a key to my house. Surely, he got tired of waiting for me and paging me while I ignored him. But, when I returned, Lee had waited me out. He was still in my house. The fighting started all over again.

There were times I drove him to LA and tricked him out of my car. During one of the last fights we had in that house, the window saved me again. When the police came, they told him to leave.

He asked, "Why do I have to go and not her?"

The police said, "She has kids and we're not going to ask her to leave with kids."

He still seemed confused as to why my kids and I shouldn't be homeless. The situation was the same. If they took him, they would've had to arrest me too. The officer told him to get any belongings he had out of the house while I waited outside. Lee came out with a black trash bag of his stuff. Or so I thought. Later that night, when I went into my closet to change my shoes, he had taken all my left shoes. I didn't have a single matching pair.

I stayed in that house for about a year until the broker sent me a letter that said the property was sold. The owner was asking that I leave in 15-30 days. I asked the broker what was I supposed to do in 30 days? Section-8 took 30 days to issue a voucher. And then I still had to find a place and get it approved. That normally takes 90 days. The broker,

Tom, told me he would mail my deposit once I moved out. I told him if he wanted me out within 30 days, I needed my money right then.

The next day he called me. We met and he reluctantly gave me a check for my deposit. As if he didn't trust me. *Wasn't he the one that sold the condo from under me forcing me and my three kids to be homeless?* That same week, Sandi and Curtis helped me move. I had nowhere to go. I didn't have a chance to save money. My Section-8 was only good for 18 months. I had already used 12. I was not sure what was going to happen. What owner was going to take a Section-8 voucher for 6 months? On my way out I got a nice parting gift; I was pregnant.

Chapter 27

Mad, Homeless, and Pregnant

I was 25, homeless and devastated. I didn't want another baby, let alone by that nut. I did what I knew to do, I moved back to the hood. I slept between motels, my father's and Sandi's floor when I could. I asked my father if I could keep some of my furniture at his house. He agreed.

It was Thanksgiving time; my aunt invited my kids and me to her house in Moreno Valley for dinner.

During dinner, Annette asked me, "Where are you going to move?"

I told her, "I'm still looking."

"Oh, cause your daddy told me you and your men can't move in his house," Annette said.

I looked at her and asked, "WHAT MEN?"

Hell, even if I wanted another man I couldn't because of the nut I can't get rid of. It had been six years since I was pregnant, what a way to kick it off. *I was mad. I was also thinking if I hadn't given you so much of my dope money, maybe I would have a house.*

I stayed from motel to motel; it all depended on how much dope we sold. Paying for a motel room cost more than having an apartment. I remember a few years before, Yvonne told me about shelters that were helping with permanent Section-8. I didn't really consider it until things in the motel got shaky. *As I told you before Lee couldn't get along with anybody.*

One afternoon as I was coming out of our motel room, guess who was arguing with a prostitute? *Yeah, you guessed it... Lee.* I walked up in the middle of the argument. She was saying she was Sally from the Valley and she would call her pimp. As Lee continued to argue with her, I stepped in front of him and punched her in the mouth. I think my belly fooled her because she was in shock. I guess she was thinking who fought while they were pregnant? *Um me.* My hand was bleeding and so was her mouth. I had teeth prints in my right hand. She ran off yelling she was calling her daddy. *Oh, by the way, she wasn't calling her biological daddy, "daddy" meant her pimp.*

I waited for her to come back with her pimp. He was there in no time. He pulled up in the motel parking lot, and as he got out the car, he looked and called my name. "Alicia?" It was my brother Curtis's childhood friend, Ray. He turned to Sally and said, "Do you know who that is?" By the look on her face, she knew that wasn't good news for her.

Ray slapped her up and made her leave. That night when I went to bed my hand was swollen. After two days, I couldn't get the swelling to go down, so I went to Dr. G. He had been my doctor since I was 15. When I went into his office Rita the receptionist/nurse immediately took me to the back.

She took one look at my hand, frowned, and asked, "What happened?"

Rita knew I had been in a fight. I tried to lie. She told me my hand wasn't swollen it was infected. I guess the teeth marks on my knuckle gave it away. I went ahead and told Rita the truth. She told me that human saliva and blood was not a good exchange, especially from a prostitute that might be HIV positive.

"HIV?" I never thought about that.

She reassured me that I would be all right especially if I stopped fighting. She called Dr. G in and told him what happened. He then drained the fluid from my hand with a needle and gave me medication for the infection.

That wasn't the only time I saw my doctor for war wounds. Whenever I could, I tried not to stay at the motel. Lee seemed to be angry that I was spending nights at Sandi's house. One morning after staying with Sandi, I met him at my father's. My father had left for work. Edwin gave me his key to get in. Lee started to complain about being homeless. I told him it wasn't my fault no one liked him. The fight was on. The argument started in the living room. I was seven months pregnant; I couldn't keep my balance. I ran into the kitchen. There was not one knife. *Who doesn't have knives?* Lee hid them. I ran into the bedroom and tried closing the door. He pushed through the door. He picked up a VHS tape hit me in the head, and it shattered. I'm not sure how long we fought, but it seemed like I was trapped in that house for years.

After repeatedly hitting me and pushing me to the ground, I knew I had to do something, because he was going to kill me. I got up from the floor and ran back into the kitchen. He didn't follow me because he knew I was trapped. The front door had a deadbolt lock and he already took the key from me. I looked around. *What could I do?* There was nothing in there to use to defend myself. Then I saw bleach. This was going to be my ticket out.

I opened the bleach, put some on my hand and around my mouth. I pushed the dishes that were on the counter to the floor and laid on the floor. Lee heard the noise and came running in. All he saw was me, on the floor and an open container of bleach. He called the ambulance. That was my ticket out.

As they carried me out on a stretcher I could see Lil Bone looking from his front yard. When I got to the hospital, I was in labor. The nurse was very nice to me. She immediately told Lee he had to go. She knew something was wrong. The hospital paged Dr. Freeman. He arrived and told me they were going to give me something to stop my labor. He looked up, saw Lee sitting on the empty bed and repeated what the nurse said. He told Lee to leave. He also knew something was wrong.

I had never seen Dr. Freeman look so concerned; normally when I saw him he was telling inappropriate jokes, but not this time, he stayed in the room until Lee left. I was hospitalized for a few days and it allowed me to rest. After I was released I went right back to Lee.

Staying at my father's was no safer than the motel. *Wouldn't you know that on the night I decided to stay something crazy happened?* I was sleeping on my couch and a crashing sound happened. I jumped up as fast as I could. Which, wasn't that fast with my big belly. Scared out of my mind I grabbed my gun from under my pillow. Shaking I grabbed the couch to get up. It was my homeboy, B. Somebody forgot to lock the door. He was high off Sherm. I thought I was going to go into labor.

He was ducking behind the couch telling me they were after him. I screamed, "B, what the hell are you doing?"

He kept saying, "Homegirl help me. They coming for me."

I kept yelling, "Who's coming for you?"

He kept looking around saying, "The gangsters."

When I got completely off the couch, he tried to push past me to go into the hallway to the other rooms. I told him he had to go. I got him out the house. He went next door to Bone's house and started grabbing on his door. I couldn't go back to sleep. I kept thinking I had to do something, so I decided to go into the shelter Yvonne had told me about.

The next day I went to the church with Annette and called the shelter, which was no longer doing permanent housing. I kept calling shelters. Finally, I found one and got an interview. I went to the interview and they accepted me. The shelter was called Gramercy Place Shelter. The good thing about this shelter was they only took single parents and married couples with kids. No boyfriend or baby daddy's, so that eliminated Lee.

When my family heard I was going into a homeless shelter, they were shocked. I don't know why, considering no one asked me to move into their house, well except Sandi. The problem with her living situation was she was living in a small two-bedroom duplex with her four kids. I couldn't do that to her; I was going to the shelter no matter what. Plus, she was always at church, so we lived two totally different lifestyles. I had to get my stuff together because the shelter had a curfew. I kept telling myself anything is better than the motel, prostitute fights, and the homies crashing through the door at one in the morning on Sherm. Lee whined like the punk that he was. He had the nerve to ask me if he could stay at my father's house.

I told him, "Hell I can't stay at my father's house. If I could I wouldn't be going to a shelter dumb ass."

I told him to move in with his dad. I had become very good friends with his dad. He was a nice man. He knew his son was crazy and unlike Lee's mother, he never made excuses for Lee's behavior. My curfew at the shelter was 10:00 p.m. Lee dropped me off and picked me up every morning. The cool part was I took my kids to Sandi and she got them to school. At first, it was a hard adjustment. A month later, Kai moved into Gramercy. I was good. I had my homie across the hall from me. We helped each other.

Not a month after I had moved into the shelter Lee was starting to work my nerves. At Gramercy we had to do chores and attend parenting classes. He couldn't understand why I couldn't just leave. You know we argued about that too.

One morning, I was waiting for him to come and get me and he never showed up. I thought he didn't come because he was mad. I wasn't getting kicked out for this fool. While I was sitting outside on the steps, to my surprise, Ed drove up. My heart dropped. I knew it! Someone had finally killed this idiot because he's always fucking with people. I braced myself for who finally shot him.

As Ed walked up I asked, "Is he dead?"

Ed said, "Almost. Lee got into a fight with a man at the motel; the man almost beat him to death. He's in jail. I'm here to take you to your car."

I went back inside, got Baby Dee, and went to my car. Then I went to the Glass House. That's where they took inmates that needed medical services. I had never been to the Glass House before. When I got there the visitation was via TV. I asked Lee what happened and he kept giving me different stories. He told me that the man at the motel accused him of not paying rent.

"What rent? What were you doing sleeping at the motel? You said you were going to stay with your dad. You couldn't keep a room before. That's why I'm in the shelter now."

Lee couldn't give me a straight answer. During the whole conversation his head was down until I finally told him to hold his damn head up. Lee looked up into the camera. I almost went into labor. His face was disfigured and he had stitches.

I asked, "What the hell happened?"

He couldn't answer, so I kept cussing him out until I left. *I was mad. What the hell did he get himself into? And to top it all off,* the man at the motel was pressing charges.

I went straight to the motel to talk to one of the girls to find out what happened. When I got there, Cinnamon told me, "The man that beat Lee is the motel manager. Lee didn't pay for the room for the last two nights."

"Nights?"

Cinnamon said, "Yeah. Lee had been staying in the motel. Lee and the Indian man began to argue. Lee knocked him out, and then told the man he would be back later. When Lee came back that night the Indian man was ready, and he beat Lee until he was screaming for help. He dragged Lee all over the parking lot until the skin on his back was raw. A few of the homies were walking by and wouldn't help because they hate Lee. Lee tried to get a gun and the man beat him some more. The man took the gun and called the police."

I went back to the shelter. Lee stayed locked up for a few days and the charges were dropped. When he got out, the swelling had gone down. He had stitches on both sides of his nose and ear. They had to stitch those parts back on to his face. *Ouch!* Lee was silent for a couple of days, and then he was back to his old self. When we got into an argument, I told him I was going to get the Indian man that smoked his peace pipe to beat his ass. Every time he messed with me that was my go to line. He was hot, but it was funny to me. I told him to go fight a man and leave women alone. *Yes, you got it, he had no comment.* Lee couldn't explain how he could afford the room now, but I wasn't leaving Gramercy. I stayed in the shelter doing what I needed to get that voucher.

There were a few times Lee tried to make me miss curfew to get kicked out. He wouldn't take me back on time and, so I called Sandi. She would pick me up, so I could make curfew. I wasn't going to let him ruin this, like everything else. I met weekly with my caseworker Norma. I had to save 70% of my income, so I could have money to move. All of a sudden Lee had money. *How is his broke ass coming up?* Lee came to get me one morning. We went to have breakfast. He had a pocket full of money. We parked to eat, he said he had a girl working for him. *Hold up homie, I don't believe in pimping women.* I had homeboys that had girls working for them, and in my opinion, they were punks. Any time you had to have a woman sell her body so you could eat, you were no hustler, you were bitch.

I started cussing Lee out. He stopped me, "I'm not pimping her."

"How much product did she get?"

"She doesn't smoke dope."

I dropped my fork. "So you ain't pimpin and she's not buying drugs from you? Why would she be working for you, you can't protect her."

He had nothing to say. *Something wasn't adding up, I'm no damn fool.* Lee told me to eat; I told him no thanks especially if the money came from her. He said he wanted me to meet her. I was so mad I could feel my baby moving, she must have felt my blood pressure shoot up.

"No thanks," I told him.

He said, "I got to pick up my money from her."

I looked him dead in his eyes and told him, "I don't give a fuck. I don't want a dime." We left the hamburger stand and went to the Full Moon Motel. I stayed in the car as he jumped out to go to the room to get his money. Afterwards, he went to the manager's window and she came out of the room. She was a Hispanic girl about five feet tall. She looked like a leprechaun she was so little. She saw my car, came close, mad dogged me, rolled her eyes, and went back to the room. *Wait, wait did this chick just come out and roll her eyes at me?*

I yelled out the window, "Hey bitch who you rolling your eyes at?"

She kept going like she didn't hear me. I got out of the car and followed her into her room. She never expected me to get out of the car. Neither did Lee. When I walked in the room, I saw their clothes.

I looked at her and asked, "Bitch, you fuckin Lee?"

He walked into the room just as I asked. I took the iron off the dresser and hit him in the head. She was no longer bad. I guess the stomach fooled her too. Before I could get to her, she ran out the room. I kept screaming, "You fuckin a prostitute? I'm pregnant with your baby muthafucka! I'm going to kill your ass." Lee kept saying, "No."

As he was trying to duck, I grabbed anything not nailed down to throw at him. I threw the lamps, turned over the bed, busted the mirror, and began to kick and throw their clothes out the door. The motel manager came running to the room. When he saw the damage he told me, "Mama, stop it." He called me Mama because he didn't know my real name. I wouldn't stop; I was in full rage mode.

He said, "Mama get out of here and don't you ever come back."

I didn't care. *This nigga is fuckin' with prostitutes?* That was an issue for me. My father slept with prostitutes and both of my brothers messed with prostitutes. I hung around prostitutes, so I knew what that life looked like.

I screamed, "I don't mess with nigga's that buy pussy." I had no respect for tricks, men that bought pussy and no respect for pimps, niggas that used women.

I went outside. Anyone and everyone that had a room was outside for that sideshow. I got in my car and cried all the way back to the shelter. Lee paged me all day. I didn't call back. When Kai got to the shelter, I told her what happened. She said Cee told her he saw a Mexican girl in my car, but she never thought anything about it. I called Timmie because I needed a gun. I knew Lee wasn't going to give me my gun to kill him and his hoe. Timmie told me Lee had brought my car to him to get my sounds checked out, and he had that girl in my car. Timmie said he never knew she was a prostitute. I cried all day. My eyes were red and puffy. I couldn't rest. It was about 8:00 p.m. when I asked Kai to keep the kids.

I told her, "Fuck this, I'm about to go get his ass." All this time, he was fighting me, calling me a hoe, saying I wanted to screw other niggas, and he didn't even have the respect to get another woman? This nigga went out and got a prostitute?"

I drove back to the hood and found Lee. We parked down Figueroa. I begged him to tell me the truth or he would never see me gain. I grilled him for hours until he admitted it. He had slept with her once and she started working for him.

I said, "Yeah right, once? You ain't that good in bed."

I couldn't believe it. He kept trying to apologize; saying he wasn't going around her anymore. I told him to get the hell out my car. I had to go back to the shelter. I threw him out, and as I was driving something told me to go back. I turned around and parked around the corner from the motel for about an hour when I saw Lee go in and go into a room. I got out the car and knocked on the door.

Veronica looked through the window, "Oh my God, Lee she's here."

He told her don't open the door. I started cussing and told her if she didn't open the door I would stalk and kill her. I reminded her she was in my hood and the other girls would tell me everything. I could hear them argue. Finally, she opened the door. I went in like a mother bear robbed of her cubs. I grabbed Veronica, slammed her to the floor. She was screaming for Lee to help her.

All he kept saying was, "I told you don't let her crazy ass in."

"Hold up you doin' a prostitute and I'm crazy?" *Whatever.* The beat down was on. I dragged her through the room slamming her into walls. She couldn't handle me.

Lee stood back telling me to stop. "Yeah, right," I told him. Finally, on the last slam on the floor, I sat on her and smashed her head on the floor. I felt someone touch me. I turned around, it was Coco, one of the girls. I think Coco was going to jump in.

I looked at Coco and with tears rolling down my face, and told her, "Bitch if you touch me I promise you, I'm going to kill you."

I couldn't stop crying. Coco knew me; she knew I would kill her and go do my time. She left the room. *You know who showed up next, the motel manager.*

He came in shouting, "Mama didn't I tell you not to come back. You come back again Mama. I'm calling the police on you."

I slammed her head on the floor one last time and rolled off her. I had no strength left. I was physically and emotionally defeated. All the years of him telling me that no one wanted me with my three baby daddies, welfare, high school dropout self, it hit me. He was right; not even a Sherm head wanted me.

I went back to my car and cried for hours. Kai was paging me 911. I knew the shelter manager was looking for me. I called the shelter crying and said one of my family members had an accident. Because I was crying hysterically, they believed me. I got back and told Kai what had happened. I got into the bathtub to rest my tired body. I had more teeth marks in my hand. As I got out of the bathtub I looked down and my entire right toenail had come off. I didn't even feel it when I was fighting. I knew I would in the morning.

That morning Kai took the kids to Sandi. I couldn't move, I was emotionally numb, and my body was sore. My mind was jacked up. *Now what?* I kept thinking I knew he wasn't shit, but a prostitute? Lee's father paged me. I called him back, he told me he was checking on me. He couldn't believe Lee did that. I told him I was alright. *But the fact was, I wasn't alright.*

Lee stayed away for about two weeks, which was an all-time record. He kept leaving messages at the shelter that he wanted to talk with me. Finally, I met him at my father's house. He promised that he would never see Veronica again and told me that she was gone. As he was lying through his teeth, I went into my trunk. What did I find? Welfare papers with her name on them. I read them. She had a son and she was 21 years old. I was 26 and I told him that she was a damn kid because he was 36.

Just as I started to cuss him out I thought I saw Veronica walking down Figueroa going into the New Bay Motel on the corner of my father's street.

I told Lee, "Get the fuck out of here. I just saw her."

He said, "You're crazy. I told you she's gone."

I started walking across the street to the motel. He followed me telling me that it wasn't her. I went into the motel looking for her.

I started yelling, "Veronica, I just saw you."

As I was yelling, Coco opened her room door and said she wasn't in the motel. I didn't trust her. I knew I wasn't crazy.

Then Cinnamon came out of her room and said, "Licia that bitch is a liar. Veronica is in room five. I told that little bitch not to be back in your car after I heard you whooped her ass. I didn't want to tell you about Veronica the day I told you about Lee's fight because I wasn't sure what was going on between them. Lee had her in the motel the night he had the fight with the manager. I told her that you didn't know about her, and when you found out she was in your car, you were going to get her."

Lee stood there looking stupid because Cinnamon wasn't scared of him. I went to room five banging on the door. A girl I had never seen before answered and I pushed my way in. Veronica was sitting on the bed.

I told her, "I told your ass to get out of my hood and every time I caught you I was going to beat you."

I rushed in, grabbed her off the bed, and the fight was on. Lee and Cinnamon were at the door.

Cinnamon was yelling, "Get that bitch Licia 'cause I told her ass."

Lee came in and grabbed me as I pinned her to the bed. I couldn't get him to let me go. I was crying and begging for help. Help to kill this hoe. And, as I was screaming for Lee to let me go, a man came into the room. He was a young black man who was the new hotel manager. I had never seen him before.

He came in, "What the hell is going on?"

I looked at him crying like a baby and I asked him, "Tell Lee to let me go."

The man turned to Lee and asked, "That's your baby Mama?"

Lee said, "Yes, she crazy."

I yelled, "Yea crazy for beating this bitch ass that you fucking."

The man looked at Lee, "Let her go."

I still had Veronica pinned to the bed. Lee was holding my arms.

I looked up. The man told Lee, "If you don't take your hands off her, I'm going to knock you out."

Lee looked at him. I guess it was that Indian defeat he thought about, and let me go. It was on. I punched her so much that I was weak and could hardly swing anymore. I then grabbed a flashlight that was on the bed and began hitting her in the face with it.

The man said, "Ma, that's enough."

"Enough? I'm going to kill her."

The man told Cinnamon to get me. He turned and told Lee, "You ain't shit for fucking a prostitute and taking her side."

I stopped because I respected him for standing up to Lee. I told Veronica this was the last time I was going to tell her to get out of my hood. If I caught her for whatever reason I was going to get her. I left the room and walked by Coco. I told her if she ever crossed me, again, I would personally shoot her in her head. After that, I was no longer cool with Coco and she stayed away from me. As for Veronica, I never saw her again.

Chapter 28

Something is in the Air

S andi heard about my fight and as usual, she asked me to come to her house to relax. She said I needed to get away from 85ᵗʰ and the shelter. When I got to her house, I forgot she was graduating from a CNA program. I told her to take Annette to her graduation; I would watch the kids. I was beaten up on the inside and really didn't want to go. I watched as she got dressed. I was proud of her. I had made nothing of my life and it was looking like I would be nothing-- just like everyone said.

On her way out, she had a plant and asked me to bring it in and water it. I brought the plant in and when I sat it down, I noticed her CD player. I opened it. There was a CD in it. Not my usual NWA or Tupac, but at this point I didn't care what it was. I hit play. It was a song by Yolanda Adams called, "The Battle is Not Yours." *Did Jesus love you, Alicia?* I couldn't stop crying. I was a disappointment to everybody. *Did God love this disappointment?* I felt something I had never felt before. Something I never felt during the times I went to church. Something I didn't feel when I was baptized. I played that song on repeat for hours. When Sandi and Annette came back, I was still listening. I didn't know how to describe what I felt or what had happened. I told Sandi I liked that song, but I couldn't explain what I was feeling because I didn't know what it was. My heart was comforted. I felt peace. *Was God talking to me?* I didn't want to leave, but I had to go back to the shelter.

After two months of being there, I got my Section-8 voucher and I found a place back in Harbor City. I never wanted to live in LA again. Lee was bugging me because I wouldn't let him move in. I moved into a two-bedroom townhouse, and for the first time, I was happy about the baby. I hadn't had a baby for a long time and it was a girl. Sandi had already given me her name, Rayven. I began to get clothes and furniture.

One morning, Lee came by and complained.

"You care more about a baby that isn't here than me."

I told him, "You damn right, go be with your hoe."

Lee went back to LA. I was no longer interested in going to LA. Later that day Kai came and took me to the Burlington Coat Factory to get Rayven's bed. It was beautiful. It was hunter green and royal blue. I spent half the day putting it together. When Lee came back and saw it, he was mad. We started arguing over the bed. *What did he do? No, he didn't hit me.* He looked at my baby's bed and began to kick it. I screamed for him to stop. I tried to pull him back, but I had no strength. By the time he stopped, I was on the floor holding my stomach crying.

I told him, "I'm going to pay you back for this as soon as I have my baby. I promise you I'm going to pay your ass back, I promise you!"

Kai came back the next day. We took the bed down. It wasn't all destroyed. We took the pieces back to Burlington coat factory. I spoke with a sales person and told him the bed was damaged when I took it out of the box. He looked at me as I tried to avoid eye contact with him because I was holding back tears. *How could I tell him that my baby's father destroyed the bed with his bare hands?*

He knew I wasn't telling the truth. He said, "Give me a minute."

As he walked away I didn't think he was going to help me. I was expecting him to come back and turn me away. He went and got the replacement parts for the bed and told me good luck with my baby.

When I got home, I put the parts up because I didn't want Lee to destroy the bed again. I tried to stay out of his way. I just needed to have this baby. Lee would say things like he hoped the baby didn't make it. At all cost, I tried not to fight him. Everyday he called me all kinds of names. I stopped responding. I realized he was looking for a reason to fight and make me lose the baby. I was almost due. I was excited. I guess he smelled happiness.

I had not forgotten the experience I had at Sandi's house while listening to the Yolanda Adams song. I still didn't understand it. One morning, I was sitting in the living room. It was peaceful. As usual, Lee came in and picked a fight with me. I tried to walk away. He pushed me so hard I fell to the floor. I tried holding on to the coffee table to get up when he started punching me on the side of my head. I kept trying to get up and fight, but I couldn't keep my balance. I held on through the punches and got to my feet. He snatched my chains off my neck. I managed to turn around. I threw my body into him. We fell onto the couch. I was swinging, biting, kicking; whatever movement my body would allow. It stopped with him finally getting me off him. As he pushed me back to the couch he slapped me in the face. I couldn't move. He went into the room, grabbed my car keys, and left. We had many more fights like this up until I had Rayven.

I was 26 when I went into labor on February 12, 1996. Sandi and my cousin BeBe came to the hospital. I was in so much pain. I looked toward Lee to hold my hand and the idiot just sat there looking completely lost. He didn't even want to stay in the room with me. He kept walking out, so Sandi and BeBe took over. My legs were spread wide and I didn't care who saw. Sandi did everything from helping the nurse pull Rayven out, to cutting the umbilical cord, and washing Rayven. After the delivery, I asked Sandi if the hospital was going to pay her. Rayven was beautiful. I went home and was happy.

Once again, wherever joy seemed to be, Lee did whatever he could to kill it. When Rayven was about a month old, I started working out doing sit-ups.

Lee laid next to me with a smirk on his face, "What are you doing?"

I told him, "Getting my body back in shape, so I can pay your ass back."

He laughed loudly, "What you mean?"

I calmly explained I was no longer pregnant, and it was time for me to cash his check. The laughing stopped. He knew I was serious. Every chance he got he tried to discourage me from doing sit ups. *My thoughts on the matter, NO THANK YOU, SIR! I have a check made out with your name on it. I'm about to drag your ass through the MUD, all dollars and no cents.*

I started going to Yvonne's house, leading him to believe that I was going out. I had nowhere to go with a newborn, but he didn't know that. This was the beginning of the check-cashing process. I started looking at my pager even when no one had paged. He would look over his shoulder and ask if someone had paged me. I would say, no. I even started giving my number out.

The baby weight fell off. My stomach was flat and I was back in my tight jeans. He was now trying to be nice. *Oh, no sir I wasn't going to put a stop payment on that check after the way he had dogged me out.* He tried to take my keys one night when we were fighting. I stabbed the both of us with the keys. I was no longer pregnant, so he couldn't throw me to the floor anymore. There were nights I stayed at Yvonne's and didn't come home. When I came home a few days later, he would try to figure out where I'd been.

It was now his turn to suffer. At night I could hear him cry. I laid there thinking aloud, *"It's just the beginning. I'm not done with your ass. You're going to feel what I felt."*

On one of his many nights of crying, I snarled, "I don't want to hear that shit."

He rolled over and said, "Bitch, you don't give a fuck about me."

I told him, "Yea, you right I don't give a fuck about niggas that fuck with prostitutes."

He jumped up in fight mode. I jumped up with him. He ran up on me and before he could swing I hit him dead in the nose. The fight stopped.

He began screaming, "Bitch, you broke my nose!"

With that, I didn't want to waste the opportunity. I jumped on him full force. We fought in that small room until Rayven was screaming. He couldn't do anything with me. The hit in the nose had him. I didn't sleep that night because I knew it wasn't over.

The next morning, I took the kids to school and came back to get Rayven dressed so we could leave. That's when he confronted me about the fight. I was sitting on the bed with Rayven in my arms, as I laid her down and turned to face him, he swung and missed me. His punch landed on the bed right by Rayven's face. She started screaming. I grabbed her and pushed past him to the kitchen. Before he could grab me, I had a kitchen knife swinging it full force. I kept yelling you almost hit my baby. I stabbed at him and missed. He ran out the door and I locked it.

I didn't know that he was leaving in my car. I didn't know that when I went to the kitchen he grabbed my car keys. I was mad and stuck. I paged him all day. He wouldn't answer. I walked to get the kids from school. Later that night I paged Kai. She came and got me. We were going to steal my car back. I told Kai I had an extra key, but I didn't have an extra car remote. I told her I would figure it out. Kai took me through the hood and within 15 minutes we found my car. We crept up to my car and Kai let me out. She parked on the corner so Lee couldn't see her car just in case things went bad. I opened my car door and the alarm went off. I kept trying to start it, but it wouldn't turn over. Lee came running down the apartment stairs. When he saw it was me, he stood there and started laughing. He knew the car wouldn't start without the remote box. He stood there for a minute still laughing. I looked under the steering wheel column and saw a box. I snatched it out, turned the key and the car started. I needed an American Express commercial: one car key $2.00 dollars, kill switch unit $50.00 dollars, the look on his face: Priceless.

I drove off cussing out the window with my middle finger in the air. I laughed all the way back to Harbor City. I knew he couldn't get a ride back that night. The next day I had a new alarm put in my car. Lee was pissed. It took him three days to talk someone into giving him a ride.

When he finally made it back to Harbor City, the fights were on again. He had no keys, so he hopped the gate and waited on my porch or, he would climb up my balcony. *Mind you, I lived on the second floor.*

He would wait until I returned then force himself into the house. *I know you're wondering, why not call the police? I tried to get past the no-snitching rule. I tried it once, and it didn't work for me.* Rayven was two months old when we were having our usual fist fight. This particular time, I took off and ran out of the house. I left Rayven and started running down Pacific Coast Highway with no shoes and short pants. I didn't know where I was going, but I was going. As I was running, I looked behind me and Lee was behind me with Rayven in his arms. I saw a police car passing by. I flagged them down. They stopped to find out what was going on. I explained to them what happened. They said there was nothing they could do. *"What the hell?"*

I told the officer, "He's chasing me with a two-month-old in his arms. You don't think something's wrong with this picture?"

I told the police I wanted him out of my house. I told the officers he wasn't on the lease, and I asked if they could escort him out. The officers told me if he had one piece of mail coming to my house then he lived there. *Were they serious?* It took me years to do this and this is what I get? I told the police he was outside with a t-shirt, no shoes, and a baby in his arms. Their response? "It's his baby, too." *Ok, I was done.*

He followed me back to the house with Rayven in his hands, just smiling because he knew I couldn't legally put him out. The police had given him ammunition to use. He had mail there. So, if he called the police and said I locked him out, they would tell me to let him in. In my mind, I didn't give a damn. His ass still wasn't living in my house. I was sick and tired of Lee and the fighting. My body was beat up, and it was starting to show.

One day, I couldn't walk my niece Nae to school. I had my daughter Whitney walk her to her kindergarten class. The school was across the street from my apartment. I stood at the top of my stairs and watched them until they disappeared. I waited for Whitney to come back. She had walked Nae before, but this time, she had not come back. I kept checking on Rayven and coming back to the stairs. Finally, I said enough is enough. Something wasn't right. I ran into the bedroom grabbed Rayven and my gun. When I returned to the door, Whitney was there out of breath. She was screaming a man in a van tried to make her get in. Whitney outsmarted him. She played as if she was going one way and she double backed. She described the van. I took her and Rayven to the car. I looked for that van for over an hour. I was going to kill this pervert. I couldn't find the van, so I went home and called the police. They came out and said that a man in a gray van had raped a few girls. He was a serial rapist. I didn't know that over the last couple of weeks this was going on. I called Sandi. She left work and came over immediately. Of course, I really had no time for Lee's stupidity; a rapist had just chased my baby.

That night I sat on my bed and began thanking God that the rapist didn't get Whitney. Lee was trying to start his usual argument. I told him I didn't want to hear it. My mind was somewhere else. I felt helpless. There I was arguing and fighting with the village idiot who was no help in my house, just dead weight.

That Sunday, I got up and got my kids dressed because I was going to church. I was thankful that God had protected my baby. As I got up Lee jumped up and asked, "where you going?"

I said, "I'm going to church."

I think it almost killed him. He couldn't believe it. When I showed up at church, I think my sister almost had a heart attack. It wasn't Christmas or Easter. That day I sang praises. As I sang, I saw my sister Sandi crying. She passed out. I started crying. I thought, "Oh my God, she's crying just like I had done so many times throughout my life."

After church, she explained that she wasn't sad at all. She said she was grateful. *Grateful?*

"Grateful for what?" I asked

She replied, "Jesus has forgiven my sins and washed me clean."

I had no idea what she was talking about. The next Sunday I got up, went to church, and I had a good time with the women. When I came in with the kids, they grabbed Rayven, so I could enjoy the service. The pastor was preaching a sermon that fit my life perfectly. It was as if he lived in my house. *Did my sisters tell him what was going on with me?* I sat in the back because I felt like the pastor was speaking directly to me.

The following Sunday, I got up to get dressed for church, and this time, I had a surprise, Lee was up and dressed.

I asked him, "Where the hell are you going?"

He said, "Church."

"Church? Church with who?" I replied.

He told me he wanted to go with me. I told him, "No, you want to see if I'm screwing someone in church." I thought this because he already told me that was the only reason I went. When we showed up, I think my sister almost had two heart attacks. During the service, I could feel him watching me. I was irritated. I couldn't enjoy what the preacher was saying because I was watching Lee watch me. That Sunday I left church angry. I went home, called my sister, and told her I didn't have a good time because Lee was there.

She told me, "Licia he needs Jesus, so let him come."

I told her, "He's just coming to spy on me. I'm sure Jesus is in other churches. Why can't he meet Jesus somewhere else?"

My sister asked me not to discourage Lee from coming to church. *Was she hearing herself?* He was just following me. Sandi said if Lee was following me, he just may run into Jesus. Well at this point, I needed Jesus to meet him at the door because I was sick of his ass. Going to church made me feel good. No one had to beg me. I was experiencing peace and it was angering Lee. When we got into arguments, I would just let him say what he wanted and I was still content. I wasn't cussing with him. I was trying to do what the pastor said. Plus, my mind was beat up.

At first, going out to the club was a problem; now he was complaining about me going to see Jesus. My decision to attend church regularly was cause for an argument. As if we didn't have a million other stupid things to argue about. I didn't care, I was enjoying church. Something was different when I went. I would come home with a peace I couldn't explain. The church arguments became more frequent and violent. One day, I decided I was going to take the kids out of the house. I wasn't going to argue over going to church. I had Baby Dee, my niece and nephew. As they were playing in the room, we began to argue. I didn't want to hear what he had to say. I still had some type of peace. I sat on the couch not giving him my usual response. I wasn't cussing. I wasn't angry. That made him want to hit me. He grabbed me off the couch and we started fighting. This time, I was fighting with the intent to kill him. I had peace and his ass was fucking with me. The fight started in the living room. We fought our way into the hallway. We were throwing punch for punch. I was small since I lost weight. I wouldn't let him grab me because if he did I knew it would be over for me. The kids came into the hallway crying. I yelled, "Go back in the room!" As I turned to throw another punch, Lee was already in mid-swing and hit me in the jaw. I felt a crack. I started spitting up blood. I grabbed my mouth. The blood wouldn't stop. I touched my jaw and it moved from one side to the other. I knew it was broken.

Lee was running up as I held my jaw, I said, "My jaw, you broke my jaw!"

I couldn't stop throwing up blood. It was so bad, he stopped the fight. He yelled to the kids to get their coats. We had to go to the hospital. Bay Harbor Hospital was down the street from my house. We pulled up to the hospital and Lee told me to page him when I was done.

I walked into the hospital. The nurses came running when they saw me. I had blood everywhere. They got me a wheelchair and they took my information. Then, they asked what happened? I told them it was my cousin. The nurse asked, "What's his name?" I said it was a girl. They took me in for x-rays. Once they were done, the doctor came in and asked what happened? I stuck to my story. The doctor told me my jaw was broken in two different places and a woman did not have that type of strength. I had nothing to say, plus, I couldn't talk anyway. After that, I don't remember much.

I woke up to loud voices. Wait, I recognized those voices.

"THANK YOU LORD that she's alive, that you kept her."

The voices were harsh, who was praying for me? I came out of seda-tion. It was Sandi and Annette. They were at my bedside praying over me. I heard them praying before, and it never sounded like this. I looked around the room, Lee was sitting in the corner with his head down. I looked at Sandi and apologized for fighting in front of the kids. *Wait, that didn't sound right. What was happening?* I was talking through my teeth my mouth was wired shut.

Sandi kept saying, "Don't try to talk. We're just glad you're alive."

Annette agreed with an angry tone in her voice. *What was going on?* They were sending Lee a message letting him know that they knew he did it, even though I wouldn't tell.

My sisters came home with me when I was released. Annette wanted to take Rayven because I was on medication. I had just had my baby, I didn't want her to go. Annette said she would take her for a few days, and my cousin BeBe said she wanted to help with Rayven or, Ray Ray, as she called her. When I got home, the blood was still on my floor. My sister asked me to come home with her. I said I was going to stay in my own house. My two sisters were watching me like the sisters on *The Color Purple*, like Odessa watching Sophia. Every move I made in the house they watched me as Lee sat there with his head down. I told Lee he had to leave. He whispered in my ear that he wanted to take care of me. He was real nice because *The Color Purple* sisters were ready to fight. My sister Annette decided she was staying.

Lee left and came back the next day. When he came to the door, he said he wanted to help me. I told him no. I stepped out of my front door. I had my car keys in my hand. He asked again, who was going to take care of Rayven? My mouth was wired shut; I was too tired and weak to argue. As we stood at the top of my steps, he began to argue. He looked down and tried to snatch my car keys out of my hand. I had my back toward the stairs and as he tried to snatch my keys I fell backward. I grabbed the banister and Annette busted out my screen door full of rage. I guess she saw what happened.

She said to Lee, "You trying to fight me?"

Lee looked and quickly said, "I'm not trying to fight you."

She asked again, this time, tears were running down her face. She was ready to fight, but Lee wasn't.

Ahh yea, we about to beat you, fool. Lee hurried up, walked down the stairs, and left.

My sisters kept Rayven for a few days. I wanted my baby back, so they brought her home. We had a small fight about Rayven being with my sisters. A small fight meant he pushed me and I didn't do much of nothing because my jaw was wired. I was afraid of what would happen if he hit me in my mouth again. Every day, I drank milkshakes. I had to get my weight up. I knew I couldn't win with a broken jaw.

I was embarrassed to go to church with my mouth wired, so my sister Sandi talked me into going to women's fellowship at my cousin's house. It was close to Easter and they blended some food. They laid hands on me and prayed. I was feeling God in my heart because I was surrounded by women that really didn't know me, but still showed me love. I wasn't embarrassed anymore about my jaw being wired. They acted as if my mouth was normal. When I went back home that night, I was tired. My mind was at peace. I laid there. I remembered something Sandi had always told me.

"Alicia, if you pray God will hear you."

That night, I thought about all the love the women at the church had shown me. Now I was back here sleeping with the enemy. Then I did something I had never done before, I rolled over on my knees. Lee started looking at me as if I was crazy, but I didn't care. I had shot at him, dragged him down the street with my car, stabbed him, told the police on him, hit him in the nose, slept with someone else, and none of these things worked to get rid of him. That night I decided to give Jesus a try. When I was on my knees, he just sat there watching me.

After I got off my knees, he said, "Oh you praying now?"

I told him, "Yea I'm praying you out of here."

He looked at me and laughed. The next night I did the same thing. But, this time, my prayer was different. My prayer was this, "Lord I don't know you, but my sister told me you hear us when we pray. Jesus If you get him out of my house I'll serve you."

Later that week I went to LA to meet Kai. Lee dropped us off in downtown. Kai was pregnant and we were going to get her baby some things. I paged Lee. He never responded. I paged again and nothing. Finally, Kai and I called for a ride. When I got back to the hood I went on 94th and Figueroa. My homie Lou told me that Lee had been taken to jail. Lou gave me my car keys.

I asked him, "Jail? Who was Lee messing with now?"

Lou said, "Nobody, he went for dope."

"Dope? He didn't have any dope."

That night Lee called me and confirmed what I knew; his broke self didn't have dope. Lee said the undercover agent said he saw him selling dope, so he was arrested. I thought wait maybe I was wrong.

I asked, "How the police gonna keep you with no evidence?"

That week I went to see Lee. They weren't going to let him go. *You asked me did I run down the street with my newfound freedom? Did I throw a party? No.* I called my sister and asked her to have her pastor call me. I wanted to get Lee out. *I know what you're thinking, what was wrong with me?* I didn't realize God had answered my prayers. The pastor called and I told him, "I need your help, my boyfriend is in jail."

Pastor said, "Ok was he working?"

"No, Pastor."

"Did he want to work?"

"No."

"Did he go to school?

"No."

"Did he want to go to school?"

"No."

"Did he come to church?"

"No."

"Did he want to come to church?"

"No."

The pastor then said, "Well there's nothing we can do for him."

Chapter 29

Metamorphosis

The party was now on. I started going back to LA to see my friend Timmie. While at Timmie's I met a guy named Benny. I called myself cashing that check I promised Lee. When he called from jail I was not home. Eventually, Benny started coming over. I made sure Lee knew Benny was there. Lee cried on the phone. I didn't care because all I could hear was that check clearing through the bank of "*Payback is a Bitch.*"

Benny and I started hanging tough. He was very different from Lee. He was nice. He cooked and had a job - imagine that. *Now please don't get me wrong, Benny was Blood affiliated.* I was happy because he wasn't controlling or crazy. We talked on the phone for hours about Lee. He was cool.

One morning, I got up to go to LA to meet him and I couldn't get up. I was nauseated and tired. I called Benny and told him that we had to meet later. I experienced the same thing over the next couple of days. At the end of the week, I laid in bed; tears began to roll down my face. All I thought to myself was wait, I'm pregnant. I laid there. *This can't be possible.* I was supposed to get my tubes tied after I had Rayven, but my doctor told me to wait and then come back for the procedure. Finally, I went and took a pregnancy test. It was positive. I came home and wouldn't get out of the bed. I asked Sandi if she could get the kids because I was sick.

When Sandi dropped the kids off, I met her at the car. She said, "The Lord told me what's wrong with you."

I told her, "Yea, I'm just sick." And walked away from her car.

I delayed going to get an ultrasound because I knew I was pregnant by Lee and I was depressed. I knew the ultrasound would tell me how many months I was. Heck, I already knew how many months. That equaled another baby by Lee.

When I went for my ultrasound, as the tech was punching buttons, rubbing the ball on my stomach. I thought I saw two babies.

I said, "Hey wait, I see two babies."

The tech looked up, pushed her glasses on her face, smiled and said, "Oh yeah. You're having twins."

I cried, and cried, and cried. When I got home, I called my cousin Angel. She said, "Baby, just come on home."

Still crying I said, "I am home."

She told me, "Come to my house."

I did. I cried and cried and cried. What was I going to do with four kids and pregnant again by a fool? I told Benny. He was so excited. I asked him, "Why are you excited?" He said, "because I'm having twins." I told him he wasn't having anything. I was already pregnant when we slept together.

For weeks, Benny refused to believe me. This was a first, a man begging to have a baby with me. I told Benny how many months I was and he didn't care, he just wanted those babies. The next time I went back they told me the sex of the babies, boys. Benny really wasn't going to walk away. He called me every morning and every night. I just laid in bed for days. My sister started picking up the kids. I still hadn't told her.

It was a Friday and she picked up the kids. When she came to my apartment I opened the door and let her in. Immediately, I went and got back in bed where I had been all day. And then, I heard water running. I got up. Sandi was cleaning my house and cooking. I got scared Jesus had told her because she was cleaning my house and cleaning was not her best gift.

My brother Edwin called me that week because he hadn't heard from me. I told him I was pregnant.

He said, "So do you need me to take you?"

I asked him, "Take me where?"

He said, "To the abortion clinic."

I hesitated and said, "I don't know what I'm going to do. I haven't decided yet."

He replied, "Why the hell not? You don't want no more babies and don't be listening to those damn church people. They're not going to help you."

I told him I was thinking about what to do. Before he could go into his cussing phase, I hung up. He called every day for a straight week. Asking if I made an appointment and if I wanted him to take me to the abortion clinic. I laid in the bed depressed, wrestling with the thought of the abortion clinic. I was weighing out my options. I also remembered how sad I was the last time I did it. I was in the bed on a Sunday night still wrestling with the decision, abort or not to abort. It was then that I heard the Lord speak to me. God whispered to my spirit, "Come into church and bring the babies with you."

I went to church the next Sunday. As the pastor was preaching, I heard God call my name. *I heard him!* I got up and gave my life to the Lord. I was excited. I was at peace. I now understood what Sandi was trying to explain to me for years.

I went home, called Benny and I told him it was over. I was saved. I wasn't going to be sleeping with him anymore. He still begged me to reconsider. There was nothing for me to reconsider. I was done. I heard God. When Lee called me, I told him that I was pregnant. He began to make plans and fake promises when I interrupted him. I told him I was saved. He was happy about me being saved because he figured I wouldn't be running the streets. It wasn't until I told him that I wasn't going to be bothered with him anymore that he had a problem. For months Lee called and tried to get me to change my mind.

On January 6th, 1997 at the age of 26, I went into labor while I was at church. Annette took me to the hospital and the next day I had twin boys, Marcus and Marquise. I was so happy. I finally had peace in my house and a church family.

When the twins turned a month old I took Marquise to the county jail to see Lee. When Lee saw that something was different about me, he began to fuss and hit the glass. He was trying to get me to argue with him. He started cussing me out. Everyone in the visiting area was watching us. I told him that I would not put up with being called out of my name anymore. I was not going to allow that around my kids.

Lee started yelling through the glass, "You must have a nigga because you're acting funny."

I told him, "I don't have a man, but I do have a Heavenly Father and his name is Jesus."

I got up and left the county jail. That month I applied for an emergency voucher from Section-8. A month later, I moved back to LA and changed my number. The twins were about three months old when Lee got my new number. He called me collect saying that he wanted to see his kids. I told him that his father could pick the kids up and his father could monitor the visit, but he could not come to my house. Lee then asked me about the guns. I told him I sold them and bought the kids toys.

"Toys? Toys?" he yelled. "Where are my guns?"

I politely interrupted him, and said, "You have no guns. I decided I no longer want that life. I won't have any guns, drugs or anything else in my house that doesn't please God."

Lee started threatening me. "I know where you live and how to get you," he said.

I told him, "Where I live is not a secret, you're just not welcome here."

Lee started cussing me out and in the middle of the conversation, I stopped him and said, "The old Alicia no longer lives here. As a matter of fact, she's dead. If you're going to call and cuss me out, you at least have to pay for the call." I hung up the phone. *I wept, wept, and then I wept some more!!*

I couldn't stop crying. For the first time in my life, I was weeping for a different reason, many reasons. I was free and I could feel the changes deep within me. It didn't matter anymore who believed me or who believed in me- I was finally starting to believe in myself.

Lee did 18 months in jail. After he was released, he tried to contact me and I refused to see or talk to him. He came by my father's house asking about the kids. My father's response to him was always the same. "Are you off drugs and do you have child support money?" His answer was always the same. I'll tell you the answer. "No." When Lee's father died, it severed all ties between him, the kids, and me. I have seen him from time to time in the neighborhood and when I do see him, I keep it pushing. It has been over 20 years and he's still the same troubled man. He's still has the same mindset and the same vices. It's sad, but it's no longer my reality.

Although I now had a new beginning God took me back to where it all began. It began with the first man that I had ever loved, the first man that broke my trust, and the first man that broke my heart into millions of pieces -- my father. He broke my trust by unmercifully beating me and he broke my heart by accusing me of killing my mother and allowing her memory to die on a couch 23 years ago. After getting saved, I started going to church every Sunday. On this particular Sunday it was Father's Day and the message was "Traumatized Mind." The pastor said, "You're not in this state by chance, something happened."

He continued, "It's not that you're not touchy feely and you don't like to be touched, something happened to you." The pastor called everyone who had experienced some type of trauma up to the altar for prayer. My body took me up there -- almost like I was in a trance. I made my way to the front of the church and stood before the altar. I stood directly in front of the pastor. Pastor prayed for me and looked me in my eyes and said the word 'forgiveness.' Immediately my father came to my mind and just as I was about to cuss in my head, the Lord whispered into my spirit, *"Forgive Him."*

When I walked away from the altar I decided I no longer wanted to be bound by unforgiveness and anger. I no longer wanted to harbor bitterness, sadness and hatred in my heart. As I left church, I saw some women selling flowers for fathers and I bought one. After church I went straight to my father's house. He wasn't there. It didn't matter, I knew what I needed to do. I left the flower with a letter on his door. I wished him a Happy Father's Day and told him I loved him. *That day I forgave my father for breaking my heart.* Next, I forgave myself for all the years that I was disrespectful toward him and for hating him. I asked God to do a new thing in my heart and mind. I was taught to never forgive and I didn't realize it was unforgiveness that had clogged my heart and suffocated my emotions. I realized that forgiveness was the oxygen I needed for my soul and for the first time in 27 years-- I had the ability to breathe. And this breath felt like a promise for a new beginning.

> *If any man be in Christ, he is a new creature. Old things are passed away, behold, all things become new, 2 Corinthians 5:17*

Now that the metamorphosis cycle has been completed, the rest of the journey begins. It begins with a profound sense of purpose that has been assigned to you and me. It's a journey of self-love and forgiveness that will enable others to be touched by our lives. This portion of my transformation is merely a stepping stone to where TRUE manifestation will be revealed. Just like the butterfly touches the petals of flowers, branches of trees and rocks in a stream, so will my Metamorphosis change lives…

Today, I choose to love myself and my life, regardless of my past. My perspective on life has totally changed. You may ask "how?" I now love life. There was a time when I didn't love myself. I didn't value my life or any other life for that matter. I didn't look forward to having a future because I had already decided I wasn't going to live anyway. But now I love me and although things aren't always perfect, I trust God to get me through and I appreciate the hills and valleys of my story. For those like me, I'd like you to know that situations change and I love you. Celebrate the fact that not many people have survived what you've been through. You are STRONG! You're also smart, courageous, and beautifully designed by God to be His masterpiece. I believe in you. I thank you for believing in me.

I hope to see you on my continued travels *"A Butterfly's Journey"* coming soon.

Oh yeah, and if you're ever in a small city called Pasadena, and you so happen to come into a little church on a hill, you'll encounter a butterfly with magnificent wings praising God a little longer, a little more intentionally like her life depends on it.

And that's when you know you've encountered
METAMORPHOSIS!!!

Acknowledgments

To Sneak, Gwen and Petrie who are no longer with me, through the good, bad and the ugly thank you for helping me survive the streets. To those that looked out for me when I was a 15-year-old runaway, you know who you are, thank you.

To my father, God has allowed me to see your pain. Things haven't always been great between us, but the power of God's forgiveness outweighs any hurt, pain or sorrow. I love you.

To my Uncle Mike who is no longer with me, when I was 7 you told me, "Alicia you are the smartest little girl I've ever met. You can do anything you put your mind to." Thanks to your outpouring of love and encouragement. I've put my mind to many things including writing this book. I'll always love you.

To my sisters Theresa, Cassandra and Robin we have laughed and fought as all siblings do, but the greatest thing you did was introduce me to Christ. I thank you for your countless prayers. You couldn't have given me a greater gift. I love you.

Tameika my sister and sister in the Lord, we started off as enemies, but God knew we would have a deeper friendship and sisterhood, you stood with me. I love you.

Madolyn, we met at USC in 2002 and from the first day we spoke you told me I would do big things. You pushed me, and every time I was exhausted and wanted to give up you told me how amazing I was. I don't have enough words to thank you.

I love you.

Pastor Jon DeCuir, when we first met I was exhausted and just passing through, but you yielded yourself and encouraged me. There were times that after we spoke on the phone I simply hung up and cried. After our conversations I wiped my tears and did what you asked me to do. You always gave me truth even at the risk of me walking away. And as a result of one of those hard conversations you helped me birth my vision, *The Metamorphosis Experience.* You told me I would be great, and you were right.

I love you.

Darryl (PD), what can I say except, God knew when to send you into my life. You have pushed and challenged my thinking. You loved on me. Since God has allowed you in my life, you have been one of my biggest fans. There has not been a day that you did not tell me how smart, anointed or beautiful I was. When I had doubts about pursuing my dreams YOU reminded me that I was the butterfly who was destined for greatness.

Thank you man of God.

I Love You.

Bio

A licia Cass dropped out of high school at the age of 15. She went back to school at 28 years old and obtained her high school diploma. At 34, she earned her Bachelor of Science Degree in Sociology with a minor in Children and Families in Urban Settings from University of Southern California (USC). Proudly, at 37 years old, she completed her Masters in Social Work (MSW); also from USC while raising her children as a single parent. While at USC Alicia received numerous accolades. She was a Norman Topping Scholar, which is a high honor that provides scholarships to first generation college students who demonstrate strong community service and outreach. She was also a USC Black

Alumni Scholar, received the USC Ambassador Award, USC Trojan Recognition Award, and USC McDuffie Award. Alicia was a member of the USC African American Honor Society and a recipient of the USC Henry Lederman Award. Currently, Alicia is a social worker and a doctorate student at the University of Southern California.

Alicia's story of triumph and overcoming obstacles has been heard first hand at her various speaking engagements and in documentaries. She's spoken at local churches, juvenile halls, colleges, and organizations such as: Project Unity, Going Straight Ministries, Love and Order youth department, Loving Your Disabled Child, Barry J. Nidorf Juvenile Hall, Central Juvenile Hall, Long Beach City College, University of Southern California, Women and Youth Supporting Each Other (WYSE), Stanford University (WYSE), University of California of Los Angeles (WYSE), USC Anthropology Gangs class, USC Social Work Gang class, USC Reentry Conference, Project Kinship, Los Angeles Transitional Housing, DCFS Foster Youth, The Esther Project, Visionary Youth Center, Jackie Robinson Youth Center, SEP Coaching, LDL Foundation, Service Works LA. Alicia is a mother of 8 and grandmother of 4.

CPSIA information can be obtained
at www.ICGtesting.com
Printed in the USA
FSHW021440121118
53731FS